COOK+CORK

HARRY MILLS + CHRIS HORN

COOK+CORK

A CHEF AND A SOMMELIER SPILL THE SECRETS OF FOOD AND WINE PAIRING

photography by HAYLEY YOUNG / illustrations by STACEY ROZICH

HEAVY
RESTAURANT
GROUP

Contents

Printed in China

Design and layout: Kate Basart/Union Pageworks
Project management: Elizabeth Cromwell/Books in Flight

ISBN: 978-0-692-75100-8

Heavy Restaurant Group
120 Lakeside Avenue, Suite 300, Seattle, WA 98122
info@heavyrestaurantgroup.com
www.heavyrestaurantgroup.com

Wines and Recipes

This book is dedicated to our wives,
Keita Horn and Kristin Mills. Without them,
we'd still be talking about writing a book.

Introduction

Talk is Cheap, Advice is Free, or Why We Think You Should Read This

Here's our wish: that people become so comfortable with wine in their lives that picking up a few bottles at the wine store is as natural as a trip to the hardware store, the dry cleaner, or the organic produce section of the grocery store. Our wish is that sitting down to eat means opening a bottle of wine. Our wish is that food and wine pairing is no longer a vague or fatuous concept, but a natural impulse based on simple understandings of what can happen when liquid meets solid.

Right now, the world is being bombarded by large-scale industrial wine production on one side and the residual effects of wine snobbery on the other—and we don't want either to win.

We want *you* to win. Win by finding a reliable source for wines made by people—either with intent or in the name of tradition. We want you to win by learning how to make food with wine in mind—so that when it comes to pulling a cork or twisting a cap, there's no trepidation or gnashing of teeth. We want you to fall in love with pairing wine and food in the same way that we have.

Drinking wine should be fun. After all, we don't drink wine to get sober.

Our first order of business is to fill you in on some of our backstory: the personal and professional reasons that

led us to the point of wanting to write a book in order to advocate and evangelize a thoughtful and healthy approach to wine and food.

Following that, we'll talk about flavor and also introduce you to your Mind Mouth (you have one, but maybe didn't know it). We'll also suggest some simple things you can do to understand the basic structures of wine: body, acid, and tannin.

There are guidelines as well as historic food and wine–pairing truths to introduce—important stuff, but not as fun as actually eating some food paired with the right wine. So we've detailed a number of food and wine experiences you can replicate with little or no cooking whatsoever. These are not only the gateway food and wine pairings—they are the experiences

we go back to time and time again to remind and ground us to the fact that no matter how clever a chef or wine guy might be, there are tried, true, and historical pairings that are bigger than all of us.

And then we'll introduce you to your Wine Wardrobe: the toolkit of wines you should have in your house at all times in order to outfit just about any dish you might be putting on the table. A distillation of the wines we use every day at the restaurant when pairing our food. Wines that you simply need to have in your life.

Several times during the course of putting this book together, we've reminded ourselves to consider it more or less an exercise in dispensing the kind of advice you would want to give to a good friend. The kind of insight that would, if we were talking about the stock market, elicit an investigation from the SEC on grounds of insider trading. Because our jobs afford us the luxury of a specialized point of view, let's go ahead and talk about some professional truths we see every day—even though there might be some stuff people would rather we not talk about.

Here is the simple truth, the thing we are all up against: wherever you look, someone is trying to sell you something. I (Chris Horn, wine guy. Thanks for reading this far.) was born into a world of constant bombardment by advertisements. When I think about growing up, I can recall as many television commercials as I can television shows—as many jingles as Top

It's best not to take oneself seriously.

40 songs. But I had it good compared to my kid, because the average hour of television when I was growing up contained 20 percent commercials. Today, taking into account longer breaks and clever product placement, the new estimate is now a bit above 33 percent. And that's just TV.

Sales pitches used to be as obvious and quaint as a billboard on the side of a scenic highway, but now we live in a world where something that *looks and feels like a magazine* is actually a catalog of "articles" meant to get you to buy stuff. Advertising has always been a wolf, but now it's in sheep's clothing.

And then there's the Internet, otherwise known as a world of marketing disguised as "informative content." Take into consideration that much of what you see is based on your own personal traffic—every minute of net browsing supplies information about what you like to the people looking to supply you with things you may or may not need. The term *World Wide Web* was at first an apt metaphor for connection, but it has evolved into a startling expression of entrapment.

Even when doing a web search for "food and wine pairing," I get a website that has the message, "Discover what food pairing can do for your brand." For the record, that idea is not only terrible, but total crap.

We used to fear Big Brother—the constant surveillance of our every move—but these days, instead of the big government, it's big advertising that follows us relentlessly.

So here's our truth: we are not selling anything. (Well, this book perhaps. But if you're reading this, then there's a chance that the transaction has already taken place, and we thank you.) In this book you will not read about specific wineries, since no winery is bankrolling this. As much as I would like to say, "You need to eat Dungeness crab with Abeja Chardonnay," I won't.

Because of the world we live in, where honesty seems constantly in question, I feel compelled to declare: **This book is not sponsored by any winery or wine region.**

And while it may elicit ire from the close-minded and criticism from those who are threatened by an informed public, this book is purposefully not definitive. (But if you follow the advice within, we guarantee you will be a happier human being.)

Two Kinds of Advice

When it comes to the wine side of things, I'm going to give you Specific Broad Advice. Yeah—that sounds both contradictory and insane. Here's what I mean:

Back when I was 13, I had an epic sleepover with my brother Pat and my older cousin Brad. They (being three years older than me) gave me a seminar/motivational symposium on how to kiss girls. The advice was specific yet broad, and (at the time) incomprehensible. It's like a person trying to talk about their favorite song without the ability to sing; it's easy to understand the passion, but the rest is impossible to comprehend.

And I suppose I listened to some of their advice—but it ultimately didn't matter. Once I experienced that first kiss (which was predictably tragic and hilarious) I was game to try again despite my utter lack of success.

The right food and wine together is more than just melody—it's Lionel

Richie/Diana Ross–level harmony. Every time we come across an amazing food and wine pairing, it becomes my new favorite song. But I don't want to *tell* you about how great this specific Bordeaux is with the steak frites, I want you to experience it. And yes—I'm comparing food and wine pairing to both music and kissing. Three things you should have in your life. Every day.

My hope is that the people who pick up this book throw caution to the wind and just kiss the girl. Pairing food and wine at home won't always be successful, but I want to get people to start ignoring the bullshit on the back of the bottle and start exploring for themselves.

What you should expect from my chef and co-author: Springboard Advice. In most cookbooks, recipe format is a paint-by-numbers list of ingredients and steps to help you re-create the professionally styled food photograph on the opposing page. And while you'll see recipes in here, they are not meant to be the end of the story, but a starting point. He's not going to construct boxes, but launching pads.

And finally, parts of this book will sound quite raw—and maybe on the edge of not being well written. That's intentional. We're not professional writers any more than you're a professional cook. So let's start with forgiving each other.

There's No Wine in Baseball

A roadmap doesn't have to list every alternate path; there are a thousand ways to get to a destination. These are ours—and sometimes it's the quickest route, and sometimes it's the scenic route—but however we get there, we want this trip to be pleasurable.

Let's go from vague analogy to something a bit more concrete: I know nothing about baseball. Well, almost nothing. I suppose I have a basic idea of the rules; how long a game is, how many outs are in an inning, how many strikes before you're out, and what the seventh-inning stretch is—though I couldn't tell you why in the world they do the seventh-inning stretch.

You could say I don't know anything more than I need to know in order to go to the ballpark and enjoy watching a game.

The Sommelier's Job

Wine is a liquid that needs its solid. There are flavors in wine utterly unlocked and liberated when introduced to the right food.

Which is really the sommelier's main job. Flavor liberator. Flavor manager. Flavor concierge. Sommeliers don't make wine, winemakers don't grow grapes, farmers don't run wine programs. But we'd all be nothing without each other.

Mine is the last step—which is the only reason the world has bothered to elevate it. We close the loop; we end the journey. We know our food, and with it, we pair wine.

The winemaker has to trust the farmer to grow the grapes correctly, just as the farmer has to trust the winemaker to produce the wine.

Trust the sommelier. My job does not involve the growing or producing of wine; my job is to know what I need, buy the right wine at the right price, and find the right person to drink the wine—at the right time.

But baseball is more than just a game to some—it's a religion. Part of that religion seems to involve knowing as much about the history, players, and statistics of not only one's own team, but of the entire subject. Major League Baseball gets bigger every year, to the tune of thirty teams playing 162 games each (4,860 total) followed by the playoffs and the World Series. Baseball is known by some, mastered by few—but it can be thoroughly enjoyed by anyone willing to watch a game.

So wine is like baseball?

Yes, to a point. Wine is also a subject that includes a great many details: grape varietals, geography, winemakers, and new vintages every year. Like baseball, wine is also known by some, mastered by few, and can be enjoyed by those willing to pour a glass.

Where wine and baseball differ is this: Have you ever sat in a baseball stadium and watched somebody manually scoring the game? I have—and I have no idea what it involves. But that person taking notes does, and though I have to believe he is experiencing the game a little differently than I am, it doesn't bother me or change my experience in any way.

People are not intimidated by the baseball expert. People aren't intimidated by the car expert, the jazz expert, the horse expert, or the plumbing expert either, for that matter. But people are different when it comes to wine. And the shame of it is, I think that prevents us from wanting to know much about wine beyond how to pull out a cork and what sort of score it got from some critic.

Wine is unlike baseball because it's always been less about *playing* and more about *knowing*.

I want people to approach enjoying wine in the same spirit as going to the baseball stadium. It doesn't matter if you can name the starting lineup of your home team. You can still cheer when somebody hits a home run. You don't need to know the subregions of the Loire Valley, but you can really enjoy a bottle of Sancerre. Both are complex, yes—but you don't have to know everything about them to have a fantastic experience.

So how do we make wine more like a game? How do we make people want to play with wine on a daily basis without self-consciousness?

Here's what I say: The true game of wine is pairing it with food. It's a game that is easier to learn than you think—but like anything else, you'll need the right equipment to play. We'd like to give you the tools.

Introductions, or Who the Hell Do We Think We Are?

The word *chef* used to be a pretty innocuous job title. My French isn't that great, but it's my understanding that it all started as *chef de cuisine*, which more or less means "person in charge of food." However, in this day and age, the job of chef has been elevated to an echelon of fame just a few ticks below rock star. We now have TV channels dedicated to chef personalities and competitions. Cookbooks followed by book tours. Branded pots, pans, and mixers. Frozen and canned foods in every grocery store. A couple of decades ago, the only chefs most of us had any familiarity with were Julia Child and Chef Boyardee (and the Swedish Chef from the Muppets, of course—though his influence never quite made it to the dining room table).

Fast-forward to today: Depending on your exposure to the back of the house (the term we restaurant people use to refer to the kitchen), when somebody uses the word *chef*, a number of different types of human beings come to mind. The zany made-for-TV chef. The snooty chef with the puffy hat. The temper-tantrum chef with the abusive language. The tortured perfectionist chef painstakingly plating microgreens with tweezers. While they sound like clichés, I've worked with all of them at one point or another, so I can vouch for their existence. They all have a certain level of entertainment value. I can see how they make good TV.

But there's a more common kind of chef who doesn't make for great TV. That's the one who chose to do the job for few other reasons beyond a love of food and a need to feed people. An objective look at the life of a chef—not on TV but in reality—will steer most people down another road. It's a career path that involves such highlights as repetitive motion syndrome, knife accidents, and regularly endured second- and third-degree burns, all in a stiflingly hot work environment. And don't ask for a break.

It takes a certain kind of crazy to work in a restaurant. It takes twice as much to work in the kitchen. And

it takes a certain specialized stack of skills to be in charge of that kitchen.

When I first met Coach (my chef and the coauthor of this book), he was the opening sous chef at the Seattle location of the Purple Café and Wine Bar. I knew little about him beyond the fact that he had taught culinary school for almost a decade. And that everybody in the kitchen kept calling him Coach. I found the idea rather refreshing.

The nickname wasn't arbitrary: he runs the kitchen staff as a team, appreciating the importance of each position and the value of each person. Understanding how to produce food is one thing—understanding how to keep your people producing consistently great food while keeping morale high is another. He's got that uncanny ability to point out errors in performance while making everybody feel like *it's going to be OK*. There are all sorts of no-BS chefs on the planet, but few who manage to enforce standards without creating a punitive environment. In Coach's kitchen, expectations are as clear as the instructions.

Here's the common chef and sommelier relationship: Sommeliers love food. Chefs love food. Sommeliers love wine. Chefs say they love wine but don't make food with wine in mind, then drink mostly bourbon and beer.

I've the rare opportunity to have a chef who loves wine as much as I do. I have a chef who insists on building recipes based on the culinary traditions of wine-producing countries. I have a chef

That's Chef Harry "Coach" Mills on the left. Sommelier Chris Horn on the right.

who will present a plate and declare the wine he had in mind while creating it. I have a chef who blind-tastes wine along with my sommelier team. I've got a chef with an academic background who is as comfortable learning as he is teaching. And so I get to learn along with him.

The contents of this book are the natural result of two restaurant people with an agenda to get the world to fall in love with food and wine. One happens to be the chef, and one happens to be the sommelier—and while our expertise is seemingly separated between the front and the back of the house, what we care about most is the moment those two things collide.

There are two voices here, but only one agenda.

I arrived at the Seattle Purple Café location as a sous chef before I even had a company chef jacket. I was in my tenth year of restaurant work, but it was my first restaurant opening. I only knew that I wanted to work hard and impress people. There were so many people and so many new faces.

I immediately disliked Chris Horn. At least I thought I did . . .

He was walking through the restaurant holding a laptop like it was a manila folder, swinging it about with pronounced gravitas and confidence. I thought he worked for the contractors. I had never worked in a restaurant that had a sommelier before, and it never occurred to me that this cat could be the sommelier. Up until then, my experience with sommeliers had been old men wearing a silver cup around their necks and intimidating guests more than helping them.

Once I found out he was the sommelier, I meant to get to know him. I was lucky enough to grow up with wine. My pops is a big collector, and so wine has always been a passion of mine—as is learning as much about it as possible. I relished the idea of having a real-deal sommelier in my work environment every single day.

I was working my ass of with the cuisine. He was building a wine list. It was a new restaurant. We were grinding. There were late evenings when we gave each other a sidelong glance, but "getting to know each other" time in a new restaurant is based entirely on necessity, and it was just too intensely busy for that to happen yet.

The environment of a professional kitchen is not for the faint of heart. Coping with the working conditions requires a certain clever roguishness. Eventually, a good number of questionable jokes and pointed insults had been exchanged across the pass. I knew he was one of us, in spite of the tie.

The kitchen has always taken a strange shine to Mr. Horn, and if certain people don't, I make sure that they do. In fact, much to his chagrin, often when he walks on the expo line in the kitchen, he is given a bellowing proclamation (unrepeatable here), followed by a standing ovation by everyone in the kitchen. While he hates it, I love it. I want my staff to show him respect, even though most of them have very little comprehension of what he does. They just love to give him the ovation. Respect comes in many forms.

What he does is build wine lists full of strange and unusual wines from all over the world, bolstered by a few recognizable labels for those who are a bit less adventurous. Because Purple is a wine bar in Washington, many people mistakenly think that we focus entirely on Northwest wines. Not true at all. Those Northwest labels are phalanxed by wines from France, Italy, and Spain, along with Croatia, Slovenia, Greece,

Another busy lunch at the Seattle Purple Café and Wine Bar

Macedonia, Uruguay, and other far reaches of the planet. These wines are hard to source, but Horn spends the time to get them. This gives us a panoply of flavors to play with for pairing with every single dish on our menu. Horn calls it his toolbox. We firmly believe we have one of the best toolboxes in the country, and Chris is always looking to make it even better.

Chris also brings his incredibly high standards to the restaurant, to help less experienced and more youthful employees learn how to help each and every guest incorporate wine into their meals. Every wine bar should be so lucky to have a sommelier like Chris. I'm just glad that we've got him. It truly allows us to collaborate on menus, rather than me dropping one off on his desk, or him telling me to "make food for Oregon Pinot." For wine dinners, we're often in the kitchen tasting,

spitting, and making final tweaks to dishes moments before they go out to the guests. I know of no other chef/ sommelier team that takes it as far as we do to assure that each pairing is truly remarkable—and we never guess. You'll learn in this book what can happen when you guess. Disasters can happen when you get lazy and take a guess.

As my mind drifts from writing this introduction, I'm already mentally into my next project, which is to write a menu for four diners in the secret room inside of our famous wine tower at Purple. I will draw very light sketches, highlighting what is in season and what dishes I think we can execute out of the back kitchen during a roaringly busy Saturday night rush. My next step? I'm going to go see Mr. Horn about some wine. Then we will put all of the principles in this book to work. It's one of my favorite parts of my job.

Wine is a Lot of Things

WINE IS HISTORY: the history of the people, and the history of the land.

WINE IS GEOLOGY: the specific expression or voice of the earth in which the grapes grew.

WINE IS GEOGRAPHY: aspect, angle, latitude.

WINE IS SOCIOLOGY: the traditions of production and the traditions of cuisine, interconnected and grounded by one another.

WINE IS PERSONAL: the result of a person or group of persons with a single vision, goal, and purpose.

WINE IS WEATHER: but we use the word *vintage* instead.

WINE IS FASHION. Wine is marketing. Wine is popular culture.

WINE IS PERISHABLE. Wine is future vinegar.

WINE IS ONE of the only things that has the chance of improving by sitting on a dark, cold shelf for decades.

WINE IS MAGICAL.

In wine you can taste all these things: history, geology, philosophy, meteorology.

But for all the magic that wine can be on its own, it will always, always, *always* be better if it's consumed in the context of food.

How It All Started

Opening a restaurant is arguably the most masochistic endeavor we humans willingly take on—it's akin to building a house of cards in a wind tunnel while wearing boxing gloves. Having been involved in and witnessed many restaurant openings over the years, it's a wonder anybody survives, patrons included.

A mere twenty-four hours before the first planned service, most restaurants hold little resemblance to the final product—meaning the dining room usually lacks basic things like tables and chairs. Everything that *is* in the building is covered in sawdust, and the dishwasher is cycling nonstop in a futile attempt to keep up with the settling of debris. The point-of-sale (POS) system hasn't been programmed and/or isn't working right—and even if it were, the staff hasn't had enough training to confidently ring in a glass of milk. Not to mention that half the wine coming in the door is the wrong price or the wrong vintage, and the chef is tweaking all the dishes you thought you had paired earlier that week because suddenly the produce guy can't get arugula. You pull sixteen-hour days for two weeks, and it still feels like you've gotten nowhere and you're never going to make it. Emotionally, it's like speeding by a motorcycle cop while doing double the speed limit—you know you're screwed, and it's going to cost you, but you can't even conceive of hitting the brakes. I get a little stressed just typing this out. Post–Restaurant Opening Stress Syndrome isn't widely recognized by the mental health community, but it should be.

So it was under this sort of duress that I went ahead and guessed.

There were about fifteen items on the menu that still hadn't been paired, but the pairings were due so that the menus could be printed. Needless to say, I couldn't get around to actually trying things out—either the kitchen couldn't get the dish together, or I didn't have the right wine in the building yet. So I did what I suspect the vast majority of restaurants in the world do on a daily basis: I made a number of educated guesses. I had no choice—but I also had no fear. After all, I was a food service professional with years of pairing a number of different cuisines under my belt. I simply imagined what the dish tasted like based on the chef's description, recalled a variety of personal and professional experiences, and probably checked the Internet. (Never ask the Internet, by the way. More on that later.) All in all, the menu copy looked good, and while a part of me knew it wasn't ideal, we were under the gun. Also, did I mention I was a confident restaurant veteran?

And I would have totally gotten away with it if it wasn't for that pesky Chenin Blanc.

In my Mind Mouth, the idea of this specific South African Chenin Blanc with the white anchovies was a wine pairing slam dunk; the Chenin had a fatter style to match the mouthfeel of the oil, and there was a touch of residual sugar to deal with the salt and the spice—the choice was easy, bordering on obvious.

About a week into the opening, the general manager, Dan, caught me by the end of the bar. "Say, Horn . . . have you tried the white anchovy pairing?" I hadn't, but I assumed he wanted to congratulate me on being a food and wine–pairing genius. "You might want to give it a try," he said.

I did give it a try. I took a bite of the fish—a preparation in the spirit of classic Spanish tapas. It was fresh, salty, and delicious. Then I took bite of the fish and chased it with a healthy swig of the South African Chenin Blanc.

The result was tongue slaughter. The pairing took perfectly fresh flavors and accelerated them all the way to late decomposition. The wine made my mouth feel as if I'd just consumed a fistful of rotten fish. It was utterly vile, and to add insult to injury, I couldn't seem to get the taste out of my mouth for what felt like days.

I know what shame tastes like, I guess.

When I look up the bottle today, the Internet recommends, "This wine should be served slightly chilled as an aperitif, or with lighter seafood dishes." Yeah, I tried that and look what happened.

From that point on, the decree has been that every food and wine pairing in our restaurant was to be road tested by human mouths. No more guessing—guessing about food and wine pairing should always be the first step of the process rather than the last.

The Back of the Bottle

Here's part of the problem with food and wine pairing as a *thing*: turn around the average bottle of wine in the store and read the back label. "Goes well with red meat, cheese, and spicy and earthy foods." (I have found this on many a bottle of Bordeaux—there must be an export manager who has convinced the Bordelais that we choose our wines based on the back label, and that every dinner table in America will have one or more of these things on it nightly.) Or check the back of a bottle of Cabernet from Australia: "Perfect for spicy Mediterranean dishes or lamb curry." When is the last time most of us put together a proper lamb curry? How about a spicy Mediterranean dish? And if you've ever had spicy food with a tannic wine (like an Aussie Cabernet), then you know that the marriage of those two elements actually intensifies the spice heat.

Here's a crucial thing to know about the back label of a bottle of wine: it has to be approved by the Alcohol and Tobacco Tax and Trade Bureau (known generally as the TTB). The process of getting a Certification of Label Approval is neither easy nor speedy, so the declaration of simpatico between Cabernet Sauvignon and the lamb curry was written well before the grapes were even harvested—even before the wine was bottled, stuck in a box, and sent across the ocean. In fact, once a label gets approved, they will use that template, unedited, for many vintages—because leaving it alone means avoiding the bureaucracy of changing it.

Since August of 2006, we have paired thousands of dishes. Every day at 3:30 p.m. the chef team meets us at the end of the bar (that same place where I got the news of the grand fish failure) to pair the specials. Additionally, the sommelier team maintains a dry erase board of every dish on the menu and the preferred pairing. Our nightly e-mails detail the day's pairings, and everybody contributes to the end result.

This painstaking pairing methodology has influenced the way I approach buying wines for the restaurant, and I would like to think that it has influenced the way the back of the house approaches the creation and execution of cuisine. Because we're in the same boat—I want my wines to taste good, and they want their food to taste great.

Coach in his natural habitat: the Purple Café kitchen

Drink Whatever You Like with Whatever You Like, or *The Story of Prawns and Cabernet*

When I was a culinary school instructor, we always wanted to put food and wine pairing into the curriculum, but we were restrained by the fact that we had a large number of students who were underage. A lot of us instructors had a very good grip on the subject and we really wanted to share this knowledge, but the school was adamant about the potential liability of even having the underage students *smell* wine. To be honest, it was the right call. You have to taste both the food and the wine for all of this stuff to work.

Fortunately, we got to teach a continuing education series every summer for high school home economics teachers. (Do they even teach home economics anymore?) They would come to the school and take six classes of four hours each on pairing food and wine. It was the greatest win-win of the whole seven years that I taught school. The teachers would get some continuing education credits, and we instructors would get an absurd amount of extra pocket money for teaching the courses. Unlike our normal college-level courses, there was no testing or grading—and culinary students were volunteering to clean everything! It was great. Even more absurd is that somehow we convinced whomever was in charge of this thing that teaching a whole course on food and wine pairing was pertinent to bettering the teachers'

ability to educate their students. In actuality, we were teaching these fellow teachers about how to enjoy themselves, and we were somehow getting credit on paper for doing something far more important.

So we had carte blanche with this curriculum, which prompted us to think about classic wine and food pairings that we could show the class as examples. Then a brilliant colleague of mine, who was our dining room instructor for the school and the cagiest of old restaurant veterans, came up with the idea of illustrating utterly awful wine pairings as well. The idea being that if you experienced how bad it could be, you could dismiss that "Drink whatever you like with whatever you like" mantra that was being disturbingly bandied about in the late '90s (probably by wine producers who, back then, were making some of the least food-friendly wines of all time). We wanted people to know that while they *could* drink whatever they wanted with whatever they wanted, it could taste really, really fucking bad.

We thought about it, but oddly, there wasn't a big list somewhere of pairings to avoid—only pairings to try. This is one of the examples we came up with: Olive Oil–Sautéed Prawns with the biggest, richest California Cabernet Sauvignon we could afford to pour.

I tasted this nauseating pairing right along with the students every year. I really wanted to remind myself of just how horrific a food and wine combination could be. (It was usually a good wine too, because we would use the same wine and pair it with grilled rib eye later in the class.) It was metallic, fishy, shrill, bitter, overly tannic, and absolutely cringeworthy. It was bad enough to come just short of making you want to gag. The mouth tended to flood with saliva, which felt like a physiological defense mechanism

kicking in—the body's way of saying, "I'm going to flush this nastiness out." Some of the students told me that they couldn't shake it off for a half hour or more, despite an onslaught of mineral water.

Oddly, despite the fact that we had just done them harm, the home ec teachers were absolutely enlightened by the exercise. They thanked us. They had been buying into the "drink what you like" hype, but they had never pushed it as far as prawns with Cabernet Sauvignon. Many of them had never considered food and wine pairing until they'd signed up for our class, and those who had mostly admitted that they were reading the back of wine labels to figure out what to pair with.

All winemakers want to sell their wines. They don't want you to believe that you can't drink one of their wines with every meal. Many people trust the words about food and wine pairing on that wine label, but few consider the motivation behind those words.

Intrigued? Read on.

What You Drink with What You Eat Is a Fairly Big Deal

What's the big deal, really? We hear it all the time—if you like the food and you like the wine, what's the big bother?

Well, here's what I think: if you take pleasure in your life with any amount of seriousness, then why settle for something less than awesome? It's like an audiophile shrugging his shoulders about his crappy six-by-nine-inch speaker with a shoe box for a cabinet and saying, "I like the song, so who cares about fidelity?" It's like a great script and a terrible cast: "We love Shakespeare, so who cares if the actors were weimaraners in period dress?"

What you drink with what you eat is a big deal.

Let's break some things down: There are hundreds of beverages on earth more delicious than milk. That known and agreed upon, there is no other beverage to consider when offered a vulgarly portioned slice of chocolate cake at a birthday party. It is natural to reach for the milk when the cake is cut—in fact it's a question of personal safety if one is hosting a birthday party for a gaggle of elementary school kids. (Can you imagine the fallout of ruining your kid's fifth birthday party by forgetting to pick up that extra gallon of 2%? I'm almost positive Stephen King wrote a story about it.)

So yeah, milk and chocolate cake—the people demand it, and no other option approaches reasonable. In fact, it's entirely *un*reasonable to expect chocolate cake without milk.

But for some reason, wanting people to drink Chablis with their oysters is seen as some brand of elitist snobbery.

Can something be both delicious and snobby? Our thesis is that it cannot. If putting the right food with the right wine results in inarguable pleasure, then it is patently not snobbery.

So let's agree that a food and liquid pairing resulting in a positive flavor experience repeated over the course of many years is not snobby but *awesome*—and should not be reserved for birthdays, but inculcated into how we approach everything we eat.

Milk, Cake, and Cookies

From a chef's point of view, the pairing of milk with sweets is perfect for a reason. We hear about lactic acid when referencing milk. It is true. Milk is acidic, and acid balances salt, fat, and starch. Milk *seems* rich (and it does contain a small amount of fat), but it actually cuts through richness. Which is why you can often drink a whole glass of milk with cookies and cake, even if your adult mind doesn't like the thought of drinking a glass of milk.

Unless . . . your glass of milk contains two shots of espresso, and it's hot, and it's served in a paper cup. Then a glass of milk is OK. I used to say that I didn't drink milk; I only used it as an ingredient. I thought I verified this by how little milk I purchased for my home. It turns out that I buy my "drinking" milk on the outside, at coffee shops. I think a lot of us do.

This page and next: Two of the world's finest food and beverage pairings. You wouldn't want anything else with chocolate chip cookies, and you shouldn't want anything else with oysters.

What this love of milk and coffee means flavor-wise is that you're playing the lactose, or milk sugar, angle. Milk sugar balances bitter coffee. Add additional sweetness to that combination if you like, such as syrup or sugar, and it will soften the bitterness and the acid of the coffee even more. Personally, I like the internal balance of just whole milk with the coffee. Whole milk is sweet, rich, and acidic. That combination to me is perfect with acidic and bitter coffee. Adding more sweetness like sugar or honey adds complexity to this flavor, but the coffee flavor loses intensity at the same time. This process is known as rounding off flavors. Using fat to soften acidity, or sugar to diminish bitterness are but a few of the techniques employed by this philosophy. Rounding flavors off is not always desirable, but it can also be done with deliberate intention.

Finely made chocolate chip cookies are one of the best pairings for a glass of milk, neat (I love the idea of ordering milk neat). First, the milk has to be cold. Second, the milk should be 2%. Whole milk is better than skim, but 2% is best. Acid, sugar, and fat are nicely balanced in the milk. There is sugar, salt, bitter, and fat in the cookies. A ton of flavors interacting at once.

Remember, milk is a simple beverage, as noted previously. There are hundreds of beverages on earth more interesting than milk. Can you imagine opening a meal with a glass of milk? Or celebrating a college graduation with milk? Yet this simple beverage can make chocolate cake or chocolate cookies sing.

All we are doing when trying to pair your food and wine is to give you that milk-and-cake kind of pleasure with something far more exciting to drink. So many amazing experiences await those who are willing to try new things.

We think that much of the snobbery surrounding wine drinking has been derived from the jerks who spent decades trying to make wine into some sort of private club. The cost of admittance was tons of arcane knowledge, coupled with some thespian skills that were used to fling copious amounts of bullshit at a subject when knowledge fell short. We love it when guests admit that they don't know something. It is an opportunity to transfer some of our knowledge to them and lead them to experience a whole new pleasure in life. Imagine if we were the only ones that knew about the milk and cookies? We'd be pretty uncool if we didn't share that wonderful knowledge with everyone we knew.

The Hope

Falling in love with the challenges and satisfactions of pairing wine with food is different than falling in love with wine. For some inexplicable reason there is a separation; it's like claiming to be a baseball fan while only paying attention to the infield.

Or only playing the white keys on a piano.

Or only caring about the words and ignoring the melody.

If we can do one good thing here, it would be to encourage everybody to end the separation. We all love food. We all love wine. Let's get the band back together.

Introducing The Term Mind Mouth

Sommeliers hear it all the time: "I don't know anything about wine," said as if we are owed an apology from those who have decided to not memorize vintages, geographies, producers, grapes, history, and other wine minutiae. It's akin to apologizing to your mechanic about not understanding the ins and outs of a carburetor. (I actually had to Google *car parts* to complete that metaphor. I don't apologize for it. I know nothing about cars, but I still really enjoy driving one.) (And apparently cars no longer have carburetors.)

It's not a perfect analogy—to become a professional mechanic, one has to have a natural aptitude and temperament. I know this because as one of two boys growing up, I couldn't so much as check my oil, whereas my brother has rebuilt entire engines. (It's not hyperbole—I killed two cars in college through the simple failure to add oil. My brother has successfully torn down and rebuilt an actual engine to an actual car.)

Here's the truth: by the time you reach drinking age, you've had well over 20,000 meals. While most of those experiences were likely repetitions, it's still an impressive mouth workout when you consider the trillions of flavor molecules you've encountered. It's easy to profess that just about every food texture (good and bad) on earth has been in your mouth, as well as a whole range of temperatures. And you've definitely identified some flavors that you prefer to others.

You might not yet know it, but the most important outcome of the consumption of these thousands of flavors is the creation and development of a powerful and vibrant Mind Mouth. You're already a flavor expert. You just don't know it.

But wait—what's a Mind Mouth? It's the place where you imagine the taste of an orange when I say, "Imagine the taste of an orange." It's the place where you process the menu at a restaurant to decide what sounds good. It's the place that informs your ratio of peanut butter to jelly when you're making a sandwich.

So how do we take your flavor expertise and package it in a way that

can be used every day of your life?
One step at a time.

- **STEP ONE:** Introducing you to your amazing mouth and the basic structural elements of wine
- **STEP TWO:** Enduring Coach's dissertation on FLAVOR
- **STEP THREE:** Understanding how the structural elements in wine generally react with food
- **STEP FOUR:** Reintroducing you to your Mind Mouth
- **STEP FIVE:** Putting it all together

It sounds like a lot of work, but it's not. The mouth you were born with has already done most of the work for you.

Getting to Know Your Mind Mouth

The human mouth is an amazing thing. Read it again, but slowly . . . out loud . . . and why not: make it personal. "My mouth is amazing." In addition to flavors, your mouth has the ability to detect weight, acidity, and tannin—it is a specialized flavor supercollider. Incredible things are happening in there every day of your life, quite literally under your nose.

So, on to the first three unavoidable wine terms: **body**, **acidity**, and **tannin**.

Get Milk, or What We Talk About When We Talk About Body

When we describe a wine, the subject of body is important. Sometimes we use the term *mouth weight*. I think of body as the frame or the packaging for all the flavors.

Body is also the easiest of these three concepts to get one's mouth around.

I'm uncertain whom to give credit to for this brilliant analogy, but I'd like to shake his/her hand and buy the drinks, since finding a tool to help us all speak quantitatively and definitively about any aspect of wine is the work of a genius. The clearest way to explain the body of a wine is to think about milk.

In the world of wine, body falls into three easy categories: light, medium, and full. Therefore, the easiest way to calibrate it is to actually get a hold of three glasses of milk: skim, 2%, and whole. We do this in wine classes: break out a carton of each "weight" of milk and ask people to put it in their mouths, swish it about, and think hard about how it *feels*. It's something worth doing, because it's more than just speaking to viscosity.

I have been borrowing the milk analogy for years. But it wasn't until I began to question *why* that I sent a message to Coach and asked him to put things on a scale.

Whole milk is obviously more viscous than skim—but it turns out it also weighs more. Not by much, but your mouth is an amazing place and can detect even the slightest changes in weight:

- 200 ml of whole milk weighs 7.15 ounces
- 200 ml of 2% milk weighs 6.75 ounces
- 200 ml of skim weighs 6.70 ounces

When tasting a wine, consider how it feels in your mouth—light like nonfat milk, heavy like whole milk, or that something in between. You can do it. Your mouth is amazing.

Acid Trip, or Put the Lime in the Margarita

It turns out that, in addition to being a scale, your mouth is also an acid tester.

In wine, acid is the mouth *energy*. Acid is the activator. Acid is the party starter. Acid ignites the chemical reaction that leads to flavor. (Acid is also the lime that you squeeze in your margarita.)

There are a number of natural acids in grapes that end up in your glass of wine. The types and levels of acidity vary from grape to grape, and rather than get into the science of acidity, let's just say that acid is ultimately a good thing to have around when you're eating food.

When something acidic is introduced to your mouth, your body reacts by throwing an alkaline solution onto that acid to maintain a healthy pH level—and that alkaline solution is your saliva. It's not the sexiest aspect of wine, but it's the very reason we humans have developed a cultural affinity for drinking wine with food over the last 6,000 years. (And in cultures that don't have a history of wine production and consumption, you'll find that they like to add vinegars and squeeze citrus on things, making acid a vital part of that cuisine.) Saliva multitasks as an acid neutralizer and taste turbocharger. It breaks down your food and releases the aroma molecules that we call flavor.

So—in order to fully understand acid, one has only to mix a margarita. Or go to a bar and have somebody make you one—but make sure you ask them to leave out the lime. (You'll want to request a couple wedges for the experiment, however.) Take a sip and think about how much your mouth is watering. It's likely consistent with what happens when you sip your average sweetened and acidified cocktail: your mouth is watering, but you're also perceiving sweetness and perhaps a bit of a warmness from the booze. Give your mouth a bit of time to recover, then start in with the limes. (It's best to squeeze at least the equivalent of half a lime to really feel the impact.)

You know it's going to be tart—try to ignore the strong lime flavor. What you should experience is a relatively vigorous watering in your mouth as your body is sending a larger volume of alkaline solution in order to protect your mouth and teeth from the acid in the lime.

So your mouth is an acid-testing machine. Amazing.

By the way, this experiment also applies to the Bloody Mary. Or a Cuba Libre. And any beer you traditionally garnish with a lime. It is an experiment worth repeating . . .

Tannin, or Don't be Bitter— Have a Tea Party

Tannin is mouth *texture*. Tannin is the agitator. Tannin is the dryer. Tannin can come across as a gentle astringency or full kung fu–grip mouth drama.

But what is it exactly? Like everything in wine, the answer can be as complex as it is boring. (Just ask my wife.) The short answer (that will still induce a yawn from my wife): tannins are the compounds found in the skins and seeds of grapes, as well as in oak barrels, that produce the feeling of astringency in the mouth. Tannin is something else your mouth easily detects, and is translated as a sensation of drying.

Tannins are found mostly in red wines—but not exclusively.

The fastest way to familiarize yourself with what tannins feel like is the tea test. Ever accidentally left a tea bag in your cup for way too long? If you have, then you know that the result was a dramatically strong and bitter liquid whose fate was the drain—but you also replicated the best way to understand what people talk about when they talk about tannins. If you haven't, it's as simple as it is important. Toss a tea bag in a cup of hot water, and start the clock. Take a sip of the tea after two minutes. Feel the slight drying sensation when you swallow? Now take a sip after five minutes—notice the difference in the drying sensation? The fuzzy and dry feeling is the result of higher tannins steeped into the tea. And if you're not sure yet, take a sip after ten minutes of steeping and brace yourself.

It's certainly not the most pleasurable exercise to conduct. Luckily, you only have to do this once. (Maybe go back and have the margarita after this. You deserve it.)

Review of the Big Three

What's the big deal with needing to know these three characteristics of wine?

When it comes to pairing food and wine, body, acid, and tannin are the food and wine pairing starting blocks. The first three questions in the interrogation.

I check the weather every morning when I wake up. I check to see the range of temperature, the chance of rain, and if wind is going to be an issue. And maybe it's the result of living in the Pacific Northwest, but my daily wardrobe choices are made based on the information supplied by The Weather Channel app on my phone.

So if you're going to wear the right clothes, you need to read the forecast. And if you're going to pair food and wine, you need to process the body, acid, and tannin of wine.

All things being equal—memorize these basic formulas:

- Body=Weight=Milk
- Acid=Energy=Margarita
- Tannin=Texture=Tea

What is Flavor?

Taste

Taste is perceived on the tongue. Tastes can be five things: sweet, salty, sour (haughtily, we've decided to say *acidic* in the food and wine business), bitter, and/or savory, which is what the Japanese refer to as umami. If you say something tastes like raspberries, you are likely including its aroma in combination with the berries being sweet and acidic in taste. That is what flavor is. Flavor is the *combination* of taste, aroma, and mouthfeel.

Combinations of tastes, not even considering aromas, are extremely powerful. Salty-sweet, bittersweet, and sweet-sour remain some of the most satisfying and sought-after taste combinations on earth. Oddly, only a small, but important, component of the *flavor* of a dish is ascertained by its *taste*.

Aroma

Taste is a very basic perception until one combines it with the power of aroma. There are literally thousands of different, discernable smells that we are capable of perceiving. Compare that to only five tastes, and it becomes easy to understand why sommeliers spend so much time with their nose in the glass before ever taking a sip. The problem with aroma is that we don't have a million different words to describe these many perceptions.

We, especially those of us stuck speaking English, generally don't have enough aroma words to fill a small notebook. English is not equipped with a huge number of aroma words. We tend to refer to aromas as analogous to something else, and we use lots of similes to do it. A wine smells *like* honeysuckle and pear. The words *honeysuckle* or *pear* lack unique words to describe them. When we are stuck without a word, we almost start to sound like children. As an example, we often are forced to refer to certain kinds of cheese as "stinky," which is hardly a precise term. There are others, but they are relatively analogy-driven as well: floral, fruity, sharp, hot, briny, fetid, smoky, etc. We mostly describe aromas by comparing one aroma to another to illustrate what something smells like.

Mouthfeel

Smoothness is a mouthfeel, as is crispy, and gritty, and effervescent. Some of the most powerful eating experiences we have are not taste- or aroma-driven at all. Potato chips or popcorn aren't about the taste or aroma of the potatoes or corn; they're all about the texture. Sometimes we wrap the texture of foods into our overall perception of that food's flavor. Soft, oil-poached potato chips, with the identical amount of seasoning as crispy potato chips, would still seem to have a different flavor. Truth is they would.

Chile heat is a mouthfeel. Horseradish heat is somewhere between an aroma and a mouthfeel. Chile heat actually stimulates pain receptors in your mouth, but just like a belly flop, or a snowball fight, or a tattoo brings a pleasurable level of pain, so do hot chiles for many, many cultures. If you need any more proof that chile heat is not a taste, consider this: the sensation that is often perceived the day after enjoying those same chiles is in an area of the body where we are all thankful that no taste buds exist.

Flavor

Flavor is a description of the entire olfactory experience, which is to say that the olfactory bulb (the section of our nervous system that perceives these sensations) is being stimulated with tastes and aromas, and the mouth is texturally being stimulated by mouthfeel. This total combination of tastes, aromas, and mouthfeels is the sensation we call flavor. It is one of the most complex sensations we experience, often because it is very difficult to put flavors into words.

Trying to describe the flavor of butter-pecan ice cream might go something like this: salty pecans, sweet ice cream, with a hint of vanilla. Smooth ice cream is offset by the occasional crunch of a pecan. One might then say that the "nuttiness" is perceivable, or that there are hints of caramelized sugar and butter in the ice cream. A scientist could further complicate your perception by referring to the pH level given by lactic acid in the cream, and the rich, heavy body provided by the fat in the cream and egg yolks. Now, would this description be enough to satisfy someone who had never tried butter-pecan ice cream? In some ways yes, especially if they've had a lot of ice cream in their lives.

Special Sensations and Combinations, or Balancing Acts

ACID BALANCES FAT

You'll hear us both use the term *acid* with the frequency of a Grateful Dead biography. We drop acid into just about every conversation we have about food and wine pairing—because it is arguably the most important element in the collision between food and wine.

Ever had a vinaigrette? Or a butter sauce? Or mayonnaise? These preparations are all examples of how powerful and versatile the flavor of acidity balanced by fat can be. In culinary terms we say that the acidity is "cutting" the richness. This can also be true of wine. Just because the acid is in the glass doesn't mean it isn't playing a role in mitigating a rich dish. For this reason, Mr. Horn and I like to use acidic wines for contrast pairings with rich dishes.

Next time you're in the snack aisle, look at the bags of potato chips. You will notice that there is significantly more sodium in the salt and vinegar flavored chips. The simple reason for this is that salt and acid tend to nullify each other on the palate. This is only up to a point, though—otherwise salt and vinegar chips wouldn't exist. The beauty of this relationship really shines when we start talking about wines. Foods that are often salty by design (like popcorn or french fries) tend to really shine with highly acidic wines (like Champagne or Chablis).

This flavor match can be exploited for your own nefarious purposes. We weren't kidding about that popcorn. Try the salt and acid relationship yourself, with fine Champagne. Yep, the good stuff. Butter the popcorn to the point that it is almost soggy, and use really good butter. Then douse it with some fine sea salt like fleur de sel or Maldon salt. Then alternate bites of popcorn with sips of Champagne. This is best done sitting down and in the presence of attractive people as it can easily make one weak in the knees.

SALT BALANCES TANNINS

Tannin is that mouth-drying effect that walnuts or really sharp cheese have. These effects are countered by salt. Salt tends to make your mouth water. Again this is only to a point. Things can potentially be too salty or too tannic for the counterbalance to take place. The science on this flavor relationship is still somewhat inconclusive, but we've certainly put it into effect at Purple Café many times. A can of mixed nuts really illustrates this as well. The nuts with skin still on them like walnuts or hazelnuts would be incredibly tannic without the salt. We don't notice this sensation nearly as much in the presence of salt.

Special Sensations and Combinations

BITTER ENHANCES SWEET

It would seem that these tastes cancel one another, but they don't. They work much like sweet and sour. It is like holding something white against something black. They do tend to *soften* each other, however. Coffee is less bitter with some sugar added, but the bitterness doesn't go away either. Straight sugar will taste less and less sweet by adding coffee to it, but the sweetness would purportedly never actually go away.

This concept is very well illustrated in the world of chocolate. In fact, the chocolate guys have recently taken to actually putting a number on the label of fine chocolate. This number represents the percentage of cacao in the chocolate. While not a perfect analogy, we have colloquially taken to using this cacao percentage as a *bitterness* percentage. There will be less sugar as the number gets higher. Use your Mind Mouth to mentally perceive the difference between 50 percent, 70 percent, and 90 percent chocolate. All of them are bitter, but the sweetness can still be perceived as well. They don't cancel, they simultaneously enhance and soften each other.

Bittersweet chocolate and coffee are great. Dark caramel, molasses, rum, and crème brûlée are also good examples of how much we like bitter and sweet flavors together.

SALTY ENHANCES SWEET

To me, this is the most powerful and intense taste combination on earth. Both of these tastes are known for really ramping up the overall flavor of a dish. Ice cream without sugar is a nearly flavorless custard. Add some salt and broth to it, heat it up, and you just made Sauce Allemande. (No one makes Sauce Allemande anymore, but you see the point.) Without the salt or sugar, you have virtually *no flavor*. The flavor begins to be perceived with the addition of these two very powerful tastes.

Recently, and fortunately, pastry chefs, chocolatiers, and candy makers have begun to really ramp up the amount of salt used in desserts. Sea salt caramels are everywhere now. Think of how powerful the flavor profile is. Think of the ice cream above sprinkled with just a tiny bit of fine sea salt. Odd at first, perhaps, but it definitely ramps up the intensity. My mom first noticed my obsession with this idea when she saw me sprinkling salt on a PB&J. Crunchy Maldon salt really ties the room together on a PB&J.

Payday candy bars; foie gras and Sauternes; candy corn; Thai food; stilton and Port; pineapple and ham; melon and prosciutto; and cheddar and apple are all great examples of how people all over the world have been combining salt and sweet tastes for hundreds of years. A testament to how incredibly delicious this combination can be.

General Guidelines to Keep in Mind about Food and Wine, *or* Mind Mouth Manual

CLASSIC FOOD AND WINE INTERACTIONS

The relationship between food and wine can be broken into two parts: the structural and the attitudinal.

STRUCTURAL RELATIONSHIPS BETWEEN FOOD AND WINE:

- Tannin loves fat
- Acid seeks equal(ish) acid
- Sweetness seeks equal(ish) sweetness
- Sweetness has a thing for spice
- Sweetness loves salt (and from looking at this list, sweetness gets around)
- High alcohol destroys everything we love

EXPERIENTIAL RELATIONSHIPS BETWEEN FOOD AND WINE:

- Body
- Intensity
- Flavor Spectrum

UMAMI ENHANCES EVERYTHING

Umami, from a scientific perspective, is represented by the presence of glutamates. These glutamates have an effect on the human palate that makes things taste more savory. The Japanese word itself literally has no English translation, but the best understanding of it is a sense of mouth-filling richness in the absence of fat, a sort of overall deliciousness that fills the elusive middle part of the palate. A great thing about umami is that it serves to prop up other tastes such as salty or sweet. It doesn't eclipse any of the four basic tastes, but rather enhances them. Think of soy sauce, a rich mushroom sauce, balsamic vinegar, Parmigiano-Reggiano, aged ham, or most importantly, Japanese dashi broth, which is thought to be the source of the first observations regarding this sensation.

Picture in your Mind Mouth a bowl of incredibly savory chicken broth. That umami flavor is very present (say we even added a little MSG). Now think if we added honey to it, or lemon juice, or a big pinch of salt. That basic savoriness would still be present. Umami tends to fill the middle palate and the inner cheeks, two physical areas that are a bit difficult to stimulate with food.

What Happens When You Taste Things

Think about an orange.

What happens when we taste is more than the sum of the five tastes in the mouth (bitter, salt, sweet, sour, umami) and the addition of dissolved flavor molecules wafting into our retronasal passage. When we taste, we catalog—it's how we end up with a list of favorite foods and favorite drinks. We've more than enough information to form personal and thorough opinions because we've been keeping files on everything and storing them in our Mind Mouth.

Tasting is also remembering, based on the fact that you can't stick something in a drawer without also seeing at least some of the contents of said drawer. When you eat a burger you're eating it in the context of every other burger you've ever had. How do you know that the burger in your hands is any good? You compare it to the myriad of burgers in the drawer of your Mind Mouth.

What's additionally great is that so many flavors get attached to other types of memories that fine-tune perception—like how I can easily recall (for better or worse) what a Whopper with Cheese tastes like, because back in high school we used to love to skip swim practice to run across the street and stuff our faces. (And come to think of it, I remember that Chris Accetola and I also developed a rating system for Big Macs—our discerning palates could tell when there was the proper amount of Special Sauce applied.) Remembering the thing itself often recalls the context of attached experiences.

Tasting is also social—we spend so much of our lives talking about restaurants, dinner parties, food trucks, and coffee stands. So when you taste, you are also cataloging what you might say later about the food in your mouth (even if it's as simple as what it was you ate). I dare anybody to go a week without having some manner of expressed opinion or social discussion of food. You can't. (And I think that it's because at our core we believe that flavor is a magical thing, and we can't help but want to talk to people about it.)

Tasting is also emotional—the "comfort" in comfort food. And it's not just recollecting that you love your mom's meatloaf—it's the fact that we feel food as much as we do music. (It makes me want to listen to my favorite music with my favorite food. Heck, add in my favorite people and I bet whatever I open will end up being one of my favorite wines.)

So when you taste, it all starts in the mouth with:

- Sweet
- Sour
- Salt
- Bitterness
- Umami

Which is then added to the information through molecules in the retronasal passage (your nose).

Which sends the information to the brain in order to identify flavor. But along the way, whether we're aware of it or not, we all:

- Compile
- Catalog
- Remember
- Cross-reference
- Feel

Still thinking about that orange? Good, because you're not just thinking about the color, but the flavor, texture, acidity, and sweetness. You might be thinking about how it smells when you peel it. You might be thinking of marmalade on toast. You might be thinking of when you picked some off a tree and made a fresh-squeezed Screwdriver. Or the time you left that carton of orange juice in your dorm room fridge over winter break, and the smell of it when you got back. (Oh, so that's why they ask you to clean your fridges out before you go—they turn off the power for a week.) You might be thinking of that orange-flavored gum that you chewed maniacally for years. (It was weird, but compelling.) Or an ice-cold bottle of orange soda. You also might hate oranges and have ceased reading this paragraph several sentences ago.

The point is that on the subject of oranges, you're likely a master with thousands of experiences of the flavor *orange*. And you've also got quite a thick catalog of other flavor experiences filed away in your mind, ready for recall.

So that's what your Mind Mouth is: a place where we recall flavors, textures, and experiences. A place where we can combine flavors through the imagination of flavors—so that you can precisely recall not only the singular ingredients of a peanut butter and jelly sandwich, but the sum total.

That's the approach of playing sommelier: put things together in your Mind Mouth and really give them a go. It's not just (as some say) the understanding of how certain wines react with certain foods—it's being able to also taste them in your brain.

I can hear Coach saying, "Yeah, Horn. So tell me how you can sometimes look at a dish you've never had before and kill it with one shot. How the hell did you come up with Muscadet with Mexican?"

You don't have to taste a dish to taste it in your head. (That's what we do when we read a menu in a restaurant—we pick the one that tastes the best in our Mind Mouth.) You can imagine the mouthfeel, sweetness, saltiness, spice, etc. And if you've been drinking wine thoughtfully for any amount of time, you'll be able to swish that imagined dish around with any number of recalled wine experiences and start to narrow things down. And if that dish was conceived with wine in mind, things should end up pretty good.

So stop ignoring your Mind Mouth and start participating—sit up and notice what you think about when you are tasting food and drinking wine. The next time you're having a burger, try to think of every burger you've ever eaten. Then when you reach for that glass of Zinfandel, think about every Zinfandel you've ever consumed. Now think about how they taste together. Then you're on your way to having a brand-new drawer in your Mind Mouth labeled "Food and Wine Pairing." Put it right next to the drawer that contains the information on general guidelines to keep in mind about food and wine.

And if for no other reason than to convince you of the mouth's supreme talent and ability, we'll break down the elements of wine in terms that are easily processed and understood. The first step in understanding the language of wine is the fact that your mouth already understands the words . . .

Exercise Your Mind Mouth

STEP 1: Grab your favorite cookbook.

STEP 2: Open it up to a recipe you have made in the past.

STEP 3: Read the ingredient list, refresh your memory on the cooking steps, and glance at the picture.

STEP 4: Close your eyes; taste it in your Mind Mouth.

STEP 5: Imagine washing it down with as many different types of wine as you can.

Repeat the exercise, only this time do it with a recipe you haven't made. Write down the type or types of wine that worked well in your Mind Mouth. Add the wine choices to the list of ingredients, and when you go shopping, pick those up as well.

It will feel like homework at first. Stick with it. Once you get into the habit of picking out your accompanying wine when you go shopping for dinner, you'll wonder how you managed to live without this technique.

Tying It All Together

Imagine it's your first week of training at the restaurant. You've been given a burdensome binder full of policies and procedures; menus and recipes; study guides and quizzes. You're scheduled to spend time with every department in the restaurant regardless of the duty you were hired to perform. One of those scheduled observations is at three thirty at the end of the tasting bar: Pairing.

You make your way up the stairs a few minutes early and sit down. On the shelf behind the bar are about forty bottles of red wine and a jumble of ports and dessert wines. Not visible but close at hand are a number of refrigerators stocked with an almost equal number of white wines. It's daunting to think about knowing what all those bottles are, let alone what they might taste like.

Your thoughts are interrupted by people in chef coats placing plates of food on the bar next to you. With them is some guy in a tie. The Chef Types explain in detail to the guy in the tie what the dishes are while he sticks his nose alarmingly close to the plates of food.

Glasses and forks materialize, and the Chef Types take a bite. They discuss if any seasoning or flavor adjustments are needed.

Meanwhile, the guy in the tie paces up and down the bar, touching bottles and muttering either to himself or to the wine. He whirls around and opens the door to one of the many wine fridges and squats down out of sight. You hear the sound of bottles clicking together—the sound of rummaging. When he stands up, he's holding a bottle of wine and squinting at it like a shopper who left their shopping list on the kitchen counter—unsure if the item in hand is needed.

The Chef Types become impatient and use really colorful language to express their lack of patience. *They don't got all day.*

The guy in the tie uses equally colorful language in order to convey his lack of concern about their impatience while he pours a small amount of wine in everybody's glass.

Forks go into the dish. All attempt to collect every component on the plate in order to deliver one neat, perfect bite. More colorful language is used. The only thing that stops the banter is food placed in their mouths.

Food is chewed. Wine is swigged. Flavors are swished. The guy in the tie walks down the bar and spits into the sink—a gesture normally reserved for near poisonings or sudden sickness—but he's got a smile on his face.

You sift through the curse words to ascertain that everybody is happy, and that victory has been won. The dish is good. The wine is good. But together, the experience is awesome. Confetti cannons erupt and a drill team streams through the front door. Guy in the tie is hoisted on the shoulders of the culinary team, and track two of Queen's *Greatest Hits* blares from the restaurant's sound system.

Good story—but it doesn't happen that way very often. (And when it does, there is no hoisting or soundtrack.)

Here's what really happens every day in the restaurant:

The dish is explained in detail. Ingredients. Cooking techniques. Intentions. Culinary traditions or inspirations. Finishing. Also, the chef responsible for the dish may mention what sort of wine they had in mind when conceiving it. The Dish Dossier is the first step in processing the potential flavors.

It is more or less like opening up a cookbook, reading the ingredient list in a recipe, and skimming the cooking instructions. You can go a long way toward finding the right wine before you even imagine the flavors in your Mind Mouth.

Here are things to look out for:

- ACIDIC ELEMENTS—Vinegar, citrus fruit/juice, anything pickled
- SALTY ELEMENTS—Everything from olives to anchovies to capers. If there's going to be a pop of saltiness, have it on your radar.
- FATTY ELEMENTS—You may be dealing with things as obvious as marbled meat or as subtle as caul fat used to secure a stuffed trout.
- SPICY ELEMENTS—Spice in terms of either heat or intense flavor

Then I look at the dish. It's like looking at the picture in the cookbook. I'm seeing if the ingredients came through the cooking process as expected, and that I understand the extent of those techniques. Many cooking techniques change the flavor of the ingredients, so I have to take that into account.

Techniques that can dramatically alter flavors:

- Smoking
- Grilling
- Searing
- Broiling
- Roasting

Techniques that alter flavors less dramatically:

- Boiling
- Poaching
- Steaming
- Baking

The extent to which an element on the plate is altered by its cooking method must also be taken into consideration. For instance, roasting at a high temperature will brown your meats, while slow roasting will not.

Then I smell it. Seventy-five percent of what we call flavor is our sense of smell, so from just that, I've a good idea of what is going on. (Granted, this is the thing you can't do with a cookbook—but it is something you can do while you're cooking. It might seem awkward at first, but if you smell your ingredients while preparing a recipe, you're going to have a lot more insight into the overall composition of flavors.)

If you know the ingredients, the cooking techniques, and you've experienced the aromas of the dish, you're quite capable of tasting the flavors in your Mind Mouth. At that point, we're ready to start thinking about what wines may or may not go with the dish.

Size Things Up

You want an even match. Remember the analogy of nonfat, 2%, and whole milk: the weight of the wine should align with the weight of the food. For the lactose intolerant, I've compared it to putting on a weather-appropriate coat: If it's 90 degrees outside, you're not going to put on a ski parka. If the dish centers on subtle and light flavors, you'll want your wine to be similarly weighted. Conversely, a T-shirt in a snow storm is a bad idea.

Structure

Remember the description of acidity in wine as the *energy*. You want to make sure that the energy of the food is matched with equal energy in the glass. The batteries have to be the same—you can't mix 9-volts with AAAs, or the machine won't work.

Most recipes include acidic elements, be they from citrus juice, vinegar, wine, tomato products, or dairy products. (Tomato-based sauces are a great example of a common food that is high in acidity.) When the food is particularly acidic, you'll want to make sure that the wine has an equal (or greater) amount of acidity. And since we don't walk around with pH meters in our pockets, the relationship here will be one that you have some control of when cooking. For instance, when dealing with a recipe that calls for any finishing acid—squeeze of lime, drizzle of vinegar—taste your wine with the dish first. You might find that you can reduce the amount of acidity you add to a dish according to the wine selection.

The Flavor Game

After sizing things up, it's time to start considering specific flavor elements in the dish. This is where we think about those classic interactions between food and wine that will influence the relationship of the two.

APPROACH #1: CONSIDER CULINARY ROOTS

We love the catchy "grows together, goes together" rhyme, and it's not a bad place to start. If the recipe represents (or borrows from) classic regional cuisine in a wine-producing country, check to see if there is a historical match. It doesn't always work, but when it does, there's something undeniably soulful and satisfying about traditional flavor combinations, like Coq au Vin with red Burgundy.

APPROACH #2: BUILD BRIDGES

If the dish contains flavor elements you also find in wine, give it a shot. Ceviche with a Sauvignon Blanc is a summer staple because the citrus flavors in the dish bridge to the lemon/lime/grapefruit flavors in the wine, creating great mouth harmony. When I see mushrooms in a dish, I start looking for an earthy Pinot or Gamay Noir. Rich butter sauce loves a rich, buttery Chardonnay. Pear and spinach salad with Pinot Gris. The list goes on and on—if you see a bridge between an ingredient and a wine, walk it on over.

APPROACH #3: CONTRAST FLAVORS

Build drama. Pairings based on contrast between the wine and food can be more difficult—but it's worth the effort when it works out. Take Asian cuisine, for example. There isn't exactly a long-standing regional wine tradition to draw from, and there are less obvious bridges between the ingredients of most Asian dishes and wine. Add to that one of the bigger pairing speed bumps: spice. So by getting your hands on a wine with some residual sugar, you've a perfect contrast pairing on your hands: sweet versus spicy. (Might we recommend a German Riesling?)

Chef-Free Food and Wine Experiences

On the Subject of Chef-Free Food and Wine Experiences, or Before We Dismiss the Chef

This whole thing started with the idea that a chef and a sommelier could get together and offer advice on how to thoughtfully approach food and wine. Perhaps a book that might get you to agree with the notion that—just like chocolate cake and milk—it is vitally important to have the right liquids with the right solids. Our ultimate goal: convincing you to have wine be a part of your daily life, making everything you do taste and feel better.

So we sat down one afternoon and talked about some profound first experiences that have since become part of our lives—and certain ones kept coming up:

That time in the backyard where there was much shucking and slurping oysters, and swigging Chablis and Muscadet.

Replacing butter with oaky Chardonnay when cracking Dungeness crab just hours after pulling up the crab pots.

The mind-blowing flavor of Fino Sherry when you have an assortment of salty edibles at hand.

How our 20s would have been better if we'd understood that microwaved hot dogs just needed Riesling.

The polarizing status of blue cheese and the marginalization of Port—and the impossibly awesome things that

happen when you get the two of them together.

It became obvious that some of the best food and wine pairings *don't require any real cooking*. These are what we've dubbed "Chef-Free" dishes.

And so we've gone forward with the concept of Chef-Free food and wine pairings as a vehicle to introduce you to these elemental experiences that resonate and inform everything we do.

Let it be known that Coach was responsible for writing the bulk of this section—which is extensive. It reminds me that these two subjects—food and wine—are inexhaustible. No matter how many wines I taste in any given year, it will only be a fraction of what is produced in any given vintage. And no matter how simple the question you ask, Coach will always have several pages of answers . . .

Oysters and Chablis

WHAT GROWS TOGETHER, GOES TOGETHER PAIRING

One of the fondest memories of my life was the time I was standing on Mr. Horn's back porch with a bunch of chefs and other industry types, drinking Premier Cru Chablis and slurping oysters. We all kept looking at each other, nonverbally affirming how perfect this pairing was. It got to the point that I was openly giggling and shaking my head. That experience was a revelation to me. I'd always heard that this was the most textbook food and wine pairing on the planet, and here I was, tasting it for myself and realizing that it really is a perfect food and wine experience. We'd tried the pairing before many times with Petit Chablis, but here was an incredibly well-made, admittedly expensive wine that was special. I am truly grateful that Mr. Horn invited me to share that experience.

One of the things that Mr. Horn is going to tell you is that the soil in Chablis has oyster shells in it. Chablis is perfectly suited to oysters, despite being far from any sea. Crazy permutation of "grows together, goes together." But again, it works.

That day we were lucky enough to be drinking Premier Cru Chablis and eating oysters together. (By the way, *cru* is a French term used to reference higher-quality vineyards.) It was an unusually decadent experience, and one that lived up to the hype. I felt like no one on earth was having a better food and beverage experience than we were that day. However, oysters absolutely love much less expensive and easier-to-find wines like Muscadet just as much.

Shucking oysters can be challenging, even a little dangerous. To make matters slightly more difficult, you really need to make sure that you preserve as much of the oyster's natural liquid as possible. This is known to aficionados as the liquor or the nectar. Next is to make sure that the adductor

Kumamoto

Dabob Bay

Penn Cove

Kusshi

Fanny Bay

Nisqually

muscles are severed (these are the muscles holding the oyster to the shell itself.) There are usually two: one on the top, and one on the bottom of the sealed shell. You cannot slurp an oyster without these muscles being severed because the oyster won't slide out of its shell. Once in a while, even at the best oyster bars, you get an oyster that you can't slurp out because it is still tethered to the shell by the adductor muscle. Most of us just reach up into the shell with a finger and nimbly push the oyster into our maw without apology when this happens, but it is best to make the oyster as easy as possible to eat for your guests, especially if they are already a little trepidatious about eating raw oysters.

An old saying tells us to eat oysters only in a month that has an *R* in it. This is basically September to April. Warm water makes most oysters want to spawn (produce eggs), and this creates off-flavors in the oysters—which is particularly disappointing, because bracingly cold oysters on the back patio with delicious chilled beverages sounds like just the thing for a hot summer day, in a month far from one with an *R* in it. On the West Coast, especially in the Pacific Northwest, we have taken measures to keep this from happening by getting with our Japanese friends and literally engineering oysters. This engineering includes manipulating the oyster beds to produce deep cups on the lower shell, as well as genetically

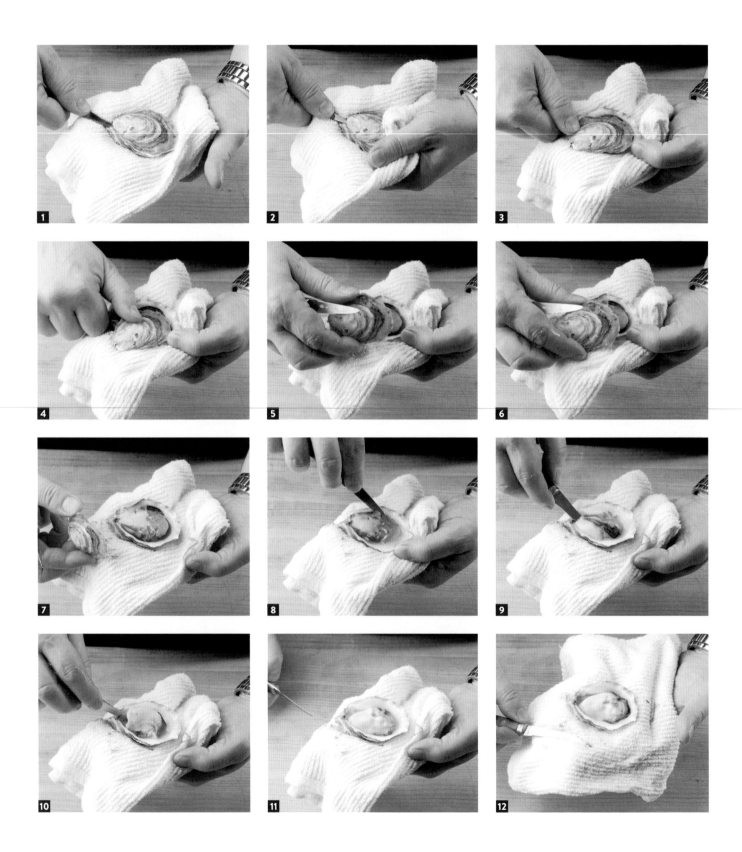

sterilizing the oysters to keep them from spawning in warm waters. These oysters taste great year-round. (The water in the North Atlantic doesn't warm as fast or as much as Pacific waters, so the northernmost bays in Canada and Maine enjoy very cold water way into the summer.)

Here's a helpful list of year-round oysters. In the cold-water months you have hundreds to choose from, but in the summer I would recommend these:

- **KUMAMOTO:** Pacific Northwest, United States; Canada
- **KUSSHI:** Pacific Northwest, United States; Canada
- **SHIGOKU:** Pacific Northwest, United States; Canada
- **FANNY BAY SELECTS:** Pacific Northwest, United States; Canada
- **MERMAID COVE:** Prince Edward Island, Canada
- **HURRICANE ISLAND:** New Brunswick, Canada
- **PEMAQUID, MAINE:** United States
- **NAKED COWBOY:** Long Island Sound, United States

Shucking oysters is not terribly difficult. You just need to be careful, as the consequences of an error can be severe. My bride, who is also a chef, accidentally stuck an oyster knife about an inch deep into the muscle between her index finger and thumb. Nasty injury for certain, and almost entirely attributed to trying to shuck oysters way too fast, in a restaurant setting. At home, the most important things are hold tight, go slow, and always be aware of where the tip of that blade is. Also, try to be aware of where that blade will go should it slip, and make sure your hand is not there. Just pad it up well with towels, be completely aware of the oyster and your surroundings, and don't rush. Let the guys doing oyster-shucking competitions go blazingly fast.

You're going to need quite a few towels that you really don't care for too much, because they're going to get filthy with mud, bits of shell, seawater, ice, etc. You will hold the oyster with a couple of layers of neatly folded towel. This is to prevent the jagged, sharp shells from cutting up your hand, and serve as some protection for the possibility that the knife takes an errant route away from the oyster.

You're also going to need an oyster knife, a deep plate (ideally an aluminum oyster pan), and a way to crush ice. We recommend something called a Lewis Bag. You just load it with ice and then hammer it with a mallet, rolling pin, or the flat side of a pan. Then you pour out the crushed ice. Pre-shucking oysters is nice, but they will dry out and start to degrade in quality once they are opened. Find a happy medium. Be a dozen or so ahead of your guests while you're shucking, then start serving and try to keep up . . . safely. Don't risk a deep puncture wound to satisfy an impatient dining companion.

If you don't wish to deal with crushed ice, then we recommend using ordinary rock salt. You can chill the salt in the freezer and it will hold a deep chill for at least half an hour. We actually think rock salt is a far superior solution to crushed ice as it does the same job (keeps the critters cold), and doesn't let your oysters become submerged in fresh water.

1 Hold the oyster firmly in a folded towel and insert the knife into the hinge end.

2 Push and wiggle the knife gently until you feel the seal between the top and the cup release.

3 Angle the knife upward toward the top shell.

4 With an angled, scraping motion, pull the knife through the top adductor muscle, all the way across the top shell.

5 Remove the top shell. If it is still stuck to the oyster, cut the muscle with your knife. Do not pull or tear at it.

6 Discard the top shell.

7 You are halfway there; you now need to severe the bottom adductor muscle.

8 In a circular motion, cut around the lower shell until you feel the bottom adductor sever.

9 Insert the flat of your knife under the oyster.

10 Preserving as much "liquor" as possible, turn the oyster over to the presentation side.

11 Remove any loose pieces of shell or dirt from the bottom shell; keep it level to retain as much liquor as possible.

12 You now have an oyster on the half shell, ready to be slurped with some tasty Chablis.

When enjoying wines so perfectly suited for these delicious bivalves, one need not embellish the oysters with anything but wine. If you really feel the need to put something on the oysters, dribble a little bit of the wine on them. It is sensational. Dismiss all thoughts of needing a mignonette, lemon, or—heaven forbid—stronger additives like hot sauce, horseradish, or cocktail sauce. You might love these accompaniments with oysters, and on the right occasion we do too, but this is a world-class wine pairing, and the Chablis, Champagne, or Muscadet will taste shrill and insipid with the addition of these ingredients.

The Wine

Most people reasonably check out when wine people start to talk about soil, but we're not going talk soil science here. I actually don't entirely understand the science, and I'm not convinced any of us do. But you don't need to have a master's degree in music theory to enjoy going to the symphony.

150,000 years ago, areas of Champagne, Chablis and the Loire Valley of France were under the ocean. We know this to be true, since the soil found in many parts of these wine growing regions is comprised of limestone, clay, and tiny fossilized oyster shells and marine skeletons.

Proof that there is magic in the world: the experience of washing down freshly shucked oysters while drinking wine made with grapes grown in Kimmeridgian soil. (That's what they call the dirt with the fossilized sea shells. . . . .)

So here's what we're doing when we drink Chablis with oysters: eating a food that comes from the dirt that used to be under the ocean, and is therefore grown in the very thing that is the food. Beautiful.

This is our battle cry for caring about food and wine pairing. No pairing is quite as soulful.

There are truths in the world of food and wine—experiences that have been repeated for centuries based on the fate that geography bestows on what appears on the menu and in the glass. We like the phrase, "What grows together, goes together," mostly because it rhymes, but partly because it's true. Oysters and Chablis is a metaphysical version of what grows together goes together.

Shuck an oyster, wash it down with Chablis. Hakuna matata.

Almonds, Olives, and Cured Meats

WITH FINO SHERRY: COMPLEMENTARY BRIDGE PAIRING

Finding excellent almonds in the United States is easier than it has ever been. The best ones I've ever tasted are Spanish Marconas from Zingerman's in Ann Arbor, Michigan. Zingerman's is meticulous about sourcing, and you can order it online. Even though as of this writing they are $9 for four ounces, you will not be disappointed by these, even if you've tried other brands of Marconas.

This doesn't mean that you shouldn't seek the best Marcona almonds in your local market. They're available in most well-stocked grocery stores now, but you can always order them online if you're unsure of your grocer's scruples about freshness. They do need to be fresh. The oils within them will go rancid quickly.

The striking thing about Marcona almonds is that they are actually sweet. Not candy-sweet, but certainly sweet for nuts. I hate to disparage my friends from California, but their almonds are better suited for baking and salads than for this very special pairing.

When you do find Marconas, use them right away; they don't improve by sitting around. These almonds are almost always blanched, fried, or roasted, but if you manage to find them raw, you should absolutely roast them drizzled with good olive oil and then lavish them with high-quality sea salt. If you buy them already processed in some way, then just slightly warm them before serving. No more than 2 to 3 minutes in a 350°F oven should do the trick (you're not re-roasting them, just warming them up). Then you'll pair the warm, slightly soft almonds with the crisp and chilled sherry. Amazing contrast.

Taking this idea to the next level, heat some duck fat in a pan and when it just begins to shimmer, toss the almonds in the duck fat for 20 to 30 seconds. No more. Then pour off the excess fat and serve them warm. Duck fat Marconas. It's the right thing to do.

What about the olives?

Most olives that you find in the jarred section of the grocery store are of relatively poor quality, and if you wish to experience this pairing to its fullest, those jarred olives

Read Your Labels, Folks

Unfortunately, as of 2007, the USDA requires that all California almonds be pasteurized, making truly raw almonds almost entirely unavailable. If you must buy California almonds, do a little research to make sure they have been steam-pasteurized versus treated with propylene oxide. This nasty chemical was approved by the FDA and USDA after just two cases of salmonella occurred, stemming from commercial almond orchards. This chemical's primary use is in the production of polyurethane plastics. It's also been used as a racing fuel, but was banned for safety reasons. Sound delicious?

will not suffice. Don't try this pairing if you can't get your hands on good olives. The olives I'm talking about are unlikely to be in your run-of-the-mill neighborhood grocery store. Spend the time to find them, perhaps in a more gourmet-style market or online.

It is no surprise that Spanish olives work best for this pairing. Arbequinas and Manzanillas are both spectacular with sherry. Don't limit yourself, though. Buy as many different kinds of olives as you can, even the oil-cured, jet-black Moroccan ones. With dry sherry, they all show different facets of a complex wine pairing.

In addition, don't worry if they have pits. Pitted olives are great with pasta (so you don't crush a molar), but when you're having Fino Sherry, just provide your guests with a means to dispose of the pits other than your houseplant pots, your garbage disposal, or behind your couch.

Be careful of premarinated olives; they are often harsh and over-seasoned. You can apply a custom marinade yourself in a matter of minutes. I highly recommend taking some decent, but not pungent, olive oil and heating it up with a bay leaf, a few strips of orange peel (without the white pith), fennel seeds, and peppercorns, then pouring the warm oil over your olives. Dried chiles, star anise, cumin seeds, coriander seeds, allspice berries, other citrus peels, and even cloves can work. All manner of woody herbs like thyme, rosemary, savory, and sage work well too. Just be careful of making your marinade too busy, and make sure the aromatics actually smell good together before you add them all to the oil. Otherwise, the sky's the

limit. Some of the tastiest olives I've ever had were Picholines marinated very subtly with tangerine peels, fennel seeds, lavender, and toasted coriander. You could perceive the flavors if you tried, but they didn't knock the wind out of you. Expert marination.

Lastly—and this is something so many people skip: please warm your olives before serving them. Just a quick toss in a sauté pan or a few minutes in a hot oven will do the trick. They should not get so hot that they can't be picked up. Just warm. Olive oil "freezes" or hardens under refrigeration. This means that olives can seem tough when they're cold (they obviously contain a lot of olive oil). Even room temperature doesn't do them as much justice as they deserve. Warm olives are also a great complement to the cool Fino Sherry.

Here are some olives we like:

- CASTELVETRANO: From Italy, these are bright green and very mild and buttery.

- KALAMATA: Greek olives, and some of the easiest specialty olives to find. Fruity and bitter.

- MANZANILLA: From Spain, these are the olives you typically see stuffed with pimientos. Shop carefully. The cheapest ones are seldom the best.

- TAGGIASCA: Italian, sweet, and fruity. Often used in olive oil production but a superb eating olive as well.

- NIÇOISE: French, but related to the tagiassca, these are small olives with herbal and bitter notes. Lots of flavor in a tiny package.

Castelvetrano

Kalamata

Cerignola

Oil Cured

Picholine

Niçoise

Salame Toscano

Coppa

Jamón Serrano

Marcona Almonds

Spanish Chorizo

Prosciutto San Daniele

- **PICHOLINE:** The most buttery, rich olive in wide distribution. From the south of France.
- **GAETA:** Citrusy with a silky texture. From the heel of the boot in Italy's Puglia region.
- **CERIGNOLA:** These large olives are available green and also an almost unnaturally bright red color. The red ones are very mild and buttery, with a firm texture. Also from Puglia.
- **NYON:** Almost always served wrinkly and cured, they have a pronounced bitterness and herbal flavor. These olives hail from the south of France and Morocco.
- **SEVILLANO:** These are from California. The manner in which they're preserved leaves an almost crisp texture.

Serrano Ham

After years of tasting and serving fine cured meat products, we have settled on the fact that the Spanish make the world's most complex and beautiful hams. Not to disparage the ham made in Italy or the United States, but Spanish jamón, when cut properly, yields perfectly gossamer slices of ham which, in a non-hyperbolic way, feel like they melt on your tongue.

Prosciutto means ham in Italian. Jamón means ham in Spanish. We try to tell people to think of these words the same way. For decades, the United States has perceived Italian prosciutto as the greatest ham available. That's because up until recently it was. Now there are incredible Spanish hams available in the US market, and they should be considered with the same reverence. They certainly are priced that way.

At the restaurant, we use jamón Serrano Paleta, which is a relatively affordable ham made from the shoulder of the pig rather than the leg. If we didn't have to charge so much, we'd use jamón Ibérico, which is the finest ham on earth. It comes from pigs that, as the time for slaughter approaches, are fed nothing but almonds, acorns, and olives. The meat is then cured with nothing but sea salt and air for up to four years.

As with any product on earth, there is a pinnacle, a product that knows no equal. In this case, the best dry-cured ham is known as jamón Ibérico de Bellota. This means that the pigs (a special breed known as *pata negra*) were fed exclusively acorns, and that the hams made from those pigs have been aged a minimum of three years. No exaggeration: plan to pay in the vicinity of $60 to $80 per pound for this product. Just remember, this ham is sliced infinitesimally thin, and the idea of buying a whole pound of sliced de Bellota seems absurd even to those of us who serve 4,000 guests a week. Go buy yourself a *tenth* of a pound and see how many slices you end up with. In other words, if you see it, buy it—even if only a little.

Cured Meats

THAT'S A BIG SUBJECT

 And not one we're going to get into terribly deeply here. Basically all you need to know to make this work is that the meats should be cured, not cured and cooked. That means prosciutto, Smithfield ham, jamón Serrano or Ibérico, or other dry-cured hams. You'll want to stay away from Black Forest, or jambon Francais, or Honey Maple. Those are hams that have been cured or brined, but then cooked, whether steamed or oven-roasted. While delicious for sandwiches and other applications, they lack the complex flavors that dry-cured products have, which are relatively essential for the pairing.

Likewise, look for dry-cured sausages as opposed to fresh sausage (the type that you purchase raw, either in bulk form or as links, and cook). Dry-cured sausages can include just about any variety that requires taking a sharp knife or a meat slicer to. Cured with salt and air, often bacterial cultures, and time, dry-cured sausages take on a lactic, spicy, fermented quality, which absolutely sings when paired with sherry.

There are many brands of these meats that we could recommend, but quite frankly there has never been a time in the world where more of these meats are being made artisanally for the commercial market. At Purple Café, we've used a least a dozen different high-quality brands of these meats

with excellent results. We just recommend that you have them sliced for you (or slice them as thin as possible yourself) as close to the time that you will be eating them as possible. They do degrade in flavor very rapidly over time, and may dry or discolor.

The Wine

In the restaurant, we garnish our Fino Sherry with olives for no other reason than getting that pairing in people's mouths. As good as the salt-on-salt experience of Fino and olives goes, the combination of chilled Fino and warm Marconas is perfection. The flavors in the wine reflect everything that is important about the almonds: nutty, salty, toasty. Same goes for meats—oxidized meat with slightly oxidized wine. Salt in the meat hits saline flavors of the Fino. Flavor bingo.

Which brings us to Fino Sherry.

First things first: Sherry comes from a sun-scorched region in southern Spain called Jerez. (The pronunciation: heh-RETH. It appears incongruous, but Jerez has gone by a number of names, some of which sound close to "sherry.") The geographical hallmarks of Jerez: its proximity to the sea and its chalky white *albariza* soil. (Great for moisture retention—a necessary function in order to endure the hot growing season.) It's important to recognize the geographical hallmark of Jerez in order to avoid imposter bottles produced elsewhere that are not even suitable for cooking with—but it's

the vinification method that is worth taking the time to understand.

Palomino is the grape. As grapes go, it's rather unremarkable. You won't see it used outside of Jerez. Not a ton of personality, but hearty enough to handle some weather. (Palomino is the grape equivalent of an extreme marathon runner, capable of withstanding duress and maintaining composure. But like watching somebody run for 100-plus miles, it's rather boring.)

Harvest happens in Jerez like most other places in Spain. Grapes are brought into the winery and the sugars ferment, resulting in a dry white wine that clocks about 12% alcohol. The winery then assesses the quality of their wines, and only the finest are chosen to be positioned in the Fino system. The first step: **fortify** (unavoidable wine term meaning to add brandy) the wine to 15%. From there, the fortified liquid

is placed in oak barrels—and here's where things get interesting.

In most parts of the wine world, oak barrels are filled to the point of overflowing in order to protect the wine from oxidation. (Unavoidable wine term: **oxidation**—the same process that produces rust and turns your avocado brown when you leave it out on the counter too long. In wine, it's the first leg on the road trip to vinegar.) In Jerez, rather than filling the 600-liter barrel to the rim, only 500 liters are added. In this oxidative state (fancy way of saying "with oxygen"), most wines would perish—but in Jerez, there's something quite magical in the air.

Unavoidable wine term: **flor**. Flor is an indigenous yeast group that lives in Jerez and thrives in a specific range of humidity, temperature, and alcoholic strength. The space left in the barrel allows it to flourish, forming a protective blanket on the surface of the sherry—protecting the liquid from oxygen while interacting with various compounds in the liquid. In winemaking, you'll generally hear about yeast converting sugar into alcohol. In Jerez, these specific, local, naturally occurring yeasts also convert alcohol and other components of wine into a myriad of aromas and flavors. It's what makes the flavor of sherry impossible to re-create (you can't do this sort of thing in a lab). The result of the flor layer is a clean, clear white wine with flavors and aromas that are difficult to find anywhere else in the world.

So if a crazy biological yeast blanket isn't enough to separate the production of sherry from most every other wine in the world, we run into another unavoidable wine subject: the **solera system**.

Please don't turn the page. It may not be as sexy as indigenous yeast blankets—but it's the other half of the sherry production story.

The bottle of Fino you buy has spent several years in a barrel—but not the same one.

The solera system is hard to explain, and try as I might (using everything from diagrams to puppets), I've never found a great analogy. It was only after weeks of agonizing over how to simply explain the solera system that it dawned on me—and I can thank my shower-averse son for the inspiration.

Key to the concept of the solera system is a technique called fractional blending. In terms we can all understand, fractional blending is what you do when you take a bath.

What? Well, part of the story is that flor giveth and it taketh away. While it creates an array of complex flavors and aromas, it also slowly reduces alcohol levels and consumes the nutrients that allow it to live. Flor is a diva, and will cease to do its job if environmental conditions (read: alcohol and nutrients) drop below a certain threshold. So the removal of a portion of the lower-alcohol liquid followed by the addition of nutrient-rich, higher-alcohol liquid ensures it will keep chugging along. It's like taking a bath. You pour a hot bath, but after ten minutes of spa soaking, the temperature has dropped enough to where you pull the plug and let out a few inches of water. Then you top off with more hot. It's like that, but with barrels of wine.

The older barrels (at the bottom of the stack) have been there for a few years, and the flor has been doing its job of interacting with the liquid, producing all sorts of amazing aromas, but the alcohol needs a little boosting to stay in the sweet spot (15.0% to 15.4% alcohol by volume) where the flor can thrive. A portion of the lower-alcohol liquid is taken out and replaced by some younger wine with a higher alcohol content. It's a complicated process—the wine world's version of spinning plates—maintaining balance in order to produce a wine like nothing else.

Here's the thing with this particular pairing—like everything in this book, we set about to examine the relationship between the wine and the food in a strictly academic mode—turning our home kitchen into our test kitchen with a myriad of meats, olives, and Marcona almonds. But it was a repeat of our oyster experiment: Instead of the scientist holding up the beaker and exclaiming, "Eureka!" we were just a bunch of idiots (again) saying the word "Dude."

Holy shit. Drink sherry.

Here is a great example of a pairing built on complementary bridges that are hallmark flavors of sherry: nuts and salt. Fino Sherry has an undeniable nutty flavor imparted by a touch of oxidation and by the distinct flavors imparted by flor—sometimes it manifests as walnuts, hazelnuts, or almonds. (And just typing this makes me want to pair Fino Sherry with mixed nuts.) Then there is the saltiness—Fino has an underlying saline flavor that some attribute to its close proximity to the sea. Throwing salty wine at salty nuts, olives, and meats creates a magically diminished salty sensation—because it unleashes all the flavors lurking underneath.

Oxidized wine bridges to oxidized meat.

Nutty wine bridges to nutty food.

Salty wine bridges to and tempers salty food.

Dungeness Crab and Chardonnay

WINE AS SAUCE PAIRING:
A Note of Personal Bias

Dungeness crabs are the best-eating crabs in the world. I know that phrase will create some indignation, especially amongst East Coasters who swear by very delicious blue crabs and stone crabs. There are also those who prefer crab species from Alaska, whether it be snow crab or king crab—also fine examples of delicious crustacean flesh. Something about Dungeness is special, though, particularly with Chardonnay. Dungeness crabs have beautifully nutty, almost popcorn-like, sweet flesh. Coincidentally, these are flavors found in well-made Chardonnay wines, whether they are from the New or Old World. For this pairing, the most important characteristic is that these wines must be oaked.

Start with Cold Crab

This is, after all, a Chef-Free experience we're talking about, so in the spirit of the exercise we will first do the pairing with chilled crab. After thirty years of eating Dungeness crab, and a lifetime of eating blue crab, I still have no preference for crab being hot or cold. Chilled crab is amazing in salads, with a handsomely crafted cocktail sauce, or even dipped into melted butter, creating a beguiling temperature contrast on the palate. For this pairing, we are going to stick with the melted butter, as it is perfect with the Chardonnay. Pro tip: Most crabs are pre-packaged steamed by the bushel, which means the smallest crabs suffer from being overcooked to ensure that the larger crabs aren't undercooked. Buy the larger crabs. They are far less likely to be stringy and rubbery from overcooking. We only recommend buying cooked crab when eating it chilled. Reheating cooked crab is likely to produce sadly overcooked crabmeat.

Suppose We Have Some Time to Cook?

First of all, even though we very biasedly prefer Dungeness crab, this method works for any species. First of all, **BUY THEM LIVE** if you possibly can. Crab meat is like lobster, and to a lesser extent, shrimp. All crustaceans have a very perishable, very tasty "liver" (known as the tomalley in lobsters). It is actually the animal's hepatopancreas. This organ works hard to break down whatever the animal eats when it's alive, but unfortunately does the same thing to its own flesh after its demise. This is why we have to keep the animals alive or cook them immediately after killing them. They literally begin to digest themselves upon death. Consider the act of keeping them alive as preserving this delicious, yet somehow dangerous organ up to the last possible second before consumption.

So now we have to cook. Steaming or boiling? Steaming presents the advantage of minimizing the amount of water absorbed by the crab while it's cooking. But what if that water being absorbed was tremendously flavorful? If it were able to impregnate the meat with extra tastiness? If that is desired, boiling is the ticket. We use both methods. Steaming the crab is perfect for when you want nothing but the pure, clean flavor of impeccably fresh crab. Boiling is great for adding all manner of aromatics to the flavor of the meat via the boiling liquid, such as wine, spices, herbs, and aromatic vegetables like leeks, onions, garlic, celery, or carrots. You can even go nuts and do it Chinese-style with fermented black beans, soy, ginger, and scallions. Or Thai-style with lemongrass, galangal, shallots, chiles, and fish sauce.

The sky's the limit. To recap, if you want the perfectly pure, immaculate flavor of crab, steam them. If you want to bring something else to the party, make a crab boil, and take them where you want to go.

Of course you'll want to take the crab out of the shell first.

The Crab Boil

Basically the crab boil is made up of anything you want the crab to take on the flavor of, and there are many pre-packaged choices out there. Having said that, here's one we like for the Chardonnay pairing:

- Leeks
- Sweet onions (Walla Walla, Vidalia)
- Celery
- Carrots
- Chardonnay
- A couple of cut-up lemons
- A fresh bay leaf
- Lemon thyme (find it or grow it—it works)
- Lots of salt
- Corn cobs (really great if you've got them around)

Put the crab boil ingredients in a large stockpot, fill with water to one inch above the contents of the pot, and boil them together for about 20 minutes. Taste the liquid. It should be excellent and flavorful. It should also be salty. If it isn't, you MUST add salt. The crabmeat came from seawater. It is inherently a little bit salty. Remember that osmosis stuff from back in high school biology? Even if you don't remember, in a nutshell if you don't match the saltiness of the liquid that you cook the crab in with the salinity of the actual crab, you will have bland crab. The liquid will leach the salt from the crabmeat so that the salinity of the crab and liquid become equal.

Boil or steam the crabs for right around 7 minutes per pound. Start your timer once the water reboils. I find that this ratio seems to work with all crabs, blue or Dungeness, large or small. Take the average weight if you're cooking a lot of crabs at once. If you're a crazed anal-retent like me, you will place the smaller crabs near the top of the pot so you can pluck them out first while the other crabs finish, thus ensuring that all of them are perfectly cooked.

If you insist on rewarming crab that you've already cooked, I recommend very gentle, ambient steam. Bring the water to a boil in the steamer, put the crabs in the pot, turn the heat off, and cover. Let them sit in that steam for 7 to 10 minutes, and they should be reheated rather nicely without further cooking them too terribly much.

Another great method to reheat whole crabs is on a real charcoal grill. Throw them on, cover the grill, and wait 3 to 5 minutes. They should be sizzling like crazy from the moisture coming out of them. This method picks up some really nice smoky aromas that Chardonnay loves. Grilled crab is a little on the dry side, and there's no way to avoid that, but the additional flavors can make up for it. I don't recommend boiling crab to reheat it, as it gets waterlogged and can wash away some of the gorgeous flavors that you strove so hard to capture with the initial cooking method.

We've Got a Live One Here!

OK, so if you have crabs that you actually caught, they won't have the convenient rubber bands around the claws that the fishmonger is nice enough to slip on for you. Crab claws are damn sharp. Think of it as more like being pinched with jagged, dull scissors. Luckily, these animals have a weakness, which is that you can grab them from behind and they can't reach their claws back far enough to get you. This is even better accomplished using some sturdy tongs. For heaven's sake, keep your fingers, young children, innocent bystanders, and your groin out of the reach of those claws or your crab feast will be supplanted by an ER run.

Make the flavorful crab-boil broth as described on page 67, then drop all of the crabs into the steamer or the boiling broth at once, and start your timer from when the water reboils. Put a lid on either operation, but leave it an inch or two ajar to let some of the steam escape. Too much extra pressure in the pot can make the crab meat tough, and/or will likely result in a messy, smelly boiling-over incident.

This dish is best served on newspaper-covered picnic tables. (What will we serve shellfish boils upon when we finally eradicate paper newspapers from our society?) Incidentally, fine Chardonnay still tastes great out of a disposable plastic cup. Don't believe me? Try it outdoors, cracking crabs, on soon-to-be-endangered newspapers. It is part of the pairing.

The Wine

 Here's why this pairing works: butter. You won't need any. If you have a bottle of overblown and oaky California Chardonnay at your disposal, there will be no need to bother with the mess of melting down a stick of butter.

I'll take it a step further: dip the crab directly into the wine. It sounds like the confluence of insanity and sacrilege, but please allow yourself to go a bit crazy and sully the glass. And if you're doing things properly, your hands are a mess anyway—it's going to be safer to dunk the crab than attempt to lift the glass up to your face.

Wine as sauce. It's not at all a revolutionary way of looking at things, but you'll feel like a rebel when doing it.

I don't know if it needs any more elaboration than this: sometimes your wine is the sauce. In order to have this work, you're going to have to seek out a Chardonnay that is "buttery."

How does "butter" happen in wine? Unavoidable wine term: **malolactic fermentation**. It's a step in winemaking embraced by many Chardonnay producers that converts the tart malic acid in the grapes to softer lactic acid. It's the difference between the acidity in a green apple and the acidity in milk—the latter is rounder, less jarring. It's not unique to Chardonnay (all red wines go through this conversion), but it has become a hallmark flavor component—and the only clear way to describe it is *buttery*. Thought to be a negative by only those who have never dipped a chunk of Dungeness in a properly slutty glass of Chardonnay . . .

Hot Dogs and Riesling

CONTRAST PAIRING

Hot dogs. Not what we typically think of as a great food for pairing with wine. Actually, a hot dog is an opportunity to use that off-dry Riesling in your fridge that Mr. Horn will insist you have on hand at all times. Think about it: hot dogs are sausages. In fact they are the mildest of sausages.

So there they sit in your fridge, the culinary embodiment of giving up. You can actually get this meal into your face, piping hot, in 75 seconds. Don't let the simplicity bother you, because the pairing with Riesling is actually perfect. Top the hot dog with what you like, but nothing should be applied too heavily. You will have the best experience if you choose raw onions, sauerkraut, and mustard. These are classic sausage toppings in Germany. This is not the place to take your dog "Chicago-style" with fresh tomatoes, neon green relish, and celery salt. You're basically pairing a German-style sausage with a German-style wine. Delicious.

The reality is that you don't have to cook like Thomas Keller to enjoy a great food and wine pairing. Good for you if you can, but in the case of this pairing you need only possess the ability to operate a microwave. This pairing is just as delicious as pairing absurdly expensive raw oysters and even more expensive Chablis, but requires no skill.

Microwaving, while not exactly the recommended culinary method for almost everything else, actually works for hot dogs. Take 75 seconds to microwave a couple of dogs, 15 seconds to put mustard on them, 60 seconds to open and pour the wine, and let's say 5 minutes to taste and retaste what seems to be an impossibly easy food and wine pairing.

You can take this pairing into the stratosphere with some good sourcing and, as always, a little planning and patience. Suppose you were to buy high-quality, German-style frankfurters that are produced with a "skin" or natural casing? This casing would insure a high-quality product in and of itself, because the economics of stuffing a hot dog versus just baking or steaming them in a mold weeds out all but the most artisanal producers. The trope around my house is that hot dogs of this quality provide "the satisfying POP of the natural casing." Not all are disciples of this philosophy, but those are the ones that married into the family.

What It Comes Down To

Pairing food and wine isn't magic, it's practice.

You can heave a ball toward a hoop as many times as you care to—but to get really good at basketball, you'd need coaching.

I suck at basketball, but that doesn't mean I don't like playing Horse.

Food and wine pairing is like HORSE?

You can be a crap basketball player but still enjoy playing the game until you're old and your knees give out. You can throw that ball at the hoop and feel the satisfaction of knowing the physics and of trying to create the swish—both additionally pleasurable when the ball goes in.

But at the very least, you're playing the game. Pairing food and wine is a game, and it's fun when you win. But even if you lose, you get better, and you end up a little less sober through the process.

There's enough out there in the world to keep us from playing games. Play this game every day, and you'll get good. Hell, you might even someday hit nothing but net from midcourt.

For the record, I hate sports metaphors.

Cooking Hot Dogs

One can cook a hot dog in a lot of different ways. To be true to the spirit of this pairing, you will microwave them. If you wish to take things out of the Chef-Free realm, then you can start applying some culinary methodology to your dogs for enhanced results.

PROPER MICROWAVING

Simple. Blast the raw (hopefully naturally cased) tube steaks at high for 45 seconds in any microwave. What would likely follow in other texts is that "All microwaves vary." That really doesn't matter. Blast the dogs at 45 seconds on high, then assess. If they aren't squeaking, literally squeaking, then blast them for another 20 seconds. You'll hear them squeaking through the door. Should you have the world's weakest microwave, blast them again. Take two large paper towels and run them under cold water. Then squeeze all of the water out of them, vigorously. Place the now hushed dogs in some bread (the more it resembles a hot dog bun, the better, but we're not pairing the bun). Then wrap the whole assemblage in the damp paper towels. Blast the whole package on high for another 30 seconds. Remove the paper towels, top with desired toppings, and start pairing.

GRILLING

Hot dogs on the grill: perfect for beer. If you want to drink Riesling with this cooking method, that's cool too. I imagine it would be delicious. I've never had wine with a grilled hot dog. I'll eventually try it, I suppose, but it's hard to keep from wanting a beer with a charred hot dog. There is something patently American about grilling a couple of tube steaks over charcoal, in a backyard, tongs in one hand and a delicious frothy beer in the other.

PAN-SEARING

Now we're talking. This is a thoughtful, cerebral way to cook a hot dog. Luckily it is rewarded with a better-tasting hot dog that is even more delicious with Riesling. Just heat up some oil in a pan. Medium heat is perfect. Put the hot dogs in the oil and slowly sear them to a crispy brown on all sides. Take your time doing this and you'll be rewarded with beautiful caramelization that only makes the pairing with Riesling taste better.

BRAISING IN WINE

You can get hyper-cerebral and braise hot dogs in Riesling. This is a guaranteed food and wine success, unless we want to analyze the psychosis of the cook who is attempting such a silly feat. I am content to be socially maladjusted and a little awkward at parties (also known as being a total food geek). However, German Riesling of any quality is likely more expensive than we want to use— I still think that the wine should be in your glass and not your pan in this instance. If you find a suitably inexpensive, perhaps New World, Riesling to try this out with, it is fantastic. Please do not get out your finest bottle of Mosel or Rheingau and pour it in a pan with a hot dog. The benefits will be far outweighed by the cost.

Anyway, to braise hot dogs, all you need to do is sear them in a pan, then add some wine, beer, or other liquid, and cover the pan. Leave the lid slightly askew so that the liquid can reduce and glaze the dogs. You're essentially combining the methods of searing, boiling, and steaming all at once.

BOILING

Simple and effective. Probably the best method for those who eschew the microwave for being a countertop space hog. Pro tip: The water must be salty. Remember that high school biology lesson about osmosis? If you don't, you'll have to trust me. The salt keeps the dogs from being bland by not letting the water leach out the salt in the dog. It will not make the hot dog salty unless you put WAY too much salt in your water. Another pro tip: Take two wooden spoons and lay them across the pot that you're boiling in. Set the buns on your new, homemade bun rack. Steam buns while boiling dogs. You should probably be drinking Riesling while you wait for this process to be completed. Food and wine pairing is thirsty business.

The Wine

 Here are some of my audacious Riesling claims:

Riesling is the most versatile grape in the world of wine.

The best Rieslings in the world come from Germany.

No other wine causes so much professional hyperbole.

There is no better value in wine than the sweet wines of Germany.

There is no better wine pairing safety net than Riesling.

As you continue reading this passage, we'd like it if you have no other takeaway than the fact that Rieslings from Germany are some of the best pairing wines you can find, period. In a world that embraces ever-increasing amounts of spice as the logical result of the popularity of various ethnic cuisines, German Riesling is the handyman everybody should hire—for the sole reason that it will get the job done. It might not be the best wine for the job, but it will rarely epically fail.

When I think of the myriad things we place on our dogs, most will find a contrast flavor in sweet German Riesling. With Riesling you have elevated levels of both acidity and sugar—two food-pairing superheroes.

Mustard = Acidic. Check.

Onions = Sweet. Check.

Sauerkraut/Relish = Acidic. Check.

Riesling with hot dogs helps illustrate what happens when your approach is to use contrast pairing. The strong elements in Riesling counter the strong elements in hot dogs. The acidity in Riesling wins the acid war. And if you happen to be using an actual German wurst (sausage) as your hot dog base—you've also managed to create a "grows together, goes together" pairing.

Blue Cheese with Tawny Port

THE CLASSIC PAIRING

Blue cheese is not for everyone. It is pungent, salty, tannic, and tangy, and the levels of these flavors can all be over the top. Those who don't like blue cheese are generally very adamant about it. It tastes rotten to them. It is unfortunate for those people, and to them I would only ask that they give blue cheese one more chance, with this pairing. The sweet, caramelly, oxidized flavors of

Saint Agur and 10-year Tawny Port

Tawny Port tames and balances even the stinkiest of blue cheeses. Years ago, we had Cashel Blue (made in Ireland) on our menu at Purple Café. It was one of the best food and wine pairings we've ever tasted. Classic contrast pairing. Salty versus sweet, acidic versus rich, sweet versus tannic. Amazing.

Buying blue cheese can be slightly challenging. You need to find good brands and get them from a purveyor that sells a fair amount of cheese to ensure good turnover of the product. If you are lucky enough to have a place like this, you are likely also to begin a beautiful relationship with the cheese monger. Then you can always ask what's really good at that given moment, knowing that most of them will work with oxidized sweet wine.

Here's a list of blue cheeses we've enjoyed over the years:

- Stilton, England
- Shropshire, England
- Cashel, Ireland
- Cabrales, Spain
- Valdeón, Spain
- Roquefort, France
- Saint Agur, France
- Bleu d'Auvergne, France
- Fourme d'Ambert, France
- Gorgonzola Dolce, Italy
- Maytag Blue, Iowa, United States
- Rogue Creamery: Caveman Blue, Oregon, United States
- Jasper Hill Farm: Bayley Hazen Blue, Vermont, United States

The Wine

In my wine and food gateway-drug fantasy, the person who claims to not like blue cheese will also claim to abhor sweet wines, and this exercise changes their lives forever.

If you don't like and/or have avoided blue cheese for most of your life, please don't skip this section. Ease into it. But don't give up. Ditto for loved ones.

My wife helped our friend Becky get over her fear of blue cheese through sincere hand-holding and baby steps. She changed Becky's life, certainly—not through trickery and coercion, but through compassion and patience. You see, one can either bemoan the fact that people make up their minds about a thing and attempt to stick to that opinion for the remainder of their lives, or one can employ the magnificent tool of social peer pressure to get them to put things in their mouths. Best to do this when they're slightly tipsy.

First step: get one of the milder manifestations of blue cheese. Maytag Blue. Gorgonzola. Saint Agur, the Neil Diamond of blue cheeses (passionate and well crafted, but easy to ingest).

Second step: stuff some in an olive. The martini is optional, but if I may recommend:

2 parts gin

1 part dry vermouth

Place the blue cheese–stuffed olive in the martini and slowly sip said martini while mentally preparing for what you might think is going to be an awful experience. Once you've consumed enough martini courage, stick the olive in your mouth and chew.

I'm not sure, but I think Becky said, "That's not so bad." If you also manage to get to a place where a gin and vermouth–soaked olive with a mild blue cheese stuffing comes across as *not bad*, repeat the exercise daily for seven to fourteen days, or for as long as it takes for you to admittedly crave that sharp and salty booze-soaked flavor bomb.

If you already enjoy blue cheese but have not had it with Tawny Port—you've been listening to Sonny without Cher.

It's important to know a little bit about Port. First of all, Port is a fortified wine that comes from Portugal—if it's from anywhere else, run away. (Don't even cook with it.) The grapes that are used to produce Port are numerous (over seventy) and unfamiliar (Touriga Nacional, Touriga Franca, Tinta Roriz, Tinta Barroca, and Tinto Cão). Understanding the raw materials, however, is not the most interesting thing about Port . . .

Things start out like most other wine. Grapes are grown and grapes are harvested. The trick to Port—the reason it's sweet—is that brandy is added to the wine before the yeast has had the chance to convert all the sugars to alcohol. The addition of brandy kills the yeast cells, creating a liquid that is high in alcohol (19% to 21%), with a level of residual sugar around 100 grams per liter. (Roughly the same as you'll find in the average cola.)

There are two branches of Port that are quite distinct from one another: one is aged in oak barrels and the other in bottles. Port aged in wood is called Tawny Port (from the color it takes on), whereas wine aged in the bottle is called Vintage Port. There are some subcategories beneath Tawny and Vintage Port, but for the sake of this discussion, we're going to stick with the major branches of the Port family tree.

Here's how to tell the difference: Vintage Port is labeled with the year it was harvested; Tawny Port is labeled in ten-year increments. Logically, ten- and twenty-year Port is the more common (and reasonably priced) Tawny Port available.

For this pairing, we recommend getting hold of a ten-year Tawny because its youthful exuberance is the necessary foil for the salty bite of blue cheese.

More details about why the pairing works so well:

- The saltiness of blue cheese hits the sweetness in the Port.
- The nuttiness of the Port is a natural match to the cheese. (Nuts and cheese, please.)
- The intensity of the cheese is equaled by the intensity of the wine.

It's one of those pairings where the wine brings new complementary flavors, contrasts flavors, and hits the intensity of the food head-on.

How To Have a Positive Relationship with Wine

Wine is Magical

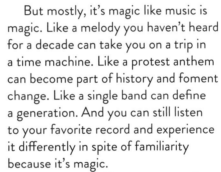

Here's something I believe to my core: Wine is magical. Every so often it's the David Blaine, big-production, prime-time television extravaganza with flashes of fire, loud techno music, and attractive-assistants-in-questionable-costumes kind of magic.

But mostly, it's magic like music is magic. Like a melody you haven't heard for a decade can take you on a trip in a time machine. Like a protest anthem can become part of history and foment change. Like a single band can define a generation. And you can still listen to your favorite record and experience it differently in spite of familiarity because it's magic.

Wine is magical because it is perhaps the only thing on earth that we store in a bottle for years before putting it in our bodies without fear that it will kill us. No—in fact, we covet those singular wines that manage to not only maintain for decades, but improve.

Wine is magical because it can express where it is grown. Other things do as well, but nothing can transport that sense of place quite like the right wine. Or it just makes your food taste better, which is a helluva trick. There may be scientific reasoning behind it, but when it's in your mouth, it's hard to think of it as science.

Here's the deal: dedicate yourself to drinking the right wine with the right food and your life will become instantly more magical—and who doesn't want to live in a world of magic?

Opinions, or Criticism— I Hate It Too

Here's the crux of the problem: the fastest way to appear as if you know what you're talking about is to have a negative opinion. It should be a bumper sticker: *I'm an expert because I think everything sucks.*

We are conditioned: most of the information we get about movies, books, restaurants, and theater comes from sources that are frothing to illustrate their expertise through several layers of cleverly worded negativity. The template for the modern day critic/blogger is to tear down in order to portray intellectual aptitude and authority. It's totally lazy. It's total bullshit.

One clear result of this: it's not uncommon in the world of wine to pile on a certain grape, region, or winery in order to strut one's status as being *in the know*. Take the ABC (Anything But Chardonnay) movement a number of years back—where the hell did that come from? (I suspect it was some clever marketing firm working for the Pinot Gris or Sauvignon Blanc cause.) I found it strange that people suddenly began to object to FLAVOR, claiming that the ubiquity of Chardonnay meant we should all cease consuming bottles of hedonistically appointed and tropically fruited pleasure bombs. Was the abundance of flavor too much for people to take, or was the madness of deriding an entire grape varietal the result of a perfectly placed marketing virus?

There's as much fashion in the world of wine as there is in clothing—I accept and celebrate that reality. I'm all for people chasing the next fashionable grape, region, or winery—it's what keeps us constantly engaged with the ever-changing wine landscape. However, when opinion is coupled to a scorched earth attitude toward entire categories of potential pleasure, it just comes off as narrow-minded, silly, asinine. It's infuriating to live in a world where misinformation and opinion so easily change the drinking habits of entire populations.

Take Merlot's ironic fall from grace: saying, "I hate Merlot" is like saying, "I hate chocolate." It makes people sound like liars, idiots, or worse.

When my kid says that he hates cheese, I remind him that it's *impossible* based simply on the fact that he has yet to taste all the cheese in the world, and therefore cannot pretend to have an informed viewpoint.

So the next time some wine-snob acquaintance claims to hate a vast swath of the wine world, you can feel comfortable telling them they sound like a snot-nosed toddler. Or at least tell them they sound like a narrow-minded amateur.

Don't Save Wine for Occasions— Save Wine for People

I've made the mistake: a bottle gets sent to the attitudinal and real

Commit to a Bias-Free Approach

When somebody asks me how to best learn about wine, I simply say: Free yourself from bias. Wine biases might include, but are not limited to:

COLOR BIAS: It's worth knowing that white wines can be produced from any color of grape. And that most rosés are made from red grapes. Drink the rainbow.

SUGAR BIAS: Sugar shows up in fruit juice, sodas, and cocktails—so why does anybody have an issue with it in wine?

REGIONAL BIAS: Maybe that place made lousy wine a decade ago. Maybe everything has changed.

GRAPE BIAS: It's like blaming a blurry picture on the camera, not the person taking the picture.

VINTAGE BIAS: Great wines are made in lousy vintages. Bobby Richardson was the World Series MVP in 1960 despite the fact that the Yankees lost.

GLASSWARE BIAS: There are some wines that would taste awesome out of a dog dish.

purgatory of "Wine to Save for a Special Occasion," which might as well be labeled, "Drink Five Years Too Late, When You're Just Drunk Enough to Forget to Remember Why You Kept It in the First Place."

Here's a personal story. When I first came down with the wine bug, I was working at a small, family-owned Italian restaurant in the University District in Seattle. Every night as service was winding down, I'd mix a vodka martini for the manager, Gary—served in (of course) a coffee mug. Upon the delivery of the coffee mug, he'd ask me what I wanted for dinner. Part of the compensation for bussing tables was free food, so I was always careful to ask for something different every night—clearly a thoughtful and mature approach to the perk.

What didn't completely register at the time was the glass of wine that Gary was putting in front of me with which to wash down my shift meal. Perhaps it was the last of whatever bottle that was left opened that night or a slow-moving glass pour that was either destined for the busser or the drain in the sink. Whatever it was, I enjoyed every gratis glass of wine with the reverence expected from a twenty-two-year-old kid who thought that free bread was also something of an adult perk—a benefit of equal gravity as free parking or health insurance.

Nevertheless, one night Gary produced a bottle and made a show of meticulously cutting the foil before pulling the cork with careful, surgeon-like precision. The look on his face was the juxtaposition of real excitement and feigned nonchalance—the same look somebody gets when they're trying to hold back on some wicked gossip that is both taboo and unexpected: smirk with raised eyebrows over shifty eyes. (When somebody smart introduces you to a thing they want you to love as much as they do, there is often a not-so-subtle omission of explanation concerning what is actually occurring, in order that you might hopefully experience it with purity and honesty. However, it's impossible in those moments not to detect the "Holy crap, is this going to be awesome" vibe underneath the "No big whoop" veneer.)

Gary was opening something terribly expensive without the intent of paying for it. But it wasn't stealing in the same spirit as a shoplifter snatching a twelve-pack of Miller Lite. No—he was lifting some fine art off the wall of a rich guy who had no idea or appreciation for what it was in order to show it to a kid who was thinking about attending art school. One part aesthetic Robin Hood, one part White-Collar Crime Division. With a dash of "I know something you don't know" thrown in for good measure.

Additionally, I'm sure Gary suspected I was both a willing accomplice and eager acolyte. (I would deny to the grave the event ever took place. Unless one day I wrote a book and happened to mention it.)

It was a bottle of Brunello from 1985. A vintage spoken of with the same reverence as some speak of the '72 Dolphins. Or the promise of the Kennedy administration. Or Fellini's finest film.

Being introduced to great wine when you've done little more than drink from jugs and wicker-wrapped bottles is like reading Richard Ford your freshman year of college. If you read *The Sportswriter* before the age of 35, you may understand the gravity of the story, but without the clarity that comes from age and experience. The first time you taste a great wine, you don't really or completely understand it—but you sense the complexity and completeness that is happening in your mouth and nose and brain. Those are wines that manage to hit your soul, and that is part of the magic that is wine.

By the way, miserable naysayer types will love to pooh-pooh this idea and perhaps fly the flag of hyperbole and overstatement. "It's just wine," people say. Fine. Live a life without magic. But here's another way to look at it: before we learned to swing our legs at the knees, swings were dull without a push. But once we understood how simple and natural it all was—once we understood the motion—it was impossible to go back to a world of stasis. Who doesn't want to live in a world where there is magic in bottles and gravity is a weak force, even to 8-year-olds.

Wine is not a matter of simply knowing or experiencing things, though. It's knowing how to experience openly while constantly acknowledging that there is always more to be known. Not every bottle will be a great book—but you can't stop reading carefully or you will miss the details.

So after that bottle of '85 Brunello, I scraped some of my busboy money together and attempted to find it at a number of wine stores around Seattle. When I did find it, it wasn't even the right vintage—and there was no way I could part with that sort of cash for a single bottle of wine. But I did find a half bottle of the '88. And according to Gary, that was a good—if not better—vintage.

It cost more than any single bottle of wine I had purchased up to that point. (And I still buy wine with a little bit of the busboy in me, admittedly.) When I finally managed to get to the point of purchase, my posture was good and I knew I was doing something *adult*.

So I did what anybody would do with a prized trophy—I displayed it.

Two Types of Wine in the World

There are two kinds of wine in the world: wines of made with soulful intent, and wines made with the intent to profit. Wine is either personal or corporate—very rarely will you find a wine that manages to straddle both.

Wines of intent are made by people with the faith that they can use their life energy to create an experience that is at once an expression of their personal vision as well as delicious enough to bring pleasure to others.

One of the more magical things about wine is that it can be both an extension of people and the expression of place—be it a family farm in Italy, a garage operation in southern France, or an 800-case-a-year winery in Washington.

Then there are wines that are built with the input of accountants, marketing managers, brand managers, and people with MBAs. Wines that are sourced from vast geographical areas through the purchasing of bulk juice, and appointed with attractive and clever labels—catchy names and graphics meant to grab your attention. Be it a tank farm in Bordeaux, a Malbec machine in Mendoza, or a vineyard in the central coast of California that measures its vineyards in terms of miles rather than acres.

Problem is, it's hard to tell the difference when you're standing in an aisle of the beverage emporium.

A short list of the worst places I brazenly exhibited that bottle:

- Middle of the kitchen table (ersatz centerpiece)
- On a bookshelf (ersatz bookend)
- Hanging from a wall (ersatz art)
- On a windowsill (ersatz tchotchke)

That half bottle of '88 Brunello lived with me through four apartments, a condo, and a house. It traveled from Seattle to Key West (where it was stored in the back of my Subaru, a hostel, and an apartment with frugal use of the air-conditioning) and back again. Somewhere in there I came to understand what proper cellaring of wine looked like and immediately placed the sacred bottle into what I hoped would be some rehabilitative storage conditions. Why was I saving it? Obviously for the *right occasion*. Right.

LIST OF LIFE EVENTS THAT OCCURRED WHILE STILL HOLDING ONTO THAT HALF BOTTLE OF '88 BRUNELLO:

- First job that didn't include lifting bus tubs
- First story published in a literary magazine
- First real wine job
- First job running a wine program
- Marriage

And those are just the big firsts that immediately come to mind. There were also a lot of great days and bad days, dinner parties and funerals. The blessed wine that was saved for either a rainy day or a special occasion kept its cork through a lot of precipitation and joy.

Landmark wines don't get drunk. And I get it—the act of saving wine for a special occasion is a great kind of life optimism—but just go ahead and exchange it with a nice bottle of Champagne in your fridge.

We should all make this commitment: drink your special bottles with special people, not for special occasions.

Additional rule: do not drink your prized wine in the hopes of impressing a new acquaintance or coworker. Dinner with the boss? Don't splurge—bring him/her something you love and can talk passionately about. Don't try to break the ice with big wine—break it with a wine that is personal. Don't just shove it in a bag and let it sit on the counter either—hand it to them label out and explain that this isn't so much a gift as a recommendation. Wine means something, so let it mean something.

Pull those corks out with people you like, in places you're comfortable being, with food you think will work. (Or skip the food entirely—though Coach will have something to say about that.) Otherwise you're doing yourself and that special bottle of wine a great disservice.

Wine is to drink.

Don't be a hoarder. I've been involved with enough estate cellar sales to know that the best stuff never gets touched by the person who cared enough to recognize its value in the first place. And I've made those mistakes myself—waiting too long to pull the cork on something that was once amazing. You will never know how special a wine is until you put it in your mouth. So put it in your mouth.

The Physical Stuff

A Few Words on Enclosures, or Put a Cork In It

I tend to complain about the pomp and circumstance that still permeates certain corners of the wine world, but there is no other subject more baffling than the continuing saga of corks versus screw caps. I want to implore that the world stop making a big deal out of it immediately. It's making everybody look silly. Take a step back. Take a deep breath. The whole cork versus screw cap thing is nothing more than *an argument about packaging.*

You can go online and find loads of science that points to the reality of global warming. You can also go online and find science that seemingly debunks global warming. Likewise, you can go online and find detailed accounts concerning the abject failure of corks as it pertains to effectively sealing a bottle of wine. But then there's an almost equal amount written about the superiority of cork-finished bottles. (By the way, the term *cork finished* is as snotty as it is inaccurate. Usually, adhering the label is the last step in producing a bottle of wine—so the very important finishing touch goes to the sticker, not the plug. I digress.)

I'm not a scientist, but here are a few things I can profess:

Corks are traditional, and therefore have a romance attached to them for no good reason beyond *ritual*. If we wanted to be truly traditional in our methods of sealing the top of a bottle, then we'd go back to shoving an oily rag in the neck with an emphatic thumb.

Corks are wood, and therefore come with some expected failures. On average, I come across a contaminated bottle 365 times a year.

Footnote: Important delineation here—there's wine that is bad because the cork failed to do its job as a sealant and has allowed the liquid to start the journey toward vinegar; and there is wine that is bad because it has been tainted by (unavoidable wine term) **TCA**. TCA is the compound 2,4,6-trichloroanisole that can find its way into corks—and it spoils a lot of great wines. Low-end estimations on the failure of corks due to TCA is 0.7%, but from personal experience as well as the amount of wines we return to distributors each week, I think the number is at least one in fifty. But say it is only 0.7%—I still find that to be an unacceptable amount of loss. If the

The difference between a decanter and a pitcher: attitude.

packaging failed on 0.7% of, say, baby food, there'd be proper rioting.

And while I'm confident the economic interests behind cork producers and distributors will develop technological advances to help diminish the frequency of TCA—I'm fine wearing the Team Screw Cap jersey for as long as I keep coming across corked wines. But that's probably because I'm a *better safe than sorry* kind of human.

Here's why, as a professional, I hate cork: *most of the corked wines in the world are consumed.* TCA is both nefarious and (for many) hard to detect.

My ongoing nightmare reality: a customer comes into our restaurant and orders a glass of wine. The wine is tainted with TCA, stripping it of its fruit flavor and rendering the liquid a rather tasteless, wet-dog-smelling inebriant. Customer (who is the kind of nice person who hates to complain about things) endures the tainted wine and leaves thinking, "The wine director at this wine bar doesn't know what the hell he's doing."

Our restaurant's policy is to snatch away any wine that is even questioned in the slightest—if there is something in the wine that doesn't taste right to the guest, it's probably corked.

And by the way, if you want to know what a corked wine smells and tastes like, feel free to stop by the restaurant at any time.

The Decanter, or Pitchering

Most wine benefits from decanting. By most, I mean 99.9 percent of all wine consumed in the world benefits from decanting. And when I say benefits, I mean it *tastes better.*

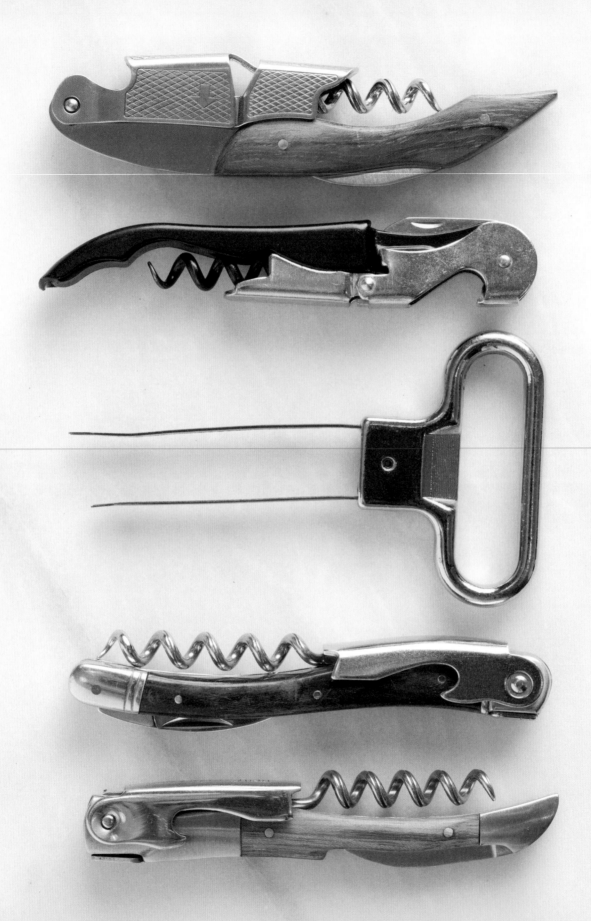

For white wines—we're invariably pulling bottles out of a 38°F environment and expecting them to provide flavor, which is both totally unreasonable and totally unfair. Here's something we learned in elementary school: when someone dared you to eat something gross (like a peanut butter and mustard sandwich) you'd suck on an ice cube for a minute in order to deaden your mouth. It's also something we learned in college: the only way to drink cheap (read: crappy) beer was to drink it ice cold. (I would also opine that the speed at which we drank said crappy beer was also to avoid putting it in our mouths at anything above 40 °F.) So get your wine out of that freezing-cold bottle and into a neutral container so there's a fighting chance of perceiving the flavor that took years to create.

For red wines—air has a magical effect on their flavor and texture. Have you ever been cleaning up the morning after a big party, only to find there is still liquid in that awesome bottle you (regretfully) pulled out when everybody was already half in the bag? If so, then you know how awesome it tasted when you poured it into a coffee mug and took a sheepish, apologetic swig—things are way better the morning after.

You hear your wine-snob friends constantly claiming that the wine has to *open up* or *breathe*. Well, they're annoying as hell, but also a little right. Think of the decanter as the alarm clock for a wine. Just like you, wine is not at its best first thing—it needs a wakeup call, a shower, and a shave—maybe a cup of coffee and a danish. It takes time for us to wake up in the morning—same for the wine. (Only imagine waking up after being shoved in a bottle for years. It's no wonder.)

Wine Keys

As a restaurant professional trying to avoid carpal-tunnel, I have a variety of methods for pulling a cork out of a bottle in my pocket at all times. (It's something I recommend to anybody who has to open more than one bottle in any given day.) My favorite is the average two-stage job you can find at most wine stores for about 10 bucks a pop. There are many rather fancy (and expensive) wine keys out in the world that are quite appealing, but here's the problem: regardless of price, the minute the knife on a wine key is dull, that thing is as good as garbage. So I don't advocate throwing money at a flashy corkscrew—it's akin to buying the most expensive screwdriver at the hardware store.

That said, I have some ties that I won't wear to work for fear of soiling them with restaurant debris. Those ties are invariably extravagant gifts given to me by people I love, because I would never spend that much money on myself. I've also got a wine key I'll never bring to work. So, what I would recommend: learn how to use an Ah-So. It's that two-pronged contraption that looks more like a close combat weapon than a cork extraction device—but you can (ironically) put it in your carry-on bag when you travel without inevitable forfeiture at the airport security checkpoint.

It's called an Ah-So because when you use it, people tend to furrow their brow and declare, "Ah . . . so that's how that works."

Besides looking cool, the Ah-So is also particularly efficacious on older corks. P.S. Don't bother trying it on plastic or synthetic corks. The density of cork alternatives prevent the Ah-So from getting in the neck of the bottle.

Here's my personal advice: don't bother buying a fancy decanter. Fancy decanters are akin to fancy spatulas—they're not better, just more expensive. I once saved an ugly '60s-era water pitcher (adorned with etched palm trees) from a garage sale for a dollar, and it's the world's best decanter. So use whatever you have around—save your money for buying the liquid, not the pitcher. (Note: If you have a wine-snob friend that you like to needle a bit, replace the word *decanter* with *pitcher*. And, yes—let's also supplant *decanting* with *pitchering*.)

How to Preserve Wine in Your House, or It's Easy. Drink, Drain, or Vinegar

But say you open a bottle to go with your dinner, only to find that for whatever reason the chosen wine is not the right fit. Stick the cork back in and open another. Hopefully the insight gained from the wrong bottle will help you choose the right one.

So then what? You don't want to waste, right? Well, you can do any number of reasonable things:

Making Your Own Vinegar

Making vinegar is not difficult at all. The only thing one needs to get their hands on is a vinegar *mother*, something that is best purchased commercially. This somewhat slimy, rubbery substance is made of cellulose and acetobacters. Acetobacters are the bacteria responsible for eating alcohol in the presence of oxygen and changing it into acetic acid, also known as turning booze into vinegar. Simply pour the old wine over the mother, wait a month, and you've got vinegar. Give it a taste after a month, because if the wine you used was a little on the strong side (14% alcohol by volume, or more) then the process will take a bit longer. If you still taste wine flavors, give it another week. In fact, if you're using really big-daddy wines like Zinfandels or Port, you might need up to two months for the first batch. Fear not, as this is the longest part of the process; from here on, it goes rather quickly.

Once your vinegar is made, you simply need to keep topping it off with more wine. Once there is enough vinegar in the pot, you won't need to wait like you did for the full conversion. You'll just be diluting existing vinegar with more wine. You usually need only a week or so for subsequent conversions to take place.

The difference between this vinegar and the vinegar you buy commercially is that your vinegar is being made with very fine wine, certainly by vinegar standards. The vinegar that you usually purchase in the store is made from cheap table grapes that were converted into the cheapest, most uninteresting wine possible, for the sole purpose of making vinegar. The wines that you'll be using would be far too expensive to produce a commercial vinegar. We recommend keeping one vinegar pot for white and sparkling and another pot for red. The results will be far superior to almost any vinegar you can buy in the store.

Vinegar is best stored in a pot or jar with a spigot on the bottom, so it can be retrieved without disturbing the mother. When you are ready to use your vinegar, strain it through a fine-mesh sieve lined with cheesecloth. Then store it in sterilized glass bottles. It will literally keep forever.

- Have the wrong wine for dessert—only a smart idea on Fridays, Saturdays, or any day you expect your boss to be out of the office.
- Stick the wrong wine (with securely placed cork) in the fridge for another night. It doesn't matter if it's red or white—you have a number of days before things start to seriously deteriorate.
- Taste the wrong wine again and work up tomorrow night's dinner. Few of us plan our weekly meals—so create the next night's recipe based on the wine you are looking to deplete.

Actually, it's more like looking at wine as a leftover. If there is leftover Muscadet, use it as an excuse to get a dozen oysters. If there's leftover Pinot Noir, use it as an excuse to make that salmon dish that invariably goes with Pinot. Leftover Zin? Grill some burgers.

It's what happens in the wine buying trade often enough—a beautiful wine is presented and left, and the only recourse you have is to build context for that wine. Because it was free—and you can't afford to drink like that—you go to the store and build your dinner around the windfall.

And what happens after a week of failed food and wine pairing? Well, you might want to have some people over on Friday to help drink the mistakes—or you can do what seems like blasphemy:

1. Make vinegar

2. Pour it down the drain

The first is unquestionably more soulful/fancy/pragmatic. Indeed—it is the liquid equivalent of composting.

The second seems like pouring money down the drain, which totally sucks. However, if you're buying thoughtfully with an eye toward economically reasonable wines, the act of pouring a third or half of a bottle down the drain should be less irksome than throwing food away.

Let's put this in honest terms: I have never, EVER managed to use an entire bunch of Italian parsley. (I have a theory that the parsley farmers are in bed with the cookbook writer—seriously: a quarter cup of loosely packed Italian parsley results in a barely dented bunch that will probably get gross and squishy in the bag two days after purchase.) If there were a tally of all the Italian parsley that's been sheepishly/queasily shoved in the compost can five days after purchase, it would be spinning numbers faster than the national debt.

We throw food away all the time. Don't sweat it if occasionally you don't finish that bottle of wine.

If we look at wine as an ingredient, we are one step closer to using it as God intended. We are one step closer to the true spirit of food and wine.

We are one step closer to a healthy relationship with wine.

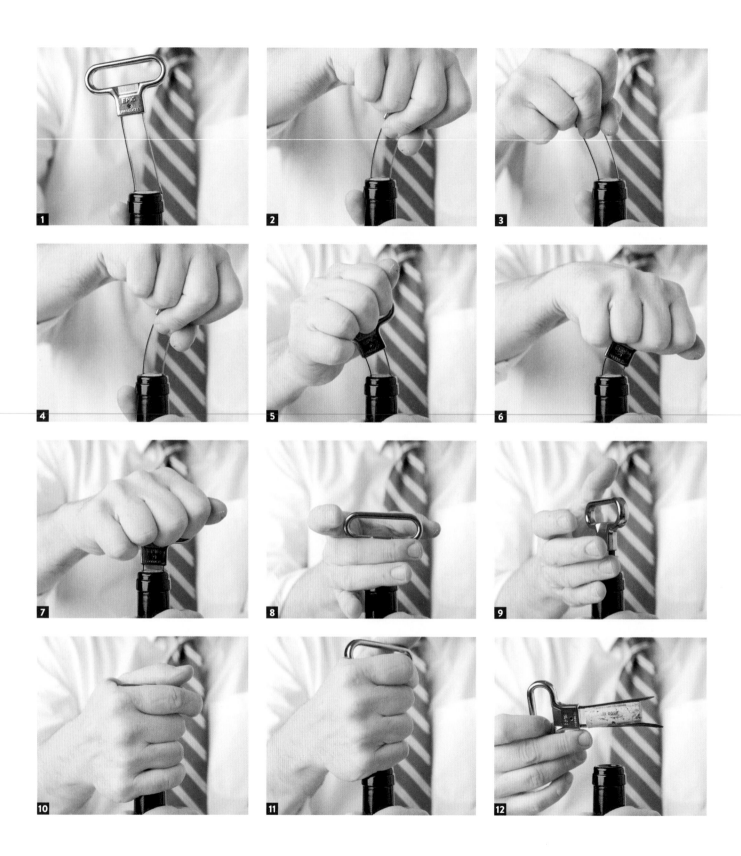

Buying It

There's a reason why my tone sometimes gets a little terse. Or accusatory. Or incredulous. It's because I take this stuff seriously—and while I know that snowing the consumer in order to move bottles is part of "good business," it ends up being counter to people really knowing and appreciating wine. I'm an informed consumer because I taste thousands of wines a year—but my mom isn't. My brother isn't. The people I know and love can't always call me when they're in the store buying wine. So, yes—I might seem to be taking it personally because above all else: this is personal. *It goes into our bodies.*

Shopping at the Big-Box Store, or Beware of the Dummy Labels

Does anybody remember going to the video store on a Friday night looking to rent a few VHS cassettes for the weekend? It was a harrowing, debilitating exercise that weighed heavy with the knowledge that whatever you grabbed was going to be a total disappointment because the movie you really wanted was already/always rented out. The malaise that set in while slowly scanning all the new releases blurred your vision and shut off your brain to the point where you'd grab just about anything to escape the burgeoning depression. There's a thing (it is a thing) called *decision fatigue*—we humans reach a threshold where the frequency and abundance of choices becomes oppressive, and we tire to the point where bad decisions are made on account of not wanting to make any decision at all.

That's what happens at the giant wine store. (In fact, they count on it.)

Faced with 5,000 different labels in a 20,000-square-foot space, what mortal could possibly make a good decision—especially when so many of those labels are completely foreign? (And by foreign I don't only mean from Europe.) The natural reaction when faced with an enormous amount of the unfamiliar is to look for something familiar—something well known to retailers. (There are enough customer surveys coupled with enough market research to know

The key to using a two-pronged corkscrew is to let the tool do all of the work. The first step is to wiggle the tines (long side first) between the bottle and the cork. Once both sides are in, simply rock it back and forth. There's no need to apply downward pressure, the motion creates a gradual entry. Once you're in, turn and pull while holding onto the corkscrew and cork. You'll look like a magician.

which labels are the most beloved and recognizable.) So when a customer asks where the (insert recognizable brand name here) is located, they get the REDIRECT.

"If you're looking for something like X wine, you should try this Y wine." And the big-box retail algebra is simple: X wine is being sold at a minimal margin (the level that leads you to believe that all the prices are as reasonable), yet Y wine is a dummy label that is being sold cheaper than X wine, but is going to garner a much larger profit for the retailer.

It's not nefarious—it's good business. People come in looking for one thing; you sell them on something similar that will be of more benefit to the bottom line. It's the American way, no?

As part of the research for this book, we took our shopping list to a national warehouse retail store and placed it in the intelligent hands of a beverage professional with the expectation that he could quickly put together a basket of the seven white wines you should have in your fridge at all times. The results were simultaneously elucidating and depressing.

Most of the wines you see in retail scenarios are not wines made by people, but by huge corporations. Additionally, most of the advice that you're being given is meant to steer you to the wines that generate the most profit.

The first advice you get is from the "shelf talkers": those dangly declarations of opinion and score often covering up the price of the bottle. They either are emblazoned with a number from a seemingly reputable wine critic or written with casual handwriting meant to look like enthusiastic advice

from the wine buyer. Sometimes they'll have both.

But here's a thing to understand about shelf talkers: they are often produced either by the winery itself or the representative of the distributor selling the wine to the store. Unlike a true third-party endorsement, the information on the shelf talker is an ersatz advertisement created to encourage you to buy a wine by masquerading as expert guidance.

And an additionally nefarious fact: sometimes the wine critic handing out 92-point scores is also in the employ of the national retail chain trying to sell you that bottle of wine.

And even if we're aware of what's going on, we all have a hard time seeing scores and not having some sort of learned reaction to them. Scores are like grades, and if one wine gets a B+ and is priced the same as a wine that got an A-, we're going to reach for the wine that somebody, somehow deemed to be superior by two points. And if the critic that gave the $9.99 bottle of Chardonnay from a sock-puppet winery a 91, we'll buy it instead of the $10.99 bottle of Chardonnay that got a 90. And because the store is going to make a higher net profit off the cheaper bottle, they'll hope you buy two.

It was difficult to find an obvious choice for our medium-bodied white wine, so the sales associate was approached for assistance and asked for a "medium-bodied white with ripe tree and stone fruit flavors." This produced a (surprise!) 2-for-1 deal on a California Sauvignon Blanc. Sure, there's a chance that the flavor in the bottle would represent the request—but the last varietal I would expect to be medium-bodied with ripe tree and stone fruit flavors would be Sauvignon Blanc. It's clear that the store employee detected some skepticism since he went out of his way to verify the choice with the store manager—it all became a game of Telephone, during which our buyer felt certain that it was a total snow job. Needless to say, he didn't buy the wine.

Conclusion: Going to a national wine retailer expecting to easily find wines of intent is akin to expecting a green salad made with local produce at an interstate truck stop.

Don't Buy Wine Because of the Label

While browsing the Chardonnay section at one of the large retail chains, it dawned on me that I hadn't heard of many of the wineries on the shelf, so I picked up a few to examine who might be behind them. Turns out that three of the four bottles I grabbed from the Chardonnay section—while seemingly bottled by different wineries—all came from the same town (Graton) in California. They were all created by what is known as an *alternating premise* or *alternating proprietorship* winery—a large, custom-crush wine factory specializing in the creation of cheap wines for restaurant chains and retail outlets. And they smartly covered all the expected retail price points: $8.99, $12.99, and $16.99. Later that night at a large grocery store, I pulled what was clearly another dummy label from the shelf to find yet another Sonoma Coast California Chardonnay with clever packaging hailing from the same town.

And what's worse is that we shouldn't even be surprised or upset by any of this. Wine is big business, and big wine creates a lot of revenue. Everybody in the wine game has the same agenda—to sell their wines—but something about *astroturfing* (the fake grassroots-support shelf talkers) and fake wineries rubs me the wrong way.

(We have an agenda too—but if you've bought this book, then we don't have anything left to do beyond getting you to fall in love with wine and making it a part of your life.)

So—might we suggest finding a local wine shop or even a local grocery store staffed with a wine steward who's tasked with wine purchasing (rather than shelf stocking). Here's something else that doesn't hurt: walking into a wine store and asking if the owner is around. The best-case scenario is that the person

Labels

Here is my personal, seemingly arbitrary, but thoroughly professional assessment of wine labels: If you hate the label, you're probably going to hate what's inside it.

I have seen perfectly charming wine labels on bottles from burgeoning wineries phased out in lieu of something with more "pop." It stands to reason—when faced with a sea of wine bottles on a shelf, it's easy to glaze over the subdued (classy) and simple (classy) labels. It's easy to spot bright colors, penguins, and ridiculous fonts.

I have also seen so many labels that seem like rip-offs from other successful labels. Maybe they copy the font, or echo the small picture below the vineyard name, or use the same color paper—whatever the thing that happens, always distrust a label that reminds you of another label. Somebody is banking on that association.

you're asking for advice also pays the rent. If the answer is a noncommittal, wishy-washy hem and haw that gives the impression that the owner is never around, find another store.

Some other things to think about when buying wine:

- Never buy a wine so expensive or precious you have no intention of drinking it. It turns that beautiful wine into slightly more than a tourist tchotchke.

- A bottle of wine is like a book. There are few books you want to read more than once. Identify those special books, and buy accordingly. If it goes with your favorite dish, pick up a case—that dish is the first reader, after all.

- If you don't know what a wine tastes like, don't buy more than one bottle—even if it's on sale. It might be on sale for a reason. It might be fine, but not your cup of tea. Either way, life is too short to drink something you didn't like a second time.

- Do not eschew any wine variety or region. You've not had them all, so your assumptions are unfounded.

Pop Wine and Marketing Methods

Falling in love with a simple, likeable, imminently drinkable wine can be like falling in love with a pop song. Something just catchy enough to grab the ear, clever enough to hold it, and simple enough to sing along to on the third or fourth listen. Pop music rarely pretends to be anything different than what it is. Occasionally, there is an overselling of earnestness, but otherwise pop music is a what-you-see-is-what-you-get proposition. It's appealing, catchy, and easy to like.

Pop wine—our term for mass produced cheap and tasty formula wines built to deliver the same flavor regardless of vintage—is also easy to like, and that's totally acceptable. In fact, pop wines can be gateway wines, the ones that got people to drink wine in the first place. What isn't acceptable is the annexation of fine wine constructs put in place to fool the consumer into thinking that they are experiencing something artisanal as opposed to scientifically mass produced.

COMMON METHODS OF FRONT-LABEL DECEPTION:

- RESERVE (No legal definition or qualification means every wine made in America can be labeled Reserve.)

- WINEMAKER'S RESERVE (It might seem like the winemaker hand-selected certain barrels for a special bottling, but that seems unlikely when the production of said wine is many millions of bottles.)

- OLD VINE (No legal definition or qualification.)

- SINGLE VINEYARD WINE (Some vineyards are measured in miles rather than acres.)

- DOMAINE (Doesn't actually have to exist to be placed on a wine bottle.)

- CHATEAU (Ditto.)

- ESTATE (Ditto.)

COMMON METHODS OF BACK-LABEL DECEPTION:

- RICH (You'll see this word on everything from Pinot Noir to Cabernet, Sauvignon Blanc to Chardonnay.)

- COMPLEX (Arbitrary.)

- LAYERED (Yes, layers of BS.)

- LONG (Palate length is one of the hallmarks of quality wine. However, there is no definition of what *long* means any more than there is a definition of the word *reserve*.)

- CRAFTED (If this word comes without the word *hand* somehow attached, then put the bottle down. And even then, it's suspicious.)

- COMMITMENT (Who isn't in business without some sort of commitment? Commitment to profit.)

- VARIETAL EXPRESSION (Basically claiming that the wine tastes like the grape it is made from.)

- SUSTAINABLE FARMING (Sigh. If the enormous wine industrial complex cannot sustain their yield year after year, their business model goes in the toilet. So yeah, there's a lot of sustainable farming out there.)

Example: *A complex, rich, long, and layered wine, crafted with a commitment to sustainable farming.*

COMMON METHODS OF RETAILING DECEPTION:

- **HUGE MARK-UPS NEXT TO PRICE SLASHING** ($30 wines for $18—what sane person would pass that up?)

- **SHELF TALKERS** (See page 90; most often written by wineries or distributors.)

- **POINTS** (Being written by paid critics or carried over from past vintages.)

- **TWO FOR ONES** (C'mon. It's like the huge mark-up on steroids.)

- **STAFF FAVORITES** (Sales-contest wines.)

- **CLOSE-OUTS** (You get what you pay for.)

Vineyard Matters

It's only been in the last couple of decades that it has become commonplace for restaurants to cite the names of the various farms being used on their menu. Where a chef sources raw materials has always been important, but this emphasis on sourcing is a fairly recent phenomenon—but one that is transitioning to the home kitchen as well. From farmers' markets to the organic produce aisle, we care more about where our food comes from today, and the proliferation of information available is a reflection of this

heightened desire to know the provenance of what we put on our plates.

In the world of wine, vintners have been putting the name of the farm on the bottle for centuries. In fact, most people that work in wine will cite that the single most important factor in the final quality of a wine is the grape that comes from the vineyard. (Any chance we can stop calling it a vineyard and refer to it as a grape farm? I digress.)

Knowing how vital the source of grapes can be should encourage you to do at least these two things:

1. Seek wines from single vineyards.

2. Once you find a wine you love from a particular vineyard, keep your eye out for other wines from that same vineyard.

For example, Dick Boushey is arguably one of the best grape farmers in Washington State. He sells his grapes to dozens of different wineries, some of which will put together a vineyard-specific bottling. When I'm browsing a wine list or wine shop, I might find a wine that I'm not particularly familiar with—but if it has the Boushey Vineyard on the label, I'm likely to give it a go.

Reason being—and this is the thing you might not know—just because a winemaker buys grapes from a specific farm does not give him or her license to use the name of the vineyard on the front of their bottle. Permission must be granted. The first step: getting the vineyard contract. Highly sought-after vineyards have waiting lists, and often the contract is not awarded on a first-come, first-served basis, but will depend on the quality of the wines being made by the winery hoping to secure grapes. The second step is (often) a vintage or two of vineyard-specific production—proving to the farmer that his raw materials are being treated expertly.

Paying attention to where grapes come from (as well as identifying the vineyards you personally enjoy) will yield a higher personal success rate. There is no better information than the origin of the raw material, after all.

How to Ask for It

This is an anecdote that may be particular to growing up in the Northwest.

For the longest time I was addicted to a particular coffee drink arrangement:

The Quad Grande Two-Pump Vanilla Nonfat Latte.

And while I still have the craving for this ridiculous beverage from time to time, I have moved on to a coffee-drink configuration that is inarguably less damaging to my health and sleep pattern. But oh, how I would impress baristas around the world with my accurate and effortless beverage order . . .

See, we all get trained (eventually) by our baristas to get things straight. There's an order—a syntax—to ordering an espresso beverage so that things can be grabbed and notated as efficiently as possible.

I imagine it didn't take long to learn that ordering *a latte with a half-dose of vanilla with two extra shots in a 16-ounce cup* came with a friendly but terse correction: "Was that a quad

Secrets for Ordering Wine in a Restaurant While on a Budget

FIRST—Commit to ordering a bottle, not one glass at a time. (While variety is the spice of life, it's no real secret that you get a better deal ordering wine by the bottle as opposed to by the glass.)

SECOND—Do order white wine or rosé. (The cost-to-enjoyment ratio on white wine and rosé is almost always superior to red wine. Simple reason—the cost of oak barrels that are employed in the production of many red wines is folded into the cost of the bottle. And since most white wines don't rely on oak to impart flavor . . .)

THIRD—Don't shy away from the cheapest thing on the wine list. (It used to be that the logic for going cheap in a restaurant was to buy the *second*-cheapest bottle of wine because the cheapest bottle is there as an economic necessity—but the second was one the sommelier actually liked. This might be the case for red wines that don't require refrigeration, but for most restaurants, cooler space is at a premium, and no wine buyer is going to give over valuable real estate to a wine he or she isn't totally proud of.)

FOURTH—Don't order the standard, popular varieties of wine. (Avoid

Sauvignon Blanc, Pinot Gris, and Chardonnay at all costs. Head toward Muscadet. Consider Pinot Blanc.)

FIFTH—Seek advice. (The easiest way to convey your economic intentions is to point at a selection that is at or around the price you're hoping to spend and simply state, "I'm looking for something in this range.")

SIXTH—Choose it before you go. (Most restaurant wine lists are online, so take the time to browse their sections pre-arrival. Make a few selections just in case the wine you ask for is out of stock, or the online menu is out of date).

Spend at Least As Much on a Glass of Wine As You Do on a Cup of Coffee

People go to crappy bars and pay sixteen bucks for two gin and tonics composed of ingredients you'd never bother with otherwise. (There's a reason they position the "well bottles" down there—it's so you don't really have to look at the label on the bottle.)

Think of it this way: if you go to a wine shop and spend twenty dollars on a bottle of wine, you're really only paying five bucks a glass.

You Are Worth It.

grande two-pump vanilla nonfat latte?" Yes. Yes it was.

And when you're in the wine store, you should get used to asking for what you want with a similar spirit—a simple but direct way to let the wine store professional understand what you're seeking. And while there isn't an officially ordained convention, I would recommend this simple syntax:

Start with **Body**.

Follow up with **Color**.

Finish with **Structure**.

Example: I'd like a light-bodied red wine with moderate tannins and acidity.

Or: I'm looking for a light-bodied white wine with high acidity.

"Wait," you say. "That seems to leave out all sorts of information like grape variety, vintage, price, and flavor—just about everything."

Well, yes. On purpose.

It's like car shopping: you go in looking for something based on make, model, and color. Those are specific criteria. But then what makes the car *yours* is the discussion and selection of the extras. The flavors, as it were.

The Language of Wine, or "Playful Yet Not Ostentatious"

Lingo. Every profession has it. Every workplace has it.

The language spoken on the campus of Microsoft does not resemble the language spoken at the florist. The vernacular of the mechanic has little overlap with words thrown around the bake shop. And it goes without saying that the front of the restaurant has a different set of terms than does the back of the house.

The problem with subject-specific jargon is that it generally repels all people who don't speak or understand that particular jargon. It alienates people, or at least motivates them to other corners of the cocktail party.

Wine-speak is another thing entirely, being as it is both subject-specific and often sounds like total BS.

For instance—I made the fatal error of using the term *typicity* on one of my first dates with my wife. At the time I think I was more focused on filling the conversational space and getting her to drink one more glass of wine than what I might have been talking about—but she tortures me to this day by dropping it at every suitable opportunity.

So let's ditch the jargon. Let's commit to this: Fruit.

While we might have different specific perceptions, I think there is general consensus about what a pear or a blackberry might taste like.

When I first started out as a sommelier, I used a helpful shortcut when trying to get people to try wine: I'd ask them what sort of jam they put on their toast. There are strawberry people, and raspberry people, and blackberry people—heck, there're even orange marmalade people—and by wrestling the discussion away from wine and into flavor, it was easier to get people to open their mouths to a glass that they might like based simply on the understanding of their flavor proclivities. Additionally, presenting a glass of California Pinot Noir to somebody who is already thinking of the flavor of strawberry means there is a higher chance that the perception of flavor and the connection to pleasure has already been made.

It's understood that we humans have the ability to discern thousands of distinct aromas that (coupled with taste and mouthfeel) we translate into what we call flavor. But my wish for those of us who want to fall in love with wine and communicate about wine stick to the language we can all understand: fruit.

Unintended Consequences of Thinking About Wine and Food Together

#1—You will become a better cook. Either from a better understanding of flavor relationships, or the fact that the beverage you're having with dinner makes the food taste better.

#2—You will cook more simply, which means there's a good chance of eating more healthfully.

#3—You'll enjoy food and life that much more.

The Wine Wardrobe

I no longer think of the wines we pour by the glass at the restaurant as the Glass Pour Program but more like the Food and Wine Pairing Wardrobe. A huge part of building that wardrobe is anticipating the types of ingredients that Coach will be putting together; in real terms, our wine menu has to be as seasonal as our food menu.

We've a pretty big wardrobe. On an average menu, there are twenty-five to thirty white wines, thirty-five to forty red wines, and fifteen to twenty dessert wines. In the summer, the whites tend to showcase more light-bodied whites and rosés; in the winter, we seek more full-bodied and oaked wines. The reds we seek in summer are attitudinal cousins of Gamay Noir and Pinot Noir; in the winter, we're more interested in finding rustic qualities, tannins, or richness. It's like storing your sweaters under the bed during the spring and trading them out with the short pants come fall. But with such a large stable, we have a lot of latitude, and we've never failed to find an appropriate pairing for the food we serve.

Even those "wine bar wines"—with the hard-to-pronounce grape names from distant lands—are chosen with food in mind. Be it the Georgian Kindzmarauli Saperavi that was paired with the duck, or the Macedonian Vranec that was paired with the stuffed dates, or that Liatiko from Greece that seemed to go with every dish last summer—wines that seem like outliers are chosen for more than just geographical or grape varietal fascination. And since we want people to drink the whole weird and wonderful world of wine, having the opportunity to showcase it in the proper context means that we're not pouring dead stock down the drain—it's going down with food.

Since it is quite impossible for you to re-create in your home the giant closet of wines we have at our disposal in the restaurant, we have isolated the styles of wine that are cornerstones of our operation. These are wines that will get you through four seasons—appropriately dressing your dining room table. Wine for every occasion and temperature. Jeans, slacks, and cut-off shorts. Winter coats and tank tops.

It's Not a Fridge, It's a Temperature-Controlled Closet for Your Wine Wardrobe

There's a statistic floating around out there that sounds at once made up and yet entirely probable: nine out of every ten bottles of wine purchased in America are opened within ninety minutes of purchase. This may or may not be totally accurate, but there is an echo of truth to it—we are a nation of people that are generally bad at meal planning.

I would like to appeal to the nation in this regard: Plan ahead, people. A great way to start is by opening up your fridge—inventory those multiple bottles of condiments—not just the mainstays like mayonnaise and ketchup, but the rarely employed bottle of orange marmalade, green peppercorn Dijon, hoisin sauce, and harissa. We afford a great amount of our valuable refrigerator real estate to condiments that we purchased for a recipe for that dinner party three months ago—we're giving away space to things that are likely to expire before we manage to consume them. Possibly forgotten jars of perishing relishes are enjoying the spaces that should be occupied by bottles of wine that will bring joy and pleasure—not elicit that discomfiting moment of "Is this still good—should I even taste it?" followed by the guilt associated with throwing away food.

World peace might not be possible, but I think we could get close if we all clean out our refrigerators to carve out space for the most joyful part any dinner—the right wine.

This is the crux of our wine-life advice: have the right wine around to open each and every day of the week. Make wine a shopping habit—when you deplete a bottle, stick it on the list next to eggs and milk. Do this, and you will likely never have to worry about having a decent thing to drink with dinner.

Wine Wardrobe Bottle #1
CHAMPAGNE

Before I knew anything about wine, I knew Champagne was *important*.
You can't launch a ship without it. You can't ring in the new year without it. And before you were old enough to drink, people gave you a fluted glass filled with sparkling apple cider to reinforce the importance of having bubbles in your hand when the best man gave the toast at your older cousin's wedding.

You should always, always, always have a bottle of Champagne in your fridge for at least these three reasons:

FIRST—You never know when something good is going to happen in your life that will need to be properly celebrated with a bottle of the *real deal*. In fact, don't consider a bottle of Champagne in your fridge to be an expensive piece of refrigerator furniture—look at it as a bottle of perpetual optimism.

SECOND—If you forgot it was your best friend's birthday or got a last-minute invitation to a dinner party, you have the perfect gift chilled and ready to go. A number of years ago, our next-door neighbors Peg and Marcus got married in their backyard. It was unexpected and charming, and we were able to pull out that bottle to drop on their doorstep as a gesture of congratulations.

THIRD—Maybe getting tired of seeing the same bottle for months on end will encourage you to drink it, because there's no better advice a wine person can give beyond "Drink Champagne more often." (Familiarity breeds consumption, or something like that.)

Microwaving some popcorn? Drink that bottle of Champagne. You won't believe how awesome a pairing it is. Take-out sushi? Drink that bottle of Champagne. You won't believe how awesome a pairing it is.

Might we also insist on trying it with french fries?

People will spend their lives drinking Champagne without ever knowing how it's made. I don't want that to be taken negatively; I have no idea how my TV works, but that doesn't stop me from watching it. And even if I were to endeavor to understand how televisions work, I don't believe it would enhance my appreciation for the shows I watch one bit. Champagne, though, is worth learning about. As complicated as it is, it's not new technology—but a method that evolved centuries before it was understood.

This is Jim. He's been a friend and coworker for over a decade. We crashed his bachelor pad to sip Champagne, listen to his extensive collection of vinyl, and make these scrambled eggs. In fact, every recipe in this book was road tested by real people in the places they live with the equipment in their kitchens.

It was magic first. Technology later.

In the name of full disclosure, I had spent probably ten years in restaurants before I even understood how it was made—all I knew is that there was a difference between Champagne and any other sparkling wines. I suppose you could chalk that up to proper marketing—the value of Champagne is not directly connected to the very process that makes it so compelling, but all the clever ways they have chosen to present it.

I'll start at the beginning. The simplest way to make wine: press grapes when they are ripe with sugar, wait patiently while yeast processes the sugars into alcohol, then stick it in a bottle. The result might not be all that great, but it would technically be wine.

Champagne starts off like any other wine: grapes are pressed and fermented—but from that point forward things get interesting. (And a little complicated. Lots of unavoidable wine terms coming up.)

First thing: The wine will grow up to become either single-vintage Champagne or multi-vintage Champagne—referred to as non-vintage or NV Champagne. In exceptional years, the winemaker will assess the quality of the base wine and put some aside to be made into the *vintage* Champagne (generally the expensive stuff that ages magnificently in the cellar). The rest of it becomes part of a Champagne house's non-vintage program, where the winemaker will artfully blend wine from many vintages in order to maintain a product of consistent quality and flavor year in and year out. (Thusly the unavoidable wine-marketing term "house style.") It's a heck of an undertaking—like trying to mix the same color of blue consistently from a random selection and quantity of diverse shades of blue.

It's an extraordinary feature of Champagne that generally goes without notice, but it's why some of us gravitate toward a certain producer. You can usually count on every bottle tasting the same as the last. I think a heathy analogy is finding your favorite cocktail. If it's made correctly, it should taste just about the same every time you order one—and there's certainly comfort in that.

The next step: adding the sparkle. Wine is put into bottles with an additional mixture of sugar, wine, and yeast, and then capped. (With the same sort of bottle cap you'll find on a soda bottle, actually.) It's then left alone for at least sixteen months, during which a second fermentation takes place *inside the bottle*.

(Quick fermentation-science note: The byproduct of yeast converting sugar into alcohol is carbon dioxide—also known as *bubbles*. But it also produces what is romantically referred to as [unavoidable wine term] **lees,** ostensibly dead yeast cells that precipitate to the bottom of the bottle. Not totally unlike the stuff floating around in certain styles of beer—think about the cloudiness found in a bottle of Hefeweizen.)

At this point of the production, we have a bottle that contains approximately twenty million bubbles as well as some lees sediment floating around. Before 1816, that's exactly what people were drinking, but thanks to the ingenuity of a certain widow, a method was invented to get that sediment out. (Unavoidable wine terms approaching: riddling and disgorgement.)

Riddling is the act of encouraging the lees into the neck of a bottle through a systematic agitation and turning in a rack designed to hold the bottle at an ever-increasing angle. It used to be a tedious (and dangerous) process done by hand, but technology has taken a two-month job and turned it into a mechanized week. There are some places that still do it the old-fashioned way, but it's rare.

Once the lees have thoroughly settled in the neck of the bottle, it's time to extract—also known as **disgorgement**. The top of the bottle is dipped in a subzero-temperature solution in order to turn the lees into a frozen yeast plug. At this point, the bottle cap is pulled off and the pressure in the bottle spits the icy yeast chunk out. A small amount of wine is lost as well, so it's time for a little top-off with a mixture of sugar and wine—which leads to the last unavoidable Champagne production wine term: the **dosage** (pronounced doh-SAHZH.) It's a vital thing to know about since it's the step that defines what category the finished wine will be.

Most Champagnes are labeled Brut—but there are other styles to consider. In the past decade, there has been a surge in interest for wines made without any sugar in the dosage phase of production—a style referred to as Brut Nature or Brut Zero. The category between Brut Zero and Brut, called Extra Brut, is also capturing fans. When you encounter these styles, I'd encourage you to give them a go.

Here's a super boring but useful chart:

CHAMPAGNE	GRAMS PER LITER OF RESIDUAL SUGAR
Brut Nature/Brut Zero	0
Extra Brut	0 to 6
Brut	0 to 15
Extra Sec	12 to 20
Sec	17 to 35
Demi-Sec	35 to 50
Doux	50 to 150

In the spirit of full disclosure, I've never seen or tasted a Doux Champagne in my life—but I fully endorse the undeniable deliciousness of Demi-Sec Champagne.

One more important thing to know about Champagne before going out in the world and getting some.

Generally speaking, there are two distinct production groups: those that buy grapes and juice from farmers and then make wine, and those that make wine from their own vineyards. Since we're talking about a product of France, we're going to run into more unavoidable French wine terms. *Negociants* are the ones that have vineyard contracts and *recoltants* are the ones that have the vineyards. (The proper terms are *negociant manipulant* and *recoltant manipulant*. But we like to shorten things: merchant versus grower is the easiest way to delineate.) Neither produces an inherently better product—they are just different. Consider the difference between a singer and a singer-songwriter: both have the potential of making beautiful music, and sometimes you wouldn't know the difference.

Other mysterious, unavoidable, but important terms found on the label of a bottle of Champagne:

Blanc de Blancs, or *white from whites*. The Champagne was produced by using only white grapes—primarily Chardonnay. There are in fact five white grapes that are allowed in Champagne, but the other four (Pinot Blanc, Pinot Gris, Arbane, and Petit Meslier) are rarely found. This is so not important, but is great knowledge to drop at a cocktail party.

Blanc de Noir, or *white from black*. The Champagne was produced using only red grapes, those of Pinot Noir and/or Pinot Meunier.

(By the way, if you have extra space in your fridge, don't be afraid to augment your Wardrobe with a bottle of rosé Champagne. Generally made by adding a little red wine to give it some

color, rosé Champagne is one of my personal wine fetishes.)

Here's one final, crazy thing to consider—the entire process of Champagne production as we know it was developed decades before there was a comprehension as to what was happening—fermentation wasn't even understood until the 1850s. And even knowing exactly how it's produced today, it still feels a little magical when you pull that cork out with the understanding that the soul of the wine—those bubbles—were created in the very bottle you're holding.

So the next time you pick up a bottle of Champagne, remind yourself that you are also holding the vessel *in which the wine was made* . . .

If you get stuck doing all the prep work, we recommend making sure somebody is in charge of dispensing the wine.

Champagne Pairing Exploration

SCRAMBLED EGGS

Scrambled eggs? Who needs a recipe for scrambled eggs? As with many things in this book, we're more focused on culinary methods than just giving you a bunch of recipes. When you know how to make basic scrambled eggs, you know how to make hundreds of different kinds of scrambled eggs. While the French style is the absolutely perfect scrambled egg method for Champagne, you can certainly serve any style that you like—just don't save that Champagne for some silly "special occasion." The reason we chose scrambled eggs as the perfect Champagne pairing is that we know you've got eggs, and we really want you to drink more Champagne.

Not Your Sunday Morning Eggs

Making scrambled eggs like the French do should be thoroughly explained, as we in the United States often make them too quickly and over too high of a flame. We're going to pair them with one of the greatest French wines, so they are ideally to be accompanied by French-style scrambled eggs, meaning eggs that end up very rich and creamy, with tiny curds (like fine-curd cottage cheese).

It should be said that this style of scrambled eggs can be off-putting for some. Many of us didn't grow up having scrambled eggs prepared this way, and there are people who will find them ghastly, exclaiming that they're undercooked, weird, or texturally challenging. That is OK. Scrambled eggs prepared in a more American style are still pretty darned tasty with Champagne, but for the pinnacle experience, the one most matching the texture of the wine itself, this is the way to do it.

The best way to serve these eggs with a glass of Champagne would be on nice little brioche toasts, as quality Champagnes often have a brioche-like aroma to them, but any well-made bread will work. I would only recommend that you don't use bread with a very intense flavor, like rye or pumpernickel, or cracked whole wheat. Brioche—a rich, fine-textured bread made with lots of eggs and butter, and sometimes a touch of sugar—is best,

but challah, baguette, ciabatta, sourdough, Como, Pugliese, or any other white or eggy bread will work very well.

Bring on the Luxe

There is also the prospect of using scrambled eggs as a vehicle for luxury products, which they do incredibly well. Most of these luxury products are spectacular with Champagne too. These include, but are not limited to:

- Duck or chicken liver pâté, torchon, or terrine of foie gras (don't warm these up, just bring to room temp)
- Smoked salmon, hard-smoked or lox-style
- Lobster meat
- High-quality sharp cheeses, such as Gruyère, Comté, Parmigiano-Reggiano, Fontina Val d'Aosta, even Brie

- Crème fraîche
- Truffles, white or black (this is actually one of the best ways to show off your fresh truffles)
- Wild mushrooms, sautéed
- Small, sweet shrimp (we like rock shrimp)
- Prosciutto, jamón Serrano, Smithfield, or other dry-cured ham
- Duck confit or rillettes
- Artisanal bacon lardons
- Pancetta cracklings
- Asparagus tips
- Tiny, young fava beans
- Freshly shucked peas or pea shoots
- Fish roe, especially salmon eggs or caviar (these should not be warmed up)

2 to 3 eggs

3 tablespoons butter (1 softened for the beginning, 2 chilled for the end)

3 tablespoons heavy cream (optional)

Kosher salt, for seasoning

Freshly ground pepper (optional)

Fresh herbs, such as parsley, chervil, tarragon, thyme leaves, marjoram, or dill, finely chopped

Luxury product, fully cooked and at room temperature if not hot

Fleur de sel, for finishing

I'm In, Let's Make These Bad Boys

Like many things in this book, scrambled eggs require a little planning and patience. Get yourself organized first, as you will be standing over the stove for a little while. Also, have every other element of your meal ready to go. The table should be set. All accompaniments to the eggs like your toast, garnishes, and side dishes should be finished and holding in a warm place. The Champagne should be chilled. You can't make these eggs in advance, and they deteriorate extremely fast, so you can't even hold them warm for more than five minutes or so. They should go right to the table. If someone in your family likes to dawdle around the kitchen at the last minute, or get up to get something right when the meal begins, it is best to give them false information about when the dish will be ready so that they are actually sitting when it is time to serve. First-timers need to experience this dish at the perfect temperature, with the perfect wine. Not all of them will like it, but those who do will have their lives changed for the better, forever.

French-Style Scrambled Eggs

Serves 1 person as a meal, 3 people as an appetizer

1. To cook the eggs, make a bain-marie (sort of a double boiler): Put about 1 inch of water in a medium saucepan and set it on medium heat. Find a bowl that fits snugly on top of the pan, and set it there. (Using a bain-marie ensures that the heat applied to the eggs is very even and very gentle. If you actually have a double boiler, that's awesome, as long as the top piece is rounded, like a bowl.)

2. Bring the water to a boil (the water should not be touching the bottom of the bowl). Turn the heat off entirely. You will be cooking with the latent heat of the water—just gentle, ambient steam.

3. Crack your eggs in a separate bowl and whisk them vigorously. Many people will strain them at this point as well, ensuring that any bits of shell, or the *chalazae* (what my wife lovingly referred to as "egg boogers" as a child) are removed. This step is unnecessary, but I would never encourage you to skip it if you're so inclined. Refinement of such a simple preparation just adds to the luxury.

4. Drop 1 tablespoon of the butter in the hot bowl, wait until it just melts, and add the eggs all at once.

5. Whisk constantly in a slow figure-eight motion. It will take about 10 minutes total for the eggs to come together into tiny, luxurious curds. Don't stop whisking or the eggs will set too quickly. If you feel that there is too little heat transfer, increase the heat by just a skosh. Resist every urge to expedite this process. We're not trying to torture you—if there was a shortcut we'd tell you. You just have to put in the time, and you will be rewarded.

6. Add the salt and pepper at this point, and add the herbs if you're going to use them.

7. Then whisk in the other 2 tablespoons of butter and some heavy cream if you're using it. These cooler products arrest the cooking of the eggs. Fold in your luxury product and taste. The eggs should be very well seasoned, very creamy, and as rich as an oil tycoon. Put a tiny sprinkle of fleur de sel on them and serve right away.

Alternate each bite of these eggs with a sip of Champagne. The acid and bubbles of the wine tend to clean as well as stimulate the palate. Each bite is almost like a clean slate, but not quite. The last bite and the last sip are pure, hedonistic flavor overload. Enjoy.

Presentation note: If you are an extreme badass, you will make the effort to find something called an egg cutter. This small tool essentially clips the top third of a whole, raw egg off very cleanly. After washing out the egg shell thoroughly, you will have a very elegant vessel to put the scrambled eggs back into. You will also need another badass piece of equipment called an egg cup to serve the dish (the English like to use such vessels to serve soft-boiled eggs). This, along with something incredibly luxurious like a truffle shaving, a spoonful of caviar, or a little foie gras, makes an exceedingly elegant small appetizer for a very nice multi-course dinner.

1 Add the eggs to the bowl all at once.

2 Carefully stir and scrape the bowl with a rubber spatula, stirring constantly until tiny curds form.

3 You can gently remove the eggs by tilting the bowl toward the plate.

4 You can also line up your warm plates and spoon the eggs from the bowl.

5 Final seasoning with sea salt.

6 Garnishing with bacon.

7 Finished eggs with final garnish of chervil sprigs.

Wine Wardrobe Bottle #2

INEXPENSIVE BUBBLES

People who say they can't drink sparkling wine because it gives them a headache are victims of the carbonated sweet wine labeled California Champagne that gets poured at too many weddings. All said, inexpensive sparkling wine doesn't have to be offensive. (Also, it's a shame that America is the only country in the world that still allows the use of the name *Champagne* on its carbonated wines.) We decided that the word *Champagne* is semi-generic—thusly allowing winemakers to use it as long as they attach a geographical designation. That's also how we get Mountain Chablis and Hearty Burgundy—even if neither contains any Chardonnay or Pinot Noir. Check out 26 U.S. Code 5388 or search the term *semi-generic* online. The US government created a word in order to allow bulk wine producers to mislead the drinking public. Marketing! (Not the first or only time that a word has been invented so that businessmen can fleece the willing populace.)

I digress.

A good place to start: Crémant. Any French sparkling wine made outside of the geographical boundaries of Champagne but employing the same production techniques is labeled Crémant. Look for Crémants from Alsace, Bordeaux, Burgundy, or the Loire Valley. These are not like knock-off Louis Vuitton handbags—they're made exactly the same way as the original, the difference being geography and the grape variety that is used. My personal preference is for Crémants from Burgundy; however, I've professionally and personally enjoyed Crémants from all over France.

This is Hun and Grace Kim. They're awesome. Plus they let us invade their stylish abode by the stadium to play with raw fish and drink inexpensive sparkling wine.

Then there's Prosecco—the most well-known sparkling wine produced in Italy. Italian wine laws have decreed the name of Prosecco protected in much the same way that Champagne is protected in France, so it's a good start to find the word *Prosecco* on the label. (There are other sparkling wines made throughout Italy, but on the basis of cost, availability, and quality, Prosecco is the current king.) The tricky thing about Prosecco is its varying degree of sweetness. Just remember (confusingly so) that a bottle of Prosecco labeled Extra-Dry is actually sweeter than a bottle labeled Brut. Here's the chart:

CHAMPAGNE	GRAMS PER LITER OF RESIDUAL SUGAR
Brut	0 to 12
Extra-Dry	12 to 17
Dry	17 to 32

Don't be afraid to venture into the Extra-Dry and Dry Proseccos—sugar is a flavor enhancer, after all. (And by way of comparison, there are over 100 grams per liter of sugar in the average cola, energy drink, or eight-ounce glass of orange juice.)

Cava, sparking wine made in Spain, gets a bad rap, and it's mostly because there is a sea of forgettable Cava out there. But here's the thing about your cheap Cava—you will not feel even a twitch of hesitation about pouring a bit of orange juice into your glass on any given weekend morning. Or better yet, dribbling in some Cassis and feeling royal about it. Which leads me to:

Why do you need a bottle of inexpensive sparkling wine in your fridge at all times? Simple—the times when life calls for a little bit of bubbly on a budget

are much more often than you presently believe. In fact, one of my go-to food and wine–pairing shortcuts is this: if it's something that goes great with beer, it's probably going to make you happy with an inexpensive bottle of bubbles.

A bag of salty potato chips with a bottle of Extra-Dry Prosecco turns out to be one of the best bags of potato chips you can have. (Stale shrimp chips work as well, by the way.)

Greasy pizza. Cheap bubbles. Right on.

Take-out fish and chips. Pass the Crémant.

I heard years ago that Champagne corks were the second-leading cause of blindness in adults. Of course, this has got to be a total fiction, but I still conjure the reality of serious eye injury when training people to wrestle the cork out of a bottle.

True story: My first restaurant job was as a busboy at the local golf club. New Year's Eve was a big deal—it was a party that went from cocktail hour all the way through to a 1:00 a.m. breakfast buffet. They would close the bar area and turn the ballroom and dining room into a glitter-covered, party-favor-infested booze palace. Lots of steaks, questionable perfume, and even more questionable dance moves. It was a long shift with the potential to be quite boring, but the money was good and it meant I didn't have to worry about what I was doing for New Year's Eve.

Right around 11:00 p.m., three cases of sparkling wine were brought to the closed-off bar area. They needed to be opened by 11:30 p.m. in order to be readied and poured for the toast. I'm not sure if it was entirely legal, but the task was delegated to the bussers.

little concerned that we hadn't finished the job of pulling the corks out of all the bottles. It had the potential to be a problem, seeing as we were up against a hard midnight deadline.

When I got to the bar, it turned out that I didn't have to worry about getting those corks out of the bottles. Many of them were now lodged in the Styrofoam-like, drop-panel ceiling tiles above the bar. However, this new development not only included the destruction of country club property, but a flood of wine that had sprayed all over the place when the corks took to the air. It was an impressive sight. Like the Daytona 500 Winner's Circle.

Lesson learned: Don't ever take your hand off the top of a bottle of sparkling wine after the cage has been loosened. The pressure in that bottle is about 90 psi—or three times that of your car's tires. Which also means—don't aim the bottle at anybody either.

The best method is to ease the cork out of the neck: hold the bottle at a 45-degree angle with one hand on the top (with the loosened cage still on the cork) and one hand on the bottom. Twist the bottle back and forth using the hand on the bottom of the bottle—you should try keep the cork still with your other hand. You don't so much pull out the cork as control its pressurized exit.

It takes some practice, but practice only means that you have to drink more bubbles.

By the way—if you don't finish the bottle, stick it in the fridge. Those bubbles should last a couple of days. (You can get one of those sparkling wine stoppers rather cheap.) And if it does go flat, use it for cooking wine.

Knowing no better, we set about pulling the foils and cages from all thirty-six bottles before lining them up in a neat row all across the bar top. It was an impressive sight. Only took about ten minutes.

I can't recall exactly why we left the bar and those thirty-six cageless sparkling wines, but our attention was drawn somewhere else. (Maybe we were fetching flutes from the storeroom?) Whatever it was, I totally forgot about the sparkling wine until around 11:40 p.m., when the lead bartender hissed that we needed to *start pouring, stat*. I jogged across the dining room—a

Inexpensive Bubbles Pairing Exploration

CRUDO:
You Can Do It!

Raw fish. At home. Isn't that generally left to the experts? Perhaps even just a decade ago we would have said *yes* to that question and found a different pairing for inexpensive bubbles, but the availability of extremely fresh fish of impeccable quality has never been better. It's time to break down the perceived wall between professional chef and enthusiastic home cook on this important category of food.

Let's back up a second. Home cooks have been serving raw fish in homes for well over half a century.

If you've ever been fortunate enough to travel to Hawaii, you might've noticed something while you were in the grocery store buying beer and suntan lotion. Even if you were in a big chain grocery store, raw tuna for *poke* and raw salmon for *lomi lomi* were right there in the fish case, waiting to be sold to home cooks who were going to serve it raw in their homes. Should you have been fortunate enough to eat in a Hawaiian person's home, you were likely served one of these two classic preparations.

Our best guess as to how you perceived this meal is, "What the hell? I'm in Hawaii, so the fish has to be fresh, right? Why not try it?" The funny thing is, salmon don't run in Hawaii at all. That fish had to have been imported from the mainland. The whole idea of eating salmon in Hawaii at all came from the mainland. Perception is reality.

The point is that Hawaiian cooks have been serving raw fish in their homes for a long time, and not all of it was "just plucked from the water this morning," as the turn of phrase goes. So conversely, why wouldn't we go to a person's home in the Pacific Northwest, be presented with a luscious plate of king salmon crudo, and be completely confident that it was safe to eat? Salmon would far more likely be just out of the water in Seattle than in Hawaii.

Crudo is the Italian (and Spanish) word for raw. In a culinary sense, it has come to mean raw fish. Think of it as the Italian word for sashimi.

This is the wall we want to break down. The negative perception of eating raw fish in the home likely has nothing to do with the home cook's ability to prepare a delicious dish with raw fish. Instead it has everything to do

with how fresh we perceive that fish to be. No matter how fresh the fish, the fact that it was prepared by a home cook can negate its perceived freshness. The applied skill for serving crudo in the home is sourcing, not cooking. Sure, there are a number of mistakes that can happen between the time the fish leaves the fishmonger and when it arrives on your plate, but generally a home cook would have to really screw up the dish for it to be perceived as not fresh. Conversely, the most talented, world-class chef on earth can't serve questionably fresh fish as a crudo dish and fool people. In general, our nose knows when fish is unsound, and there is (luckily) no way to fool it. For this reason, the "cooking method" below is going to be as much about sourcing as it is about preparation.

Crudo, a.k.a. Sashimi, a.k.a. Raw Fish

Raw fish is delicious. To many a connoisseur, fish is pristinely flavorful when it is raw. While we do feel that a good sear or char can make fish extra flavorful, we also believe that fish has the most pure and clean flavor when served raw. It is the essence of the sea: sweet, briny, and beautiful in appearance.

It is important to not think exclusively of Asia when thinking of raw seafood. While the Japanese consumption of raw fish has certainly been championed by diners worldwide, there are numerous cultures that enjoy raw, fresh fish as well. France, Hawaii, Italy, Spain, Peru, most of Scandinavia, and most of Southeast Asia have numerous raw fish preparations that are enjoyed on a regular basis. Outside of cultural

ties to raw fish, you will find chefs from nearly every cuisine on earth experimenting with raw fish and their own, personal native flavors, or even cross-cultural flavors known as fusion. Raw seafood provides a medium for creativity; this should be liberating for a home cook. Other than making sure the fish is impeccably fresh and properly sliced, the sky's the limit for how you'd like to flavor the dish itself.

Sourcing is More Important than Preparing

The key here is freshness, and the key to freshness is buying your fish from a vendor that you trust—one that you have developed and cultivated a relationship with, perhaps over several years. The fish business is tricky. To be honest, I'm surprised that anyone wants to become a fishmonger at all. It is generally not in the best interest of the fishmonger to sell you the freshest product because that product is going to last longer in the case than the fish that needs to be sold that day or risk going into the garbage. The only way that a fishmonger *really* wants to recommend the freshest fish to a customer is if he or she believes they are developing a relationship (i.e., repeat business) with that customer. If that is the case, they'll want to get you the most satisfying product every time. If you haven't read between the lines yet, that means that you generally won't get great advice from the fish cutter at the grocery store. The exception proves the rule here sometimes too, as I know a few people who have personal relationships with the fishmongers at higher-end grocers and receive

Salmon Crudo with Avocado, Pickled Fennel, and Ligurian Olive Oil

extremely high-quality fresh fish as a result, but your best bet is to go to a dedicated seafood shop. Either way, make sure the place is busy. Busy seafood vendors equate to high turnover of product, which is a better guarantee of the freshness of your fish.

In the restaurant, we share very personal relationships with our vendors, especially fish guys. We trust them, and when the rare occasion comes along that they send us something unsatisfactory, we always get restitution. We just call them and tell them to take it away. We are very fortunate that way. The difference between us in the restaurant and the cook at home is smaller than you think. Contrary to

what most home cooks believe, there isn't a special category on the fishmonger's price sheet (or in their displays) for fish that is to be served raw. In fact, "sashimi-grade" fish is a marketing term. There is no law or regulation in the United States regarding use of this term. You just have to know what the indicators for really fresh fish are, and trust the fishmonger that you've thoroughly vetted to steer you in the right direction.

We keep talking about freshness; let's review once more what that means and why it is so important. Seafood deteriorates in quality especially quickly. There are several scientific reasons for this that are not

Frozen Fish Is Not for Crudo

Sadly, you shouldn't serve raw fish that has been previously frozen. I realize this is a statement that will create tremendous added expense for our readers who don't live on the coasts. The problem stems from the fish's texture, although freshness can also be an issue. While most people understand that the refrigerator only delays or retards the process of spoilage, many seem to think that the freezer can store things indefinitely. Believe it or not, things are still spoiling in the freezer, albeit at a tremendously reduced rate. It is nearly impossible to find out how old a piece of frozen fish really is, and when you thaw it you may encounter that much maligned "fishy" smell. You just can't know until you thaw it out.

The texture of previously frozen fish is massively compromised as well. Just imagine taking a carrot and putting it in the freezer overnight, then thawing it out. In your mind you instinctively know what the result will be. The thawed carrot will be limp, soggy, and won't resemble a fresh carrot whatsoever. If you put this previously frozen carrot out on a raw vegetable platter, your guests will know that something is wrong with that carrot.

The same goes for fish. What happens is simple: the cells of fish (and carrots) are filled with water. Water not only expands when it freezes, but produces sharp, crystalline structures. This expansion and these crystals irreparably burst the cells of the fish. When you thaw it out, it will lack the firm texture that a high-quality crudo dish requires.

Lastly, beware of the term *refreshed fish*. This is a fishmonger's euphemism for frozen and thawed out. It will be sitting in the case right next to the fresh stuff, and since the word *refreshed* is similar to the word *fresh*, they hope you will buy it without asking too many questions. It is actually better to buy frozen fish and thaw it yourself than to buy refreshed fish. At least you'll know how long it's been thawed out, and complete control of the thawing process was under your watchful eye.

This is not to say that frozen fish is a horrible thing. For fish and chips, chowder, fish stew, or gentle cooking methods like steaming or poaching, a deft-handed cook can make it hard to notice that the fish was previously frozen. But for crudo and dry-heat cooking, fresh fish is critical.

terribly important to describe here, but it is critical to keep fish extremely cold to retard this degradation as much as possible. Once the fish begins to lose quality, it's over. There is no way to get it back, despite all of the tricks out there on the Internet like "saltwater-rinse it" or "soak it in milk." Fish to be served raw should have absolutely NONE of the aroma we have come to know as fishiness. It has to smell sweet and clean, with a briny aroma reminiscent of the sea. Even better, it will smell of almost nothing at all. This will be an indicator of how cold and pristinely it has been stored. Let's be honest, you'll be serving raw fish in your home or at a dinner party. You should be absolutely confident, even stoic, about serving it, and chances are that the first thing any skeptical guest is going to do to test your resolve and expertise will be to take a trepidatious sniff.

Crudo or Tartare?
Or Carpaccio? Or Sashimi?
Or Tiraditos? Or Ceviche?
Or Poke? Or Koi Pla?

Raw fish has many different traditional names and preparations. For the purpose of this writing, we are going to categorize them into two very approachable dishes that can be easily executed by the home cook—and it turns out that one begets the other. We are going to start this section with what kind of dish you wish to serve, and then tell you how to buy your raw seafood.

Crudo and sashimi might as well be the same thing. They are essentially quarter-inch-thick slices of raw fish,

cut perfectly across the grain. This requires some observation skills and a really fucking sharp knife. I mean sharp enough to shave the hair off your arm. If you are inclined to try this oft used chef test of sharpness, just hold out your arm, hold the knife at an angle similar to a shaving razor, and shave away. If it feels like the knife is scraping across your arm and no hair is being removed, it's time to get your knife sharpened. If you see a cleanly shorn spot where your arm hair used to be, then your knife is in good shape. Go wash your knife now. There's human arm hair on it. The bald spot is up to you to explain.

Slicing Crudo

Cutting across the grain requires you to be comfortable with waste, because you will end up with a lot of little nubbins of fish that don't work for your presentation of perfect fish planks. Why do you think there are spicy tuna rolls in every sushi restaurant that serves tuna *nigiri*? Yep, all of that extra fish gets diced or minced into a tartare. This is how sushi restaurants can make money with that $40+ per pound *otoro* (tuna belly) that you love so much as nigiri or sashimi.

The grain is best demonstrated with photography. The reason we cut across the grain of the fish is so that the fish is tender and melts in your mouth when you eat it. Having raw fish in your mouth that is difficult to chew can be a very challenging experience for the uninitiated. (It's important to take into account all of the apprehensions that your guests are likely to have about eating raw fish in a private home.

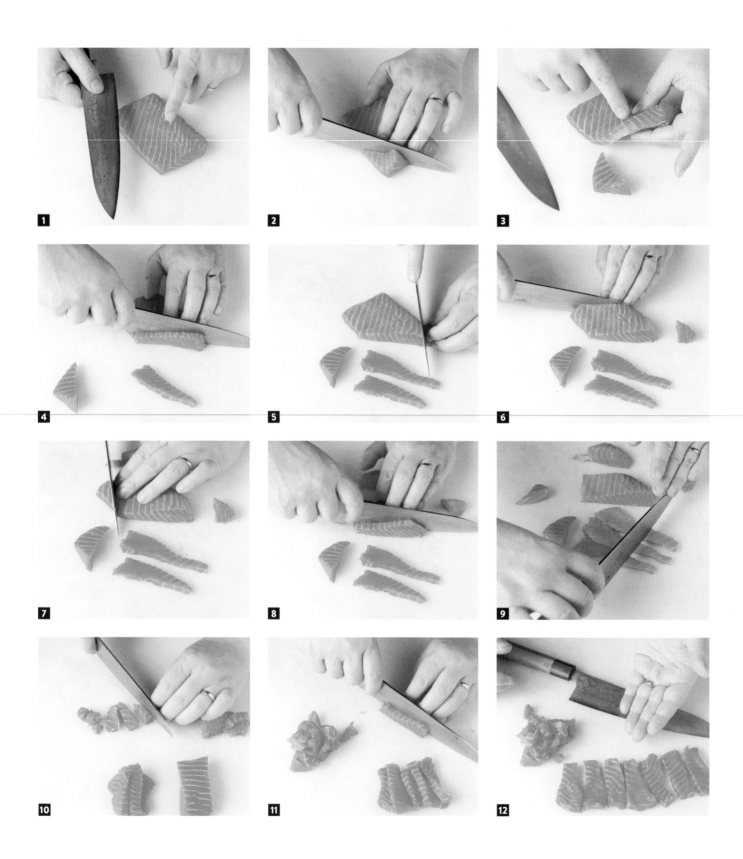

Poorly cut fish can be as off-putting as poorly sourced fish.)

Slice each piece of fish into a rectangular block as best you can. Save all of the scraps. Then look to see how the grain runs and slice directly across it into quarter-inch planks. Use a see-sawing motion and proceed slowly and gently. The word *chop* should never enter your mind when preparing raw fish. Set the planks of fish aside on a chilled plate and transfer it to the refrigerator. You will be seasoning and garnishing the fish later. Save every scrap of fish that is not darkened by the blood line or completely flush with silvery sinew. Those pieces are either bitter or inedibly tough, and should be discarded entirely.

Cutting Tartare

Tartare should be carefully cut in pieces as close to a fine dice as possible. Rough-chopping the fish on a board like you would with parsley will absolutely obliterate the fish flesh and render it into a pile of unappetizing mush. You want to slice through the tartare with just as much judicious care as you did with the crudo. You should be left with a nice, fine dice of fish flesh that is not mushy at all.

Prepping Crudo

Once your crudo is sliced, it's important to salt it a bit before you serve it. This is a somewhat polarizing instruction, but the results are usually excellent. It slightly firms the fish, and it also seasons it nicely so that the flavor is intense and savory. The best method we've used is to salt the fish just a half hour before you serve it;

then set it on paper towels and loosely lay another piece of paper towel over the top of the fish slices. This paper will wick away some of the excess moisture produced by the salted fish as it firms up. Keep everything bracingly cold during this entire process. If you live anywhere near a well-appointed Asian market, there is likely special paper available there that is specifically for this purpose. If you have access to this paper, you actually put the salt on the *outside* of the paper. The osmosis you learned in high school biology will be at work again: The moisture of the fish soaks through the paper and grabs the salt, which then soaks back into the fish without leaving granular salt on the surface. I wouldn't believe it either unless I'd done it myself. It works very well. It is also completely unnecessary, and should not be a deal breaker to you when serving raw fish in your home.

Prepping Tartare

Unlike crudo, tartare does not benefit nearly as much from this quick salt cure. Tartare, by its very nature, is far more likely to be dressed like a salad (with minimal dashes of oil and acid such as vinegar or citrus juice) than served plain—or with minimal garnishes and accoutrements. You certainly can salt tartare ahead, but through the use of the other ingredients in the tartare such as those listed below, you are going to bestow plenty of flavor. That allows you to skip the "salt ahead" step.

Serving Crudo

Crudo should be served with minimal fanfare. You have spent a lot of time and effort to get the best possible fish

1 Identify the grain.

2 Find the grain and cut a corner off, directly against the grain.

3 The grain should be evenly spaced; here's what to look for.

4 Cut slices of crudo across the grain. Your slices will be nice planks. Push the knife forward and then draw the knife back through the fish in one motion. Don't seesaw.

5 When the planks are losing uniformity, cut off another corner. All corner pieces will be reserved for tartare.

6 Remove additional corner pieces so that what remains is a nice block with the grain running one direction.

7 Final "blocking off" of the main piece.

8 Finish cutting even crudo slices from "blocked" cut of fish.

9 Trim tapering pieces to begin cutting tartare.

10 Dicing remaining pieces for tartare.

11 Final crudo cut, with finished tartare and crudo slices ready to be served.

12 Salmon: ready for tartare and crudo.

you can afford, then painstakingly sliced it and kept it icy cold. You don't need to douse it with hot sauce or extremely pungent olive oil. If you're planning to go Asian, then drenching the fish with soy sauce and wasabi is equally sinful, as you will completely mask the delicate, immaculate flavor that you sought so diligently to achieve. Save your big, bold flavors for tartare.

Here are some suggestions for garnishing crudo:

- Buttery, rich olive oil, such as one from Liguria (Italy) or the South of France
- Grapeseed oil (when the lushness of oil is desired without the intense flavor of olive)
- All manner of citrus juice
- Mild vinegar, such as rice vinegar, palm sugar vinegar, or coconut vinegar
- Aged balsamic vinegar
- Extremely high-quality Japanese soy sauce (just a few drops)
- Avocado
- Prosciutto or serrano ham
- Caviar
- Sea urchin (which also makes a lovely crudo of its own)
- Fresh herbs (not too much)
- Fresh chiles or chile flakes (remember, just a touch)
- Mild, sweet nuts like pine nuts, almonds, or pistachios
- Tomato (only at the peak of season when they're perfectly sweet
- Capers (with really oily fish)

- Egg yolk (quail eggs work perfectly for this)
- Aioli or mayonnaise (classic or flavored)
- Vinaigrette (classic or flavored)

Don't go crazy. Select up to three complementary ingredients and serve them on a plate alongside the fish—not on top of it. You've just spent a lot of money and time, not to mention cutting skill, to display this pristine fish. Covering it up with a bunch of stuff is almost like undoing your own work. If you are using highly acidic ingredients like citrus juice, or vinegar, or vinaigrette, then brush each piece of fish with a little oil. This light coating of oil protects the fish from the acidic ingredients, which will "cook" the fish over time. (See The Ceviche Effect below.)

Serving Tartare

A tartare is really a salad made of diced raw beef or fish. In our case, it is fish, impeccably fresh, meticulously cut, and kept very cold. Beyond this, there are literally hundreds of kinds of tartare out there. From the ubiquitous Ahi Tuna Tower of the 1990s, to the more thoughtful approach to tartare being applied today, there is a nearly endless realm of possibilities with this preparation. There are a couple of things that a good tartare should include, but by no means is the following list exhaustive or definitive. It should also be noted that nearly everything that goes with crudo can work splendidly when folded into a tartare.

Ingredients to Consider in Your Raw Fish Preparations

AROMATICS

These are vegetables, but ones that seldom show up on the side of a plate like broccoli or carrots. They are vegetables used for their aromatic value to flavor things. They are often made of bulbs which grow in the ground. Their botanical names are alliums and rhizomes. They include:

- Shallots
- Garlic
- Onions (make sure they're suitable to eat raw like sweet onions, or have been purged of their acridity through heat or a saltwater flush)
- Scallions
- Ramps (wild onions)
- Leeks (not raw)
- Ginger
- Lemongrass
- Galangal
- Chiles

PICKLES

Pickled vegetables are a classic addition to a tartare, and they don't necessarily have to be made from cucumber. Pretty much anything that has been preserved in salt, sugar, and acid will make a great addition to raw fish. Just chop it finely and fold it in. With ingredients this acidic, they should be added to the tartare at the absolute last minute, or should first be combined with oil to avoid The Ceviche Effect noted on page 131. These pickled products can include but are not limited to:

- Pickled ginger
- Pickled onions
- Pickled shallots
- Pickled fennel
- Capers
- Cornichons
- Pickled garlic
- Pickled asparagus
- Pickled carrots
- Pickled green beans
- Pickled peppers or chiles

FAT

Some form of fat is vital to the tartare, having some richness and keeping it from curing or "cooking" too quickly from exposure to the acid. There are many which work, but there are some that simply cannot. Butter could be a terrific addition to a tartare if it wasn't rock solid when chilled, which is the only temperature to serve fish tartare. Same goes for coconut oil, or really rich, freshly pressed olive oils. They just simply "freeze" (set up and become solid) when used to dress extremely cold fish. Here are some oils and fatty products that do work:

- Neutral oil like grapeseed, canola, sunflower, or vegetable
- Nut oils like hazelnut, almond, walnut, and pistachio
- Mild olive oil
- Sesame oil
- Avocado oil
- Coconut milk
- Olives
- Raw egg yolk

ACID

Pickles can provide some acid if you choose to use them—and sometimes that's enough, but more often than not, a tartare needs a tiny spritz of extra acidity to make it sing. This can be brought in the form of:

- Vinegar (usually a mild one like apple cider, rice, or something tropical)
- Citrus juice (any)
- Aged balsamic
- Tomatoes

Putting It All Together

So we just got a beautiful piece of king salmon. The flesh itself is fatty but also strong-flavored, even when raw, so we know it will hold up to many flavors and respond very well to acidity. We're going to use the main "loin" (fish don't actually have loins) piece for some beautiful crudo. The loin is that part of the fillet that looks like you could cut it into a perfectly symmetrical dice. Essentially the part of the fillet that is not the collar, the belly or the tail. Then we're going to cut up all of the aforementioned belly, collar, and tail parts to make a delightful tartare dish. We're also going to pair them with some Crémant, or Prosecco, or Cava.

The Ceviche Effect

One of the greatest dishes in all of cuisine is fish that has been "cooked" in acid (most often citrus juice). Fish protein has a special nature that causes it to turn opaque and firm up when exposed to high levels of acidity. Other than its flavor, the fish is virtually indiscernible from fish that has been steamed or poached. The proteins are almost identical in texture.

While ceviche is a wonderful dish, and is certainly great with cheap bubbles, this effect is also a pitfall when preparing crudo or tartare. We can inadvertently end up making a ceviche instead of a crudo or tartare. Crudo and tartare need to be assembled at the last minute for this reason—certainly if high-acid ingredients are involved.

1 Start by halving your shallot and making as many vertical cuts as possible without cutting the root.

2 Continue cutting through the shallot.

3 Finish by cutting across your vertical cuts for a fine mince.

4 Grating ginger is easily done on a microplane.

5 Peel the cucumber over a plastic-lined cutting board for easy disposal.

6 Cut the peeled cucumber into sticks before rotating and cutting into dice.

7 Begin cutting your chili pepper into planes.

8 Cut your planes into sticks.

9 Cut your sticks into dice.

6 to 8 ounces fresh wild salmon, cut into ¼-inch dice

¼ cup cucumber, peeled, seeded, and diced

1 teaspoon red Fresno chile, minced

½ teaspoon freshly grated ginger root

Juice and zest of ½ lime

¼ cup coconut milk

1 tablespoon minced cilantro

2 mint leaves, cut into very thin strips (chiffonade)

2 basil or Thai basil leaves, chiffonade

Bibb or butter lettuce leaves (optional)

If you've made the crudo on page 134, you very likely have a number of trimmings that are perfectly delectable, they just aren't nicely cut planks of fish. Fear not. As mentioned previously, when making a crudo, one is likely to make a tartare as well in order to get maximum utilization out of their very expensive fish. (Of course, you may also purchase the salmon specifically for this purpose.) This is a fun way to make tartare, with flavors slightly inspired by Asia.

Salmon Tartare with Coconut Milk, Red Fresno Chiles, Ginger, and Lime

Serves 2 as an appetizer

1. Salt the salmon and the cucumber separately and place them on a super-clean kitchen towel or paper toweling. Let sit for 5 minutes, then pat dry with more paper towels to wick away the excess moisture.

2. Place all of the ingredients except the basil and the mint in a bowl and toss thoroughly, as if you are dressing a salad.

3. Place the tartare on a plate (or shape each portion by using a ring mold). Alternatively, serve the tartare in the lettuce leaves to make little wraps. Great for parties that way.

4. Garnish by sprinkling the mint and basil over the tartare. Serve immediately, or the fish will begin to "cook" from the lime juice and salt.

Adding coconut milk to the tartare.

¾ cup rice wine vinegar

1 medium shallot, finely minced

2 teaspoons kosher salt

1 tablespoon honey

1 teaspoon black peppercorns

1 tablespoon fennel seeds

1 bulb fennel, shaved paper-thin on a mandoline

12 ounces wild king salmon fillet

1 avocado, firm but not overripe

1 teaspoon chopped tarragon

1 teaspoon chopped chives

1 tablespoon chopped flat-leaf parsley

2 tablespoons (yep, that much) Ligurian or other very mild, buttery olive oil

Small pinch of fleur de sel

½ cup ice

This is a great illustration of how a crudo can be enhanced by just a few ingredients. As we've discussed, the idea is simple: some acidity, some richness, some very flavorful, buttery oil. Finish with some anise-flavored herbs and you've got a spectacular crudo.

Salmon Crudo with Avocado, Pickled Fennel, and Ligurian Olive Oil

Serves 4 as an appetizer

1. Make the pickling solution: In a small pot, heat the rice vinegar, shallot, salt, honey, peppercorns, and fennel seeds to a full boil, then reduce the heat to a bare simmer and let simmer for 10 minutes to infuse the aromatics. Place the shaved fennel in a bowl and then strain the vinegar solution over it.

2. Let the fennel steep for 20 to 30 minutes. Taste a piece of the fennel. It should be like any pickle: crisp, salty, acidic, and sweet. If the pickle is there, add the ice. If not, let it steep for a few minutes longer. As soon as the pickles are ready, add ice to stop the process. Keep the fennel in the pickling solution until ready to use, then strain. This step can be done literally a month in advance.

3. Cut the salmon according to the instructions and photos on page 126. Remember to save all of the odds and ends for tartare.

4. Salt the fish on a plate, according to the paper towel method explained in the "Prepping Crudo" section on page 127. Place the plate in the refrigerator, allowing the fish to cure. After 30 minutes, remove the fish from the refrigerator and gather the rest of your ingredients.

5. Cut the avocado into slices equally as thick as the crudo slices. Shingle alternating slices of the avocado and salmon on a chilled plate. Garnish with wisps of pickled fennel and herbs, then drizzle the whole plate with the olive oil.

6. Sprinkle the whole presentation with fleur de sel. Serve immediately with well-chilled Crémant, Prosecco, or Cava.

Wine Wardrobe Bottle #3

LIGHT-BODIED WHITE

Unlike Champagne (the expensive type), Prosecco, and Cava—the discussion of light-bodied white wines brings in the topic of grape variety as it pertains to its geography, because where a grape grows has a tremendous influence on its flavor profile.

The flavor profile of the light-bodied white Wine Wardrobe bottle will tend to have its base in the citrus category—lemon, lime, grapefruit—fruits that bring to mind a lip-smacking tang. The tart flavors of these wines may also include tree fruits in their greener forms, such as Granny Smith apples and under-ripe pears. But what we're really counting on with the light-bodied white is the moderate-to-high acidity that will help it perform its duties as the go-to for some categories of food that are more difficult to pair.

Seasonally speaking, light-bodied white wine doesn't see as much action in the wintertime. However, if you're in part of the world where oysters are best in the colder months, it's essential.

So what is the light-bodied white going to do for us? It will be your workhorse when it comes to tackling salads and vegetable-driven dishes. Anything with a vinaigrette involved is begging for a light-bodied, high-acid wine.

My ultimate trick for the light-bodied white: if the food you are preparing calls for a finishing squeeze of lemon or lime, pull one of these out. Everything from a Caesar salad to take-out fish and chips. Tacos? Yeah, really. And it will tackle the complexity of many Mexican dishes with refreshing abandon.

There's a long list of exceptional grapes that fall in the light-bodied category, but we'll start with something familiar to most: Sauvignon Blanc.

According to the most recent reliable calculations, Sauvignon Blanc is the third-most-planted white grape in the world, meaning it enjoys the same rare air of Chardonnay and Pinot Grigio atop the mountain of grape recognition. But it also means that (equal to Chardonnay and Pinot Grigio) there's a higher probability of running into subpar examples. The charm of Sauvignon Blanc (high acidity with flavors of lemon, lime, and grapefruit) is lost when grown in a hot climate and/or subjected to new oak barrels.

So the best advice for finding a Sauvignon Blanc that tastes like a Sauvignon Blanc

is to start with historically reliable sources: New Zealand and France. In the past few decades, the Marlborough region in New Zealand has become the world's most popular address for Sauvignon Blanc—these wines tend to be dramatic, overt, and occasionally shockingly aromatic. But before the ascension of New Zealand, the gold standard was the Loire Valley of France, home to Sancerre and Pouilly Fumé. If you'd like to taste the classic, get thee to a Sancerre.

And while there are great examples of Sauvignon Blanc found in most areas with a hospitable temperature range, you're going to find variability in quality and cost.

Another grape worth reaching for: Grüner Veltliner. Grüner is the most important grape in Austria—and while it can be produced in a more opulent style, we find that the less expensive versions tend to satisfy quite well with proper acidity and liveliness. If somebody happens to recommend a one-liter bottle of Grüner with a bottle cap in lieu of a cork, hold your opinion until it's in your glass. Sometimes those bring a surprisingly high enjoyment-to-cost ratio.

Speaking of high cost-to-enjoyment ratio: Muscadet. This wine is produced from the grape Melon de Bourgogne in the far western section of the Loire Valley, which has historically been viewed as a source for cheap, insipid, grocery store wine. But like so many areas of the world where improvements in technology in the vineyard and winery collide with a group of people dedicated to producing wines with soul, the quality of Muscadet today is strikingly good. What's also strikingly good is the

price—you can find great wines for what will feel criminally cheap. (It's a great option when you're dining out, by the way—you'll certainly be getting your money's worth.)

Other excellent light-bodied white wines:

- VINHO VERDE—Portugal's (often) slightly spritzy summer-in-a-glass crowd pleaser. Often low-alcohol, Vinho Verde is the world's best beach wine. Simple and easy to drink.

- TXAKOLI—Pronounced cha-ko-LEE, grown in the Basque region of Spain. Some hold a similarity in style and spritz with Vinho Verde, but the best are simply electric— like the most interesting lemonade you've ever had.

- DRY RIESLING—Quickest way to ascertain if a bottle of Riesling is dry: check the alcohol level. If it's above 12.5%, chances are the liquid inside has a less than discernable level of residual sugar. We recommend looking for Rieslings from Germany labeled *trocken*. You'll also find some great dry Rieslings from Australia, particularly the Eden Valley. In America, New York and Washington State both make stunning dry Rieslings.

Last, look for white wines from Gascogny using such grapes as Ugni Blanc, Colombard, and Petite Manseng. They are usually very cheap and worth stocking up on for the summer.

Light-Bodied White Pairing Exploration

ASPARAGUS:

Everyone's Favorite

Asparagus is certainly the most oft-requested vegetable in any restaurant I've ever worked in for my entire career. People love, nay adore asparagus. Evidently, many wish that it was in season and delicious all year. Some people buy it and serve it year-round, but asparagus is a harbinger of spring, and undoubtedly is at its most delicious then. Here's why: Asparagus is a temperate climate vegetable, which means that it grows best in climates with four seasons as well as cool nights. When we try to make asparagus available all year, we are growing it in places with two seasons (rainy and hot), with very hot nights. Sure it grows, but it grows way too fast, and is a specter of its northern brethren. It's OK for something to be delicious for eight precious weeks a year. We can eat it with abandon then and crave it for the rest of the year, making it taste that much more delicious the next time it is available in season.

I eat asparagus at least five times a week when it's in season, which for us in the Pacific Northwest is almost always the months of April and May. If we're lucky the local asparagus is also available in June, but I don't count on it. In June, if we get it in, the stalks are often thick and meaty, which are an asparagus-lover's dream. As enticing as pencil-thin asparagus can be, it generally doesn't have as much flavor. Seek medium to thick stalks and adjust your cooking accordingly.

Asparagus has long been thought to be one of the enemies of wine. My associate will help me to utterly dispel this myth. Asparagus is actually great with wine, except maybe California

Chardonnay, which is the wine that everyone in the '80s and '90s really wanted to perfectly pair with asparagus. It likely led to this absurd falsehood about asparagus being a "wine killer."

Let's Make Some Asparagus

METHOD ONE (IF A STRIKINGLY VIBRANT GREEN COLOR IS DESIRED)

This is a vegetable that really experiences a loss of color with some methods of cooking—and there are times when you just can't serve asparagus that is army-tent green. Fortunately, there is a way to present asparagus with a vibrant green color every time. The added benefit of this method is that you can control the final flavor of the asparagus spears, because you are basically just warming them up before you serve them with the seasonings or accompaniments of your liking. If you choose to warm them up at all.

- Boil a LOT of water with a LOT of salt. The amount of salt should almost make you uncomfortable; it should be very salty to taste. I hate to sound overly chefy here, but the amount of salt depends on how hard or soft your water is; generally we use ½ cup to a gallon of water and then adjust to taste. The goal is to put flavorful water into bland asparagus. This uses the same process of osmosis that most of us vaguely remember from biology class in high school, but it actually works with food. Given enough time, the water will be as salty as the asparagus, meaning the asparagus will be well-seasoned and the water will be less salty than when you started.

- Drop some asparagus into the boiling water and stand there. Don't walk away. The water will likely stop boiling unless you're using a very large pot.

- The window of perfect doneness is very short-lived, and asparagus can vary from being as thin as pencils to as thick as your thumb, which means we can't really give you a "Cook for X minutes" instruction here. Have your spider (strainer) and your ice bath ready. Also have the pan/plate/platter on which you plan to "land" or hold the asparagus at the ready.

- The only way to tell if the asparagus is done is to take out a piece and check. After the water reboils, pluck one out and try it. Don't get caught up in some faux-Italian concept of doneness called al dente. Italians do not hold vegetable cookery to the same level of doneness that they do pasta. Well-cooked vegetables have the most flavor. Partially raw vegetables do not. The asparagus should be easy to bite through. One's molars should not need to be engaged in the process.

- Pro tip: If you're going to grill the asparagus later, remove the spears in a state that's just shy of what you would like the final doneness to be.

Daniel Patterson of Coi restaurant in San Francisco is the first person I know of to write something that a lot of us chefs have known for a long time, which is that you don't need to shock your asparagus in ice water. He writes about this in his brilliant cookbook, entitled *Coi: Recipes and Stories*. He's right, you do risk losing flavor by plunging hot vegetables in ice water. While I think that this is sage advice for professionals, I don't find it practical for home cooks or for professionals with limited refrigeration. Ideally, we professionals have the luxury of large walk-in coolers, as well as large sheet pans where we can spread several pounds of asparagus out in a single layer and get them straight into the fridge. If you're fortunate enough to have this luxury available to you, I encourage you to try this method. In fact, I implore you. The difference in flavor is noticeable.

But if you're like most of us and have to use ice, don't leave the vegetables in the ice bath. This is how flavor is lost. Cool the spears and remove them immediately. Otherwise, through osmosis, the flavorless water will leach from the flavorful asparagus (the exact opposite of what we discussed above with the extremely salty blanching water). Don't leave asparagus in the ice water.

The most important part of this method is what we call "bringing it up" in the industry. How are we going to get these already cooked asparagus to the plate, hot and delicious? My favorite method is the grill or a screaming-hot (hopefully wood-fired) oven. Just salt and oil the asparagus, and kiss them to the heat. Remember, they're already cooked, so don't leave them on or in the heat for too long.

Another method is to serve pre-blanched asparagus lavished in butter, olive oil, or duck fat, with shallots, garlic, ginger, or any other aromatic vegetable. Then herbs or spices. A very complex asparagus dish can be crafted by thoughtfully "bringing them up" in a sauté pan.

METHOD TWO (IF A VERY INTENSE FLAVOR IS DESIRED AT THE EXPENSE OF COLOR)

Sometimes it's OK to serve asparagus that isn't "restaurant green." I usually do this for people I know and love, or for people who let me explain to them why beauty is better perceived with the mouth than the eyes, at least for asparagus.

Get your oven as hot as it goes. I hope it's clean, because if not you'll need to open a window, disable your fire alarm, and turn on your fan.

- Set one of the oven racks in the middle of the oven. Heat the oven to its hottest temperature. Get your heaviest-gauge sauté pan (or any shallow pan with a handle that won't melt) and place it in the oven.

- While the oven is heating, prepare a marinade of your choosing (the easiest being salt, pepper, and your choice of oil and vinegar) and marinate the asparagus spears for about 15 minutes.

- Carefully remove the now raging-hot pan from the oven. Shake most of the marinade off of the asparagus and carefully place it in the pan. It will sizzle and spit like crazy. Get it back into the oven post haste.

- Close the oven door and don't open it for 10 minutes . . . 12 is better . . . 14 and you're a completely fearless badass, as the asparagus will likely be perfect (or they could be burnt to a crisp). Opening the oven door diminishes

the efficacy of the roast, so play a little game with yourself and don't peek unless the window in your oven is crystal clear. You can look through that all you like.

- While the asparagus is roasting, have EVERY possible bit of your mise en place ready. Hot pads. Utensil to get the asparagus onto the plate. Plates. Accompaniments. Garnishes. EVERYTHING. If you need to cook any of these things, cook them now, while the asparagus is roasting.

- Remove the asparagus from the oven. Shake it around, as it is likely very browned on one side.

- Garnish and plate. Fast. Remember, you had every single thing ready to go at this point, so getting this perfect, delicious asparagus to your hungry guests quickly should be a snap.

Asparagus: raw and blanched

¼ pound shallots, skin on

3 tablespoons neutral oil, such as canola

Sprig of fresh thyme

1 pound asparagus, as fresh as possible, woody ends trimmed

3 tablespoons butter, cultured if possible

4 eggs

Juice and zest of ½ lemon

¼ cup Italian parsley, finely chopped

Fleur de sel (or other coarse sea salt), for sprinkling

Oven-Roasted Asparagus with Blistered Shallots and Sunny-Side Farm Egg

Serves 4 as an appetizer

1. Heat the oven to 400°F.

2. Remove any loose outer papers from the shallots, then place them, still in their skins, into the oven. We recommend using a sauté pan with an oven-safe handle for this task, as it is easy to get in and out of the oven without burning yourself. Roast until they are soft and tender, roughly 6 to 8 minutes (big shallots can take up to 10 minutes). Slightly cool them, then peel and cut them into thick slices.

3. Add the oil, thyme, and asparagus to the same pan you roasted the shallots in and cook in the same way that you just cooked the shallots. Remove the asparagus spears just before they are done, toss them in the pan, and set them aside.

4. Get another sauté pan ready to cook the eggs. One that holds 4 eggs is ideal, and a nonstick coating is great too. Put 1½ tablespoons of butter into the pan and let it melt.

5. Crack the eggs into the pan and place it in the oven. (We find an oven to be the best method for cooking sunny-side eggs, as it will set the whites with ambient oven heat while keeping the yolk nice and runny.)

6. At the same time you place the eggs in the oven, add the remaining butter, the lemon juice, sliced shallots, and parsley to the asparagus pan and return it to the oven to get all those ingredients hot again.

7. When the asparagus and eggs are both done, remove them from the oven. On each of four plates, lay down the asparagus, then the shallots, then drizzle the plate with some of the butter, which should now be turning slightly brown.

8. Finish the plates with one sunny-side egg per portion. Sprinkle the egg with a pinch of fleur de sel and grate some lemon zest over the whole dish.

MEDIUM-BODIED WHITE

The first step in identifying the medium-bodied white wine is to say what it is not. It may seem like a cop-out—using the obviousness of the personalities of the sparkling, light, sweet, full, and seasoned white wines in order to illustrate the medium—but it's a surprisingly effective method. I don't think I would have passed high school biology without the ability to dissect a multiple-choice quiz, and I don't think we can effectively conceptualize the medium-bodied wine without doing this comparison.

The medium-bodied white is not as dramatic as the more overt light-bodied white, with all its identifiable leanness and citrus, high acidity, and electricity. It's also not as dramatic as the full-bodied white and its cousin, well-seasoned white, because the medium-bodied white will lack the weight, viscosity, and gravity to command the attention of the room. So if it is neither of those things, nor sparkling or sweet—you've found your medium-bodied white wine.

Here's what it *is*, though: it's the quiet majority. Of all the categories of white wines out there in the world, the medium-bodied white is the easiest to locate—and the most well-known varietal is Pinot Gris/Grigio.

Pinot Gris and Pinot Grigio are the same grape. (In Italy, it's Grigio. Just about everywhere else, Gris.) You might run into sweet styles in places like Alsace, France—or fuller styles from parts of Italy and Oregon. Generally speaking, though, there's a medium-bodied wine in a bottle of Pinot Grigio. Which is why my first strong recommendation is to skip Pinot Grigio. Not entirely—since there are some magnificent ones out there, and I would never discount an entire category of grape—but I want to encourage some adventure in your wine world.

So: cruise by the Italian white section and pick out *anything else*. The white wines of Italy from north to south are some of the most delicious and underrated wines in the world. The grapes are not household names, but some indigenous varieties have spent centuries adapting to their surroundings and forming a unique set of flavors that cannot be replicated by simply transplanting the vines to a similar climate.

This is Eric Rabena and Adrienne Kimberley. Also meet their dog Roxy, who wasn't terribly helpful with the clams, but was super cute the entire time.

And because it's Italy, sometimes the name of the grape is also the name of the place, but sometimes it's not—so this is a good place to start:

- GRAPES: Fiano, Vermentino, Greco, Verdicchio, Trebbiano, Pinot Bianco, Grechetto, Falanghina, Grillo, Inzolia, Picolit, Verduzzo, Vernaccia, Tocai Fruiliano, Arneis, Catarratto
- PLACES: Soave, Gavi

If it's white, from Italy, and you don't recognize it—try it. Sometimes these grapes veer into the full-bodied category, but you'll be glad for the introduction.

Also check out Pinot Gris's cousin, Pinot Blanc. Pinot Blanc can be every bit as appealing as its relative, with all those mouth-watering tree-fruit flavors, but with the benefit of not being so recognizable. (Especially if you find one from Austria or Germany, since they call it Weissburgunder. Or in Italy, where they call it Pinot Bianco.) That said, Pinot Blanc from Alsace is one of France's most reasonably priced experiences, and it's also easy to spot at the wine store—Alsace allows for the name of the grape to be proudly displayed on the bottle. You will also be well served if you get your hands on a Pinot Blanc from the Willamette Valley of Oregon—not as widely available, but worth seeking out.

Chenin Blanc, like Riesling, can be made in a variety of styles depending on geography and the winemaker's intent. Quickest shortcut to getting the right style of Chenin is to head to the Loire Valley and look for a Vouvray labeled *sec*. Other regions besides Vouvray worth keeping an eye out for: Anjou, Saumur, Jasnières, and Savennières.

South Africa has many thousands of acres of Chenin Blanc planted—more than anywhere else in the world. It may take some hunting and some guidance at a wine store, but we've had some luck over the years finding South African Chenin Blanc with character.

Pinot Blanc from Alsace

There's a little glitch/oddity/exception in Alsace as it pertains to bottles labeled Pinot Blanc—they actually might not contain any Pinot Blanc grapes. The grape Auxerrois is commonly used as a stand-in. Apparently, the rule is borne from regarding Pinot Blanc as a *term*, rather than a *grape*—opening up the possibility of having your Pinot Blanc contain Auxerrois, Pinot Gris, or even Pinot Noir. It's one of my favorite French wine quirks.

Medium-Bodied White Pairing Exploration

STEAMED SHELLFISH:

Not All Luxury Products Need to be Expensive

One of my favorite things is shellfish. Honestly. I love eating them, but even more I love cooking them. They provide their own flavorful sauce, which can be richly embellished or left alone. The liquid contained within mussels, clams, oysters, even small scallops, is utterly precious—to me, more precious than truffles or foie gras. Access to the flavors of those luxuries is entirely dependent on one's financial means, but the precious liquor within shellfish is available to almost anyone. Shellfish are very economical unless you're talking about enormous scallops, or oysters intended to be eaten raw. If you live away from the coast, you need to be highly selective as with any seafood, but shellfish should still not be terribly expensive. A built-in bonus is that your fishmonger wants to part with them as soon as possible or lose them entirely. It is unlikely that he or she will adorn them with a lofty price tag.

I think steamed shellfish can literally take on the flavors of any culture. I used to challenge my culinary students with this. Think about how Vietnamese mussels would taste. How about Tunisian clams? Portuguese scallops? What about Portuguese mussels but through the eye of a Brazilian? Anything goes with steamed shellfish.

Like the medium-bodied white wines we just discussed, there are a multitude of preparations of shellfish. For the purposes of getting you fed on a Tuesday night, we are going to narrow the focus to mussels and clams, as the methodology for them is virtually identical. If you happen to have access to scallops in their shells, this will work for those as well. We are also going to approach this like some of the other chapters, with an overarching method, and then some examples we know will work with the wines. Here are the basics:

Cleaning and Purging

If you've just experienced the joy of (safely and legally) harvesting your own mussels or clams (or even if you've just brought them home from the store), you'll need to scrub and purge them. Use a firm brush to scrub them free of mud, bits of seaweed, and tiny, inedible mussels that attach themselves to the larger ones. Then deposit them in a large bowl with cold running water and rinse them as best you can. Keep in mind that these are sea creatures and they don't like fresh water all that much, so don't do this for too long.

In the case of clams, which live under the sand rather than attached to dock pylons or boats like mussels, you will need to purge them of the sand and grit that lodges in their digestive systems. The best way to do this is to put them in a pan of cold water with a small handful of cornmeal. Set the pan inside your refrigerator for an hour or so. The clams will purge some of the sand from their stomachs in order to feed on the cornmeal, which will hopefully get that last little bit of sand out.

Time for a Beard Trim

Mussels have beards. They are a spindly, almost seaweed-like hairy appendage that they use to attach themselves to things or each other. These beards tend to eat about as well as you would think. Since no one wants a mouthful of beard, they need to be removed. The problem is that these beards are attached to the delicate, still-living creature within the shell, and if you roughhouse the beard you can kill the mussel. That is why it's best to debeard them as close to cooking time as possible—certainly no earlier than the morning of the same day.

We Know it Sucks, But You Have to Cook Them Alive

Dead mussels and clams can be dangerous. Being very simple organisms, they start to decompose extremely rapidly. Similar to shrimp and lobster, their digestive enzymes also start to go to work the minute they expire. The exact enzymes that make their digestion possible when they're alive starts to eat at their own flesh when they die. Fortunately there are a few ways to make sure that they're still alive and kicking so that you don't end up with a severe tummy ache or worse. (See Shellfish CPR on page 153.)

Steamed Manilla Clams with Spanish Chorizo, Spring Vegetables, and Picada

Basic Technique for Steaming Shellfish

The method for steaming shellfish is almost always the same:

1. Add a tiny bit of fat or liquid to the bottom of a large, straight-sided sauté pan that you can put a lid on.

2. Add aromatic vegetables and either sweat them, sauté them, or caramelize them.

3. Add about ½ inch of flavorful liquid such as wine, beer, vinegar, or stock.

4. Add the shellfish and cover the pan.

5. When the majority of the shellfish have opened, add finishing ingredients like butter, cream, coconut milk, herbs, and/or cured pork.

6. Taste the sauce for seasoning.

7. Serve immediately.

This method works for hundreds of varieties of shellfish dishes. Here are some examples, following the structure:

SPANISH-STYLE CLAMS

Fat: Olive Oil
Aromatics: Garlic, piquillo peppers, smoked paprika
Flavorful Liquid: Sherry
Finishing Ingredients: *Picada* (see below), chorizo, parsley, cilantro

BURGUNDIAN-STYLE MUSSELS

Fat: Butter
Aromatics: Leeks
Flavorful Liquid: White wine
Finishing Ingredients: Heavy cream, pulled ham hock, Dijon mustard, rosemary

NORMANDY-STYLE MUSSELS

Fat: Butter
Aromatics: Shallots, finely diced apples, bacon
Flavorful Liquid: Hard cider

Finishing Ingredients: Crème fraîche or sour cream, fresh thyme

SICILIAN-STYLE CLAMS

Fat: Olive oil
Aromatics: Fennel seed, garlic, lemon peel, sun-dried tomatoes
Flavorful Liquid: White wine
Finishing Ingredients: Torn basil, crispy olive oil–fried breadcrumbs, squeeze of lemon juice, drizzle of olive oil

As you can see, the possibilities are really only limited by your imagination and a basic understanding of what flavors work together. Let's do one last example, just to prove a point (although a light-bodied lager might pair better with this dish than medium-bodied white wine).

MALAYSIAN-STYLE MUSSELS

Fat: Peanut oil
Aromatics: Yellow curry paste (made of fresh turmeric, shallots, garlic, chiles, lemongrass, galangal, and shrimp paste), fish sauce
Flavorful Liquid: Xiao Xing wine
Finishing Ingredients: Coconut cream, crispy fried shallots, cilantro, Thai basil

This is why we love shellfish so much. It is truly a basic canvas upon which we can paint subtle or intense flavor profiles. The liquid released from these beauties lends a glorious natural perfume to any sauce.

Time to Sop Up the Goods

Serving shellfish without starch is an abomination. It is practically a required component of any shellfish dish. Here are some examples of starchy accompaniments to soak up all of that beautiful liquid:

- Bread
- Toast
- Bruschetta (grilled bread rubbed with raw garlic)
- Fried or baked croutons
- Rice
- Baby potatoes
- Pasta
- Hard polenta (grilled or fried crisp)
- Flatbread like naan, focaccia, pide, or roti
- Frybread

Once those shells are emptied and sitting in a shell bowl, your mission is not quite over. This is when you employ the starchy goodness. In some cases, as with rice, it is best to preheat this accompaniment, especially if you're going to plop it in the bowl with the liquid, which has now likely cooled down. Try the Malaysian recipe, and then put a big ol' scoop of hot rice in the broth. Re-garnish it with more cilantro and crispy shallots, and then tear it up. You've just successfully turned what normally suffices as an appetizer into a full-blown meal.

Shellfish CPR

1. If they're open, just pinch them shut. The muscles inside should reflexively cause them to close. Sometimes you have to hold them closed for 3 to 4 seconds, but they won't stay closed if they're dead. Toss any of them that don't stay shut.

2. Take a whiff. They should smell like the ocean. If you detect any off aromas whatsoever, you'll have to sniff each one to locate the dead or dying clam. Buh bye . . .

3. After cooking them, if there are any that refuse to open, they are likely dead as well and should be tossed. We know there are plenty of people out there, including shellfish farmers, who will tell you that the clams aren't always dead when this happens. The problem is, the results are disastrous if you're wrong. Don't risk it, please.

½ cup extra-virgin olive oil

½ cup crumbled stale bread

½ cup slivered almonds

3 cloves garlic

1 teaspoon pimentón (Spanish paprika, hot or mild)

Picada, a Very Special Thickener

Catalan cooks, in the south of Spain, have developed a very special thickening agent that is extremely versatile. It is basically a combination of breadcrumbs, sometimes nuts, and aromatics that are ground to form a fine-textured paste. The aromatics could be garlic, spices, and/or herbs. This paste is then stirred into the broth at the last minute and it thickens it, making for a significantly more substantial dish. Classic Catalan picada includes almonds, breadcrumbs, olive oil, smoked paprika, garlic, parsley, and saffron. One could easily adapt the same concept to other flavors and use the technique to thicken any shellfish broth.

Picada

Makes 1 cup

1. Heat the oil in a deep skillet over medium heat. Add the bread and fry it, stirring, until golden brown. Add the almonds and fry until golden brown.

2. Use a slotted spoon to remove the almonds and the bread from the oil. Cool and reserve the oil.

3. Add the garlic to the bread mixture and then cool the mixture to room temperature. The latent heat from the nuts and bread will lightly steam the garlic cloves, slightly removing some of the acrid bite of raw garlic.

4. Put the fried bread mixture and pimentón into the bowl of a food processor. Process to a smooth paste, adding the reserved olive oil as necessary to achieve a smooth consistency (you might not need all of it). The paste should be smooth, but not greasy or over-saturated with oil.

5. Let's take it all the way: In the interest of walking you through one of these variations, here's a recipe for Spanish-Style Clams with Chorizo and Spring Vegetables. We would pair this with a Spanish Albariño, which is an amazing wine with shellfish.

Finished picada being added to clams.

1 tablespoon extra-virgin olive oil

¼ cup finely chopped spring onions, green and white parts (substitute sweet onion or scallions)

1 pound clams

2 tablespoons dry sherry

2 ounces dry-cured Spanish chorizo

¼ cup fresh peas, blanched (or use frozen peas, thawed)

¼ cup sliced asparagus (½-inch pieces), blanched

¼ cup shelled and peeled fava beans (optional)

1 tablespoon picada (see preceding recipe)

2 tablespoons roughly chopped fresh parsley

When you are doing your shopping for this dish, note that Spanish chorizo is the one that resembles pepperoni (dry, somewhat chewy, and ready to eat); it is NOT the same as fresh, Mexican-style chorizo. Also, remember to allow time for cleaning and purging the clams before you begin cooking.

Spanish-Style Clams with Chorizo and Spring Vegetables

Serves 2 as a substantial appetizer (double the recipe for an entrée portion)

1. Clean and purge the clams per the instructions on page 150 (use ¼ cup cornmeal for the 1 pound of clams).

2. Gently heat the olive oil over medium-low heat. Add the onions and sweat slowly until they're very soft. DO NOT BROWN.

3. Turn the heat up to high and add the clams. Toss the oil and onions with the clams to heat them quickly. Add the sherry and cover the pan, reduce the heat to medium, and swirl the pan. Shake occasionally to get the clams to open. Take a peek. If the clams are relatively dry and lack some natural liquor, add a few tablespoons of water to the pan to create more steam (the liquid should come about one-third to halfway up the side of the clams). When half of the clams are open, remove the lid and keep cooking. The remaining clams will pop open while the liquid reduces and intensifies.

4. When the clams are open (discard any that remain closed), add the chorizo, peas, asparagus pieces, and fava beans. Toss to heat through. When the vegetables are nicely heated, push all of the clams and vegetables to one side of the pan and tilt the liquid into the other side.

5. Whisk the picada into the liquid. It should thicken almost immediately and release its garlicky, smoky aroma. Toss the clams and vegetables with the now-thickened broth to coat them completely.

6. Sprinkle with the parsley and serve immediately with crusty bread and chilled Alabariño.

Note: The above recipe works with other summer vegetables too. Just replace the favas, peas, and asparagus with teardrop tomatoes, diced red bell pepper, and a nice julienne of summer squash. Early autumn calls for diced, roasted butternut squash. Wintertime? Try slicing some preroasted fingerling potatoes, carrots, and parsnips and throw those in. The basic method is the same, but the shellfish dish is your canvas for creativity.

We also like a version of the above made with a splash of the medium-bodied white wine you'll be drinking rather than sherry. If you're cooking like we do when we're at home, that bottle of Albariño is already open anyway, and a second one might be needed to finish up the dish.

Advanced preparation of vegetables is more than half the battle. A battle best fought without a Chef hovering about.

Wine Wardrobe Bottle #5

WELL-SEASONED WHITE

 Oak is one of the most polarizing subjects in wine. It is also misunderstood. Reasons to put wine in a barrel, in order of importance:

1. Storage

2. Oxygen Transfer

3. Seasoning

Barrels have been around for thousands of years. It's how things were stored and shipped from one place to another—everything from fish to gunpowder to (eventually) wine. They were easy to roll, hard to break, and capable of being reused.

Turns out that there are two other great benefits to putting wine into barrels—especially those made of oak—besides efficient storage. The first is perhaps a little technical and therefore not usually discussed: the slow transfer of oxygen into wine. More important in red wine production (but also useful in whites), the transfer of oxygen softens wine—rounds out the feel of it in your mouth. Oak helps take the edges off.

The second benefit: flavor. However, I think it's worth noting that oak barrels cease imparting flavors in wine after their third use. In fact, half the potential flavor exchange takes part in the first use, which means that the primary role of oak barrels in a winery is still storage. Most oak barrels in the world are used past their ability to transfer flavors. (A well-cared-for barrel can last upwards of one hundred years.) So when talking about flavor transfer, we're generally speaking of new oak.

The narrow-minded don't consider oak flavors to be a benefit, but an abomination. I will agree that there have been (and will continue to be) criminally over-oaked wines—but I'm certain that summarily judging an oft-abused seasoning should not discredit the use of that seasoning outright. It's like avoiding salt on account of fast-food french fries. I couldn't eat fast-food french fries every day—but when I'm on a road trip, the lip-stinging over-salting at the drive-thru is the right thing at the right time.

Speaking of French, there is no better place to look for well-seasoned white wines than the Chardonnays of Burgundy. In fact, it's easy to forget that what the California producers accused of oak crimes were originally trying to emulate were the Grand Cru wines of the Côte de Beaune—it's why names like Montrachet and Corton-Charlemagne are recognized despite their relative rarity. These are wines that embrace the use of wood, and totally validate the measured use of oak to enhance and balance the raw material.

So when we talk about the well-seasoned wine, we are almost invariably heading toward Chardonnay. It's planted just about any place grapes are grown—it's relatively easy to farm and can handle a diverse range of temperatures. It's the queen to Cabernet's king. But because of this ubiquity, knowing the grape is no shortcut to knowing the flavor. And even geography doesn't entirely predict what the style of Chardonnay will be—you can taste a dozen Napa Valley Chardonnays and have twelve distinct experiences.

I remember quite clearly one of the first wine seminars I attended. It was taught by a rather famous winemaker who explained how Chardonnay—of all the grapes in the vineyard—is the blank canvas: the ultimate chance for winemakers to express themselves. He then went through many of the major elements that contribute to a Chardonnay's final flavor. It all comes down to choice—there are more choices in the production of Chardonnay than any other white grape, making the actual wine not only a result of farming, but the result of creative and artistic decisions along the way.

What's great about diving into the many steps of producing Chardonnay is that it gives a wonderful overall view of winemaking in general. (Keep in mind that these are not *all* the steps needed to make wine—that's another book, written by somebody who actually produces it. I'm not qualified to speak to everything that happens in a winery; and for the purposes of this discussion, there are enough unavoidable wine terms already.)

If a winery doesn't own any land, then the first decision made is where to source their grapes: how many vineyards to contract, and in what sorts of climates. Here in Washington, we have wonderful Chardonnay grown in cooler sites like the Celilo Vineyard in the Columbia River Gorge area, as well as great Chardonnay grown in warmer sites in the Walla Walla Valley. Winemakers will also consider what clones of Chardonnay are planted in the vineyards—for instance, there are well over thirty different Dijon clones alone, each one with different characteristics.

If a winery owns its own land, then they are faced with additional decisions such as where to plant, what rootstocks to use, and which clone (or clones) to get.

The next decision category is when to harvest. Grapes harvested early will yield a leaner fruit and aroma spectrum—higher acidity and less alcohol. Grapes harvested later will yield more robust fruit, aroma, and alcohol while having less acidity. Some winemakers will choose to harvest different blocks at different times in order to have a range of all these elements. To go a step further, there is even evidence that the time of day (and therefore grape temperature) at harvest can influence certain compounds in the grape.

Next are the fermentation decisions. First—does it take place in wood or something inert like steel or concrete? Maybe a combination? Will the winery rely on ambient yeasts to ferment the wine, or will they use a variety of commercial yeasts to get the job done, as different yeasts yield recognizably different flavors? Then there is controlling the temperature—things tend to heat up during fermentation, and keeping things cool encourages different flavor results.

Then there's the biggest decision to be made when making Chardonnay. To encourage or to prevent (huge but totally unavoidable wine term) **malolactic fermentation**.

You can go online and access the University of California at Davis course information on malolactic fermentation. It's available for free, probably because it may as well be written in Sanskrit with terrible penmanship. It's so wickedly technical that I can't fully decipher the first page of it.

But it is one of the most important decisions the Chardonnay producer makes, because the result is the flavor that is often blamed on oak: *buttery*. During malolactic fermentation, tart (Mind Mouth: green apple) malic acid is converted to soft (Mind Mouth: dairy) lactic acid.

(Note: Red wines go through malolactic fermentation as well. I've never had one that hasn't.)

Then come the post-fermentation questions: Should the winery leave the (unavoidable wine term) **lees** (spent yeast) in with the wine while it ages to impart added creaminess? If so, will they occasionally stir those lees in order to keep exposing them to the wine?

Then there's the question of aging in oak or some other sort of vessel. If oak, then for how long? Will new oak barrels be used, or older, more neutral barrels—or some sort of combination? Next comes the question of the different kinds of oak—American, French, Hungarian—each with its own distinct flavors. In fact, oak from different forests yields different flavors, so choosing a specific cooper (an artisan who makes barrels) comes into play as well. And don't get me started on the different levels of toasting the oak.

It's like those *Choose Your Own Adventure* books we read when we were kids. You can either end up at medium- to light-bodied white wine with flavors of green apples and lime, or full-bodied white wine with flavors of buttered toast and pineapple upside-down cake.

Summary of Chardonnay decisions:

- **VINEYARD**: Geography, rootstock, clone
- **HARVEST**: When and at what time of day?
- **FERMENTATION**: Vessel, temperature, yeast
- **MALOLACTIC**: Yea or nay
- **AGING**: On the lees? If so, to stir if not to stir?
- **STORAGE**: In stainless steel or oak? If oak, then from where and for how long?

There is a time and a place for all wines. Just like those drive-thru fries, occasionally it's totally right to have a tropically appointed, full-bodied butter-bomb. Sometimes wine can (and should) be a cocktail. One great reason to appoint the Wine Wardrobe with the well-seasoned white is that every so often you'll pull the cork for no other reason than you want to have a big mouthful of delicious hedonism. It's like drinking piña coladas—they're actually delicious cocktails if they are well made, the atmosphere is appropriate, and your mood is correct.

Some additional things to consider:

Chardonnay isn't the only grape that performs well in new oak. Sémillon, for example, does well with its additional seasoning powers. You can find Sémillon on its own, but in Bordeaux, it is traditionally blended with Sauvignon Blanc to give it some energy and aromatics. That practice is copied by a number of regions throughout the world—though the amount of Sauvignon Blanc will vary, so it may require a little homework.

You might have to spend a little more on the well-seasoned. Oak is expensive, which means oaked white wine will run you a bit more. (The cost will be easily offset by the other, generally oak-free wines in the Wardrobe.) You'd pay ten bucks for a daiquiri while on a tropical vacation—but there are four glasses in a bottle of wine. Perhaps that's enough fiscal justification.

There are other areas of the world that will employ new oak, but we made a promise not to recommend obscurity—so this is where I repeat the importance of getting to know somebody at your local wine store. Asking for a well-seasoned white that isn't Chardonnay may lead to something exotic and unfamiliar—but I'm quite confident that it will be delicious.

One last bit on oak—chips. When you come across inexpensive wines that have a lot of oak flavor, you're likely dealing with the addition of oak chips: the simplest and cheapest way to impart oak flavors in wine. It is exactly as it sounds—you can buy them by the bag and throw them in your tank like you're steeping tea. Is it good or bad? I guess it depends on how you feel about shortcuts. But in my experience, the evidence of one shortcut suggests many other shortcuts.

Well-Seasoned White Pairing Exploration

CREAMY PASTA

Creamy, cheesy pasta comes in a multitude of varieties, usually made with béchamel sauce, mornay sauce, or reduced heavy cream. It can be made with virtually any kind of noodle. It can be baked or served straight from the pan. It can include cheese, but it actually doesn't have to. When baked, it can be topped with breadcrumbs, or cheese, or even nothing. The universal tie that binds this wine pairing is pasta and dairy. When a rich and buttery, well-oaked wine comes into the picture, a whole new world of flavors emerges.

Quite frankly, macaroni and cheese is a bit of a monotonous dish. So is fettuccine Alfredo. They both are essentially cheese, dairy product, and starch. Of course, the dish can be embellished with all manner of aromatics like onions, garlic, shallots, herbs, and even spices like curry or lots of black pepper.

As we've discussed, acidity is critical to a great dish. It's hard to get acid into something like cheesy, creamy pasta. You can attempt to get a backbone of acid into the dish with white wine or lemon juice, but one of the side effects of this practice can be very dire. That's because the way to make cheese on purpose is to heat up milk and add acid to it. At the right temperature, and with just the right amount of acid, the milk will curdle and almost instantaneously turn into little Miss Muffet's famed curds and whey.

All of this potential monotony is assuaged by the wine pairing. All of a sudden, there is acid, and fruit, and then more buttery creaminess. That oak in the wine creates nutty, buttery notes reminiscent of caramelized, gratinéed cheese.

For this pairing, we are going to focus on two similar techniques, but these two techniques will empower you to make many, many different types of pasta dishes that will work very well with well-seasoned white wines. The first is the fettuccine Alfredo archetype, and the second is the baked mac and cheese master recipe.

Fettuccine Alfredo

Alfredo, thanks to our fast-casual Italian restaurant chain friends, is one of the most bastardized terms in all of cuisine. Everything with a white sauce is now an Alfredo. Asiago Alfredo, shrimp Alfredo, chicken parmesan Alfredo, even steak Gorgonzola Alfredo. None of these has anything to do with the original, which remains somewhat shrouded in mystery even to this day.

Regardless of which story you believe about the dish's beginnings, the original dish did not contain anything but butter, pasta, pasta water, and Parmigiano-Reggiano cheese. This original version relied heavily upon pasta water. Unlike at home, where pasta water is often poured through a colander and down the drain, in a restaurant, pasta water is used over and over again throughout the day, becoming very starchy. In the original Alfredo sauce, this starch held together a tenuous emulsion of butter and cheese, which functioned as the sauce for fresh noodles. Fresh pastas are also starchy in and of themselves, adding even more "grip" to hold this beautifully simple sauce. Alfredo without cream? A world-renowned cream sauce . . . with no cream at all? We're definitely going to go over how to make that!

8 quarts water

½ cup kosher salt

½ cup semolina flour

8 ounces fresh egg fettucine

1 tablespoon cooking butter

3 tablespoons finishing butter

1 ounce (about ½ cup) grated
Parmigiano-Reggiano cheese, plus we
like to put a plate out with the cheese
and a grater on the table so that
guests can add more if they wish

¼ teaspoon lemon juice

This recipe calls for the two types of butter: standard grocery store butter (what I call "cooking butter") and finishing butter (a higher-quality butter that is made from cream from a much more traceable and elevated provenance). Imported butters from France, Ireland, or Denmark are often far superior to American butters, though this is becoming less and less true. Find a great butter, and above all make sure it is very fresh, even if it is imported. (See page 267 for more detail.)

Cream-Free Fettucine Alfredo

Serves 2

1. Combine the water, salt, and semolina flour with a whisk in a large pot.

2. Bring it to a boil. Whisk again to make sure that no flour is settling on the bottom of the pot. You want to distribute and dissolve as much starch as possible.

3. Drop the fettucine in the rapidly boiling water and follow the cooking instructions on the packaging, decreasing the low range of the cooking time by a full minute.

4. While the pasta is boiling, melt the 1 tablespoon of cooking butter over medium heat in a medium sauté pan.

5. When the pasta has cooked, lift it from the water using a small strainer or a "spider" utensil and transfer it to the pan. Make absolutely no attempt to shake the water from the pasta.

6. Toss the pasta in the butter and water repeatedly until the pasta starts to absorb the water in the sauté pan. Test the pasta for doneness. It should be 90 percent done.

7. Add a large ladle (½ cup) of pasta water to the pan and add the 3 tablespoons of finishing butter all at once.

8. Toss repeatedly over medium-high heat. Do not let the pasta boil. You will slowly build an emulsion of butter, pasta, pasta starch, and water. Now start adding cheese with feverous abandon.

9. Never stop agitating the pan until you're ready to serve. The sauce in the pan will look almost exactly like heavy cream. Taste some of the pasta; adjust if it needs more salt. If it is too rich or flat, add a few drops of lemon juice and taste again. Keep adjusting. Your guests will appreciate that you sacrificed your appetite to get it right.

10. Serve the pasta with more Parmigiano-Reggiano on the side. Resist the urge to add cream, Gorgonzola, shrimp, or steak. Just offer a pepper mill instead.

6 quarts water

3 tablespoons kosher salt

6 ounces (1½ sticks) cooking butter

1⅓ cups (6 ounces) all-purpose flour

1 quart whole milk

8 ounces Gruyère, grated

4 ounces Parmigiano-Reggiano, grated

4 ounces fontina or mozzarella, grated

1 teaspoon lemon juice

2 pounds dry pasta (cavatappi, elbow, campanelle, penne, or other tubular pasta)

4 to 5 gratings of nutmeg

½ cup breadcrumbs (see Notes below)

2 tablespoons finishing butter

Baked Mac and Cheese

Serves 6

1. Heat the oven to 350°F.

2. Using an 8-quart stockpot, bring the 6 quarts of water to a boil. Add salt to taste, but don't skimp—the water should be salty. This water is for cooking the pasta; just let it simmer while you prepare the sauce.

3. In a separate sauce pan, melt the cooking butter until it foams. Sift in the flour while whisking vigorously. There will be a paste in the bottom of the pan that will eventually ball up in your whisk, leaving a thin veneer of flour on the bottom of pan. Pay attention to the color of this stuck-on flour. When it turns the color of blond hair, add the milk in a slow, steady stream while whisking vigorously.

4. Let the mixture come back to a full boil, whisking the entire time. You have just made Bechamel sauce.

5. Whisk in all of the grated cheeses a little at a time. Then add the lemon juice. Do not ever let the sauce boil again. You have just made Mornay sauce.

6. Boil the pasta for 25 percent less time than the instructions indicate. (E.g., if the pasta calls for boiling for 6 to 8 minutes, boil it for 4½ to 6 minutes.) Drain the pasta (there is no need to save pasta water for this preparation).

7. In a large bowl, toss the pasta and the Mornay sauce together. If it seems pasty, add milk until it is almost soupy. The mixture should feel loose to you. The pasta that you've purposely left undercooked will drink up the rest of the moisture—so if it looks perfect now, it will be dry when it comes out of the oven.

8. Taste for salt and acid. Add salt and lemon juice as needed. Add the nutmeg.

9. Pour the pasta and sauce into a casserole dish that just holds the mixture (a dish that is too shallow will burn on the sides, and a dish that is too full will spill over). Sprinkle the top of the pasta with the breadcrumbs. Dot the top of the breadcrumbs with nubbins of the finishing butter. Distribute them as evenly as possible, short of getting out a tape measure.

10. Bake until bubbly. Start checking at 8 minutes, but be willing to wait up to 20 minutes. The top should be crispy brown. Very dark in some places. That is great. Don't pull the dish from the oven when the breadcrumbs are shy of being nice and brown, as some of them will remain uncooked.

11. Let the dish rest (preferably on a rack) for at least 5 minutes before serving it up.

continued

Notes:

- Before baking it, your mac and cheese always looks like it is going to be soup. It won't be.

- You can vary the types of cheese. Just make sure some of it is cheese that melts well, like the fontina or mozzarella. Don't use all chèvre, or feta, or parmesan.

- Fresh breadcrumbs are the best, but if you have to use dried or stale crumbs it is fine; just adjust your cooking time. The breadcrumb part is entirely visual. Sometimes they brown very fast, other times they are stubborn and take a while.

- Once the mac and cheese is bubbling and hot with a crispy top, it is done. Don't worry about internal temperature or anything. There is nothing raw in mac and cheese. All you're really doing in the oven is melting and crisping, not actually cooking.

Baked Mac and Cheese with a couple of glasses of well-seasoned white wine.

Wine Wardrobe Bottle #6

FULL-BODIED WHITE

 Our sixth Wine Wardrobe selection is not unlike the well-seasoned white—just more modestly dressed.

This means the primary flavors aren't going to be driven by months in oak, but instead by warm climates and grapes with large personalities. There may be some oak used in the production of the full-bodied white, but it's not the flavor leader.

Oak often gets in the way when we seek a flavor partner for a dish. The body of the wine might be correct, the acidity of the wine might be correct—but then there's this unwelcome spectrum of flavors that messes up the program. It's not that oak will overwhelm a dish—it's just that it brings too many guests to the flavor party.

Here are some of the common flavors that oak imparts to wine:

- Vanilla
- Coconut
- Baking Spices (cinnamon, nutmeg, clove)
- Dill
- Caramel
- Toast
- Smoke

Some of these don't play well with others. That toasty/smoky component is at times a great additional flavor—especially for simple, grilled proteins—but it might also be totally distracting and out of place in the context of a vegetable dish. Baking spices are great with certain stews and dry rubs, but maybe not in a dish that incorporates a lot of fresh herbs. And then there are vanilla and caramel—flavors that can work great with seared scallops, but maybe not so much with seared cod.

So when staring down a recipe that calls for a full-bodied white wine, we just ask the question: will the flavors imparted by oak make any sense? It's often a relatively easy call to make.

What sorts of wines come fully appointed, and from where?

The white grapes of the Rhône Valley in France are a good place to start, and have been finding new homes around the world with increasing frequency and quality. Viognier is one of those grape success stories—it wasn't so many decades ago that it was practically extinct, with less than one hundred acres planted worldwide. It can now brag about being the most-planted white Rhône variety in America as well as being the official grape of Virginia. In fact, Viognier can brag about being just about everywhere now—South America, New Zealand, Italy—even Switzerland.

Viognier is known not only for its full body, but hedonistic fruit and floral aromas—if they made Viognier air freshener, I'd hang it from my

rearview mirror. And it's because of all the natural aromas and flavors found in Viognier that most producers need not rely on a regimen of oak aging to impart personality. It's already personality-plus.

With the explosion of Viognier in the world, it stands to reason that the other white grapes of the Rhône Valley would get some attention. Marsanne and Roussanne have similar extroverted personalities and are being planted in most of the places Viognier has thrived; the three are often blended together to emulate the white wines of the Southern Rhône.

Grenache Blanc is also included in the Rhône bunch, but actually has Spanish roots. A mutation of Grenache Noir, it made its way from the northwest of Spain (where it's called Garnacha Blanca) to France, where it found its like-minded friends. So when you see a Garnacha Blanca, give it a go.

Outside of the Rhône Valley grapes, you can easily locate unoaked Chardonnay. Most of these have an appealing price tag compared to oaked versions, and the better ones echo the richness and tropical flavors without the pesky wood flavors.

Full-bodied whites can come from anywhere the weather permits. It often boils down to a specific producer in a specifically warm site and a favorably warm vintage. There are indigenous grapes in Portugal, Spain, Italy, and Greece that produce wonderful full-bodied white wine experiences. However, it's difficult to broadly recommend. One more reason to make friends with a local wine retailer.

Full-Bodied White Pairing Exploration

ROASTED WHITE FISH:

A One-Sided Affair

We've all seen it. A beautiful piece of fish, like halibut, or cod, or even scallops, with a gorgeous, crispy brown crust on the surface, contrasting the silky, ice-white flakes beneath it. This should be the goal of every cook when preparing white fish. The flesh is lean, unlike red fish or oily fish, which means that we must caramelize it to produce a big, robust flavor. It also makes it very difficult to grill. Since white fish has virtually no fat of its own, you need an absolute blowtorch of a grill to keep it from sticking. We almost never grill white fish in the restaurant for this reason.

What a lot of people don't notice is that most restaurants serve the fish very crispy and caramelized on one side, but quite pale and tender on the other. Since the caramelized side is almost always served "up," or facing the guest, you may not notice that the other side has not received the same cooking treatment. This is for a good reason. While we love the deep, crisp caramelization, we also want each flake of the fish to be silky, shiny, and tender. If we caramelized the fish on both sides, the interior would be as dry as a camel's backside. Conversely, if we tried to evenly brown the fish on both sides with the goal of keeping the interior moist, the caramelization would be pale and insufficient. There are a few exceptions to this rule, such as a really thick piece of halibut or swordfish. Most of the time, with a sensible portion of fish, the one-side method is the best way to go.

What is White Fish?

Fin fish is divisible into many categories, but for the purposes of wine pairing, red fish eat far differently than white. White fish tends to be very lean, with minimal perceivable fish oil and intensity. In a word, white fish is mild. Salmon, mackerel, tuna, and sardines are red or dark fleshed, and definitely not mild. Those kind of fish respond well to the one-sided cooking method too, but are less reliable for pairing with a full-bodied white wine.

Here are some fish that we really like for this pairing:

- Pacific or Atlantic halibut
- Pollack
- True cod
- Ling cod
- Yelloweye rockfish
- Swordfish
- Black bass
- Branzino
- Flounder
- Smelt
- Snapper
- Trout
- Sea trout
- Lake whitefish

The criteria are simple: lean vs. oily, pale flesh vs. dark or red flesh, and always cooked through instead of "to order," like tuna or salmon can be. If the above criteria are met, you should consider your fish suitable for this pairing. If not, you'll need to experiment. There are a number of full-bodied whites that work with oilier fish or even red fish, but we often pair red wines with those fish and the results are spectacular.

Don't Be Afraid of Oil

One of the most interesting comments I get when I'm demonstrating how to cook food that's naturally lean concerns the amount of oil I put in the pan. Most onlookers are aghast at the amount of oil that is necessary to cook a really lean product properly. Trust me, you need it, or it will stick. Don't let it bother you, because you're not going to serve that oil to anyone. The oil is a *medium* in which to cook the fish, no different than the stove or the pan. The only difference is that you can wash and reuse the pan. The oil gets thrown out.

Most people see that much oil go into a pan and immediately start calculating added calories, fearing that the extra oil is going straight to their thighs. If that were true, then there would be no oil left in the pan after sautéing something. If that were true, then we should calculate the calories of ALL of the oil in the deep fryer for one serving of french fries.

Think of how many times you've sautéed something and there was more oil in the pan when you finished than when you started. Truthfully, there are not many proteins that *absorb* fat. As a chef, I really wish the tendency for meats was to absorb fat instead of render it out, because they would never be dry. Overcooking something would never be an issue. Braising could be done at high temperatures. We could actually aggressively boil meats and expect a good result. We can't, because meats and fish only *render* or lose fat.

With all of the above being true, there is no reason to use a tiny bit of oil when you're searing, sautéing, or pan-roasting something. Almost every cooking show on television recommends incredibly small amounts of oil in a nonstick pan for searing. This won't work if you want a really delicious, crispy brown sear. First, you should never heat a nonstick pan to the temperatures necessary to sear a piece of fish, as many of them can throw off toxic fumes at these temperatures. Secondly, if you get your stainless steel or enameled cast-iron pan to the temperature necessary to sear fish properly, you will need a fair amount of oil to get it done properly.

Pan-Roasted Halibut

Serves 2

2 trimmed halibut fillets, preferably very thick (2 inches or more), skin removed

Kosher salt

Freshly ground pepper (optional)

2 tablespoons neutral oil

3 tablespoons cooking butter (optional)

1 teaspoon lemon juice (optional)

1 tablespoon mixed, chopped fresh herbs (parsley, chives, oregano, rosemary, and thyme all work great) (optional)

Note: This formula is the exact method used in the preparation of fish in most restaurants. It should yield a very crisp crust with a silky, flakey underside. Fish is perfectly cooked when each flake wants to just slip away from the next.

1. Heat the oven to 450°F.

2. Rinse and dry the fish; refrigerate it on paper towels to wick away additional moisture.

3. Season thoroughly with salt (and pepper if you're using it). Do not skimp on seasoning. You should be able to see the salt sparkling on the surface of the dry fish. Unlike grilled fish, we don't brine fish that we're going to sear, because it's just flat-out dangerous to bring that much extra moisture to the party when using such high heat. If you have the luxury, salt your fish a full hour before you plan to cook it. You needn't put the fish back in the refrigerator at this point.

4. Coat the fish lightly with some of the oil. If using olive oil, cut it with some vegetable oil so the olive oil doesn't burn.

5. Heat an ovenproof sauté pan to very hot. Add the remaining oil and wait for it to smoke (do not heat the oil and the pan together—add the oil second). Carefully set one of the fish fillets, presentation-side down, in the pan. Wait a full minute before adding the next piece so that the pan can recover and get its heat back.

6. Set the pan in the oven. Roast for 6 to 8 minutes, depending on the thickness of the fish. DO NOT TURN the fish over or move it in any way! When the fish is done (140°F internal), pull the pan out of the oven. Only then may you turn it over.

7. If you want to feel like a badass, drop the 3 tablespoons of butter into the pan, along with the lemon juice and your choice of chopped herbs. Put the pan over a medium-high burner and baste the fish with the melted butter and herbs for a minute or two. Don't let the amount of butter disturb you, as you are going to discard anything left in the pan after this process.

8. Plate immediately; the fish doesn't need to rest.

We garnished this pan-roasted halibut with Meyer lemons, chive blossoms, high quality olive oil and lots of fresh herbs.

Wine Wardrobe Bottle #7

SWEET WHITE

The most profound of wine tragedies: The world knows not how awesome sweet wine is with food, because the world won't order sweet wine. There are entire cuisines that beg for a touch of sweetness, but without the willingness, the connection is not made. And it's shocking how some react to the idea of (unavoidable wine term) **residual sugar** in wine.

The truth of the matter is that we love sugar in every other beverage format, from sodas to cocktails to lattés. For some reason or other, we have historically derided sweetness in wine as being for dessert, or for people who don't really "know" wine.

There is a long list of misused wine jargon I would like to see go away—but if I were to pick one example, it would be the word *dry*. I would love to get my hands on a time machine so that I could stop that first uttering of the word in a restaurant, changing the course of the world forever. For no good reason, I picture a snooty British guy in a New York restaurant asking the waiter for "a glass of dry red" in front of an audience of American stockbroker types—the idea then spreading outward across the nation like a tidal wave of parrots with the ability to use only one adjective when ordering wine.

Dry is so wickedly misused and misunderstood I almost don't want to acknowledge its existence.

The source of this misunderstanding: interpreting the drying sensation of tannins in red wine as the definition of what "dry"means when we speak of dry wine. Similarly, the puckering sourness of highly acidic white wine is often perceived as dry. Neither is true. Dry is simply something that is not sweet.

Another thing worth noting: There are a lot of "dry" wines out there that actually have more than a touch of residual sugar. That super popular California Chardonnay—the one that dominated the American market for upwards of twenty years—it's got some residual sugar. In fact, many of the high-volume production wines out there are not technically dry wines. Turns out that many people really do like sweetness in wine—even if they say they don't.

Things will change, though. One day the word *dry* will join the proclamations "fine bouquet" and "nice legs" in the lexicon of antiquated wine-speak. So

here's why you should have a bottle of sweet German Riesling or something attitudinally similar around at all times:

1. It's delicious.

2. It will have less alcohol than your average wine, so you can drink twice as much if you like.

3. We like spicy foods. Sriracha and salsa are replacing ketchup in fridges across America.

Which brings us to our favorite thing about sweet whites: They are the firefighters of the culinary world.

Do this: Order some three-star Thai food—*larb gai*, say—and fetch a bottle of sweet German Riesling out of the fridge. Watch what happens. You still get to enjoy that intense spice of the food, but the fire is tempered by the sweetness in the wine. It makes your dining experience a dynamic roller-coaster of spice rather than an intense burn-out. Who wouldn't fall in love with that?

How can you tell how sweet a Riesling is going to be? Well, you can do a couple of things: You can memorize the (unavoidable wine subject)

German Prädikat System—the classification of grape ripeness at harvest—which at first seems like a cumbersome bit of homework. But if it means identifying the ballpark level of sweetness in a bottle before purchase, it will arguably save you precious life energy. Plus you will instantly know more about German wine than the average human.

If you didn't take German in high school, don't panic. For our purposes, you really only need to memorize the first bits of the Prädikat.

To be included in the Prädikat means you have made a quality wine without resorting to dumping refined sugar in the fermenter—a not-unheard-of practice in certain parts of the world. So the first level of German Riesling is labeled:

Kabinett—which is literally translated as "cabinet" and pronounced almost the same. (Simply moving the stress from the first syllable to the last will do the trick.) An easy way to think about Kabinett Riesling is that it's something you could and should have in the cabinet at all times—close at hand. Kabinett is the best place

Aging Sweet Wines

The oldest wine I've ever had the luck to swallow was an old German Riesling. (I'll leave the details out. Hearing about a great wine somebody else drank is like being told of an awesome conversation you weren't invited to.) Sweet wines have an amazing ability to live for decades because of two natural preservatives: sugar and acid. Sugar and acid

impede (unavoidable wine term) **oxidation**—the process that fades the paint on your car, turns bronze green, and makes wines lose their flavor. If you want to see these natural preservatives in action, slice an avocado in half and squeeze lime juice (acidity) on just one side. Leave the two halves on the counter for an hour. One retains its beautiful green hue

while the other is heading to what oxidized avocadoes look like. To test sugar, slice an apple in half and plop one piece in a glass of Sprite (or any sugary liquid.) Same result. One stays fresh and one turns brown. So in view of the high acidity and sugar found in sweet wines, it stands to reason that these lovely bottles can go for generations.

to start your love affair with German Riesling. And for the Wine Wardrobe, it's probably your go-to.

Next, the slightly harder to pronounce **Spätlese** (SHPATE-lay-zuh). The translation is simply "late harvest"—which can create a bit of confusion considering that the term is used to define many bottles of dessert-style wine in America. Ignore it—it only means that the harvest came a week or more after the picking of the Kabinett. The wines tend to be riper, sweeter, and fuller bodied than Kabinett—but it's a far cry from a dessert-style wine. For those who like their food a little more intensely spicy, the extra sugar might be the ticket.

Following Spätlese is **Auslese** (OWS-lay-zuh), translated as "selected harvest." Auslese grapes are picked when the grapes are very ripe, and can be wonderfully decadent—rich and full, with a rainbow of flavor (Mind Mouth: nuclear fruit cocktail). The best manage to be both viscous and lively due to the amazingly high levels of acidity. Auslese with certain pungent cheeses is a yin-yang worth experiencing,

There are several other levels in the German Prädikat (Beerenauslese, Trockenbeerenauslese, and Eiswien); however, these wines are most often used in dessert applications.

For your sweet white Wardrobe Wine, I would recommend exploring first and foremost the sweet Rieslings of Germany. Dollar for dollar, there is no better place in the world to find quality Riesling experiences.

Having said that, I've rarely gone without having a Chenin Blanc at my immediate disposal—we are particularly fond of (unavoidable wine term) **demi-sec** Vouvray. Vouvray is an area in the Loire Valley of France that produces a range of Chenin Blancs, from dry to sweet. (The levels are sec, demi-sec, *moelleux*, and doux.) I have never written a wine list without a Loire Valley Chenin Blanc by the glass, incidentally. It's one of our wine pairing parachutes.

Off-Dry

You'll hear and see the term *off-dry* from time to time. While I can't prove it, I believe it was invented to avoid incarnating the negative response to the dreaded word *sweet*. It's usually employed when a wine has just a touch of sweetness, but I try to find other ways to convey that a wine has just a touch of residual sugar. (Like saying it has just a touch of residual sugar.)

How to Tell If a Wine is Sweet

A simple way to identify the potential sweetness in a bottle of wine: look at the alcohol by volume (ABV) listed on the bottle. By law, producers have to detail the ABV percentage on the bottle with an accuracy within 1.5 percent, and most bottles that proclaim an ABV of 12.5% or higher are going to be dry. If a wine lists an ABV below 12.5%, you can bet that there is going to be some sweetness.

Here's a list of common sweet wines and their approximate ABVs:

MOSCATO D'ASTI: 5.5%

GERMAN RIESLINGS: 7% TO 12%

VOUVRAY DEMI-SEC: 11.5%

Sweet Wine Pairing Exploration

PÂTÉ:

Wait! I Thought Pâté was Something Only Chefs Could Make

All of that considered, it is important to remember that at its core, in its DNA, the most hedonistic French pâté on display in an expensive shop in Paris or Lyons is a cold meatloaf. Most American meatloaf is driven by beef, whereas most French charcuterie is driven by pork. Other than that, at its most basic level there is minimal difference between the two. Doesn't sound so fancy when you put it that way, does it? This cold meatloaf thing can be insanely elaborate, and with some research and practice, one can certainly produce some beautiful pâtés and terrines (a close cousin to the pâté). The purpose of this text is not to try to show you how to become a world-class French charcutière, but rather a home cook who knows how to cool down a delicious meatloaf and serve it that way.

As far as traditional charcuterie goes, pork is king. The meat and fat of hogs are almost synonymous with pâtés, terrines, and sausages. This is because, when charcuterie was being developed as an art, pork meat was readily available and ubiquitous—plus, pork has the ability to ride shotgun to the flavors of other meats, while still providing all of the desirable qualities of the pork itself.

Pigs are farm animals. Unlike cattle, which have to be grazed, or sheep, which have to be shepherded, pigs can be raised cheaply and effectively in a farm setting. This means that dairy farms, chicken farms, vegetable farms, and so forth can all effectively raise pigs. Hogs eat food scraps, and don't need to be vigorously exercised like cattle and sheep. Luckily for us, this created an inexpensive, easy-to-raise source of protein for the agrarian class.

Farmers brought surplus pork to the city, and a whole world of luxury pork products emerged.

Something was noticed back in those early days of rearing pigs. Pork, especially its fat, is extremely delicious. Though there are cultures that choose not to eat it, those cultures that do consume pork find it almost impossible to imagine life without bacon, or sausages, or ham. Way out in front of the world in consumption of pork is China, although Europe and the United States are also large consumers—and between the three, there is an almost 5,000-year history of pork preparations and preservation. It is ironic that the first evidence of the domestication of pigs (somewhere around 7000 BC in the Middle East and the eastern Mediterranean) occurs in two parts of the world that largely eschew its consumption today.

One of the amazing things about pork is how well it takes to curing. Some of the finest products in the food world are merely a combination of pork meat, salt, and time. This whole world of cured meats has, for some reason, taken on the Italian term *salumi*, while the rest of the world of elaborate cooked pork products has taken on the French name of charcuterie. In many ways they are interchangeable. The French certainly do not shy away from dry-curing (I'm thinking of their world-famous *saucisson sec* and beautiful mountain hams), but the tendency of the French is to prepare the products in the form of terrines, pâtés, galantines, confits, rillettes, and more.

The Italians and Spanish have a tendency to cure and ferment their pork, never actually applying heat to it. This leads to all manner of *jamón* from Spain and prosciutto from Italy, as well as dry-cured chorizo, *soppressata*, salami, *coppa*, and other such products. Due to the extremely specialized equipment and environment required to produce dry-cured products, we suggest that you buy these from

Pâté vs. Terrine

There has been a lot of ballyhoo about the difference between pâtés and terrines. As a former culinary school instructor, I can tell you that this is a vestigial result of a need to create concrete concepts in culinary schools so that tests can be administered. The problem is that the world of food is dynamic and fluid. Trying to make absolute rules and definitions regarding cuisine serves very little purpose other than to test culinary students. So for our purposes, let's consider pâtés and terrines to be the same thing.

TO MAKE A PÂTÉ OR TERRINE YOU WILL NEED:

- A terrine mold. This is the most expensive thing you'll have to buy, but it is critical, so don't do it on the cheap. Metal loaf pans will work, but they tend to cook unevenly, resulting in a tunneled or somewhat dry pâté. Enameled cast-iron or pure ceramic molds are the best.o
- A quality food thermometer

- A kitchen scale
- Ground meat
- Livers (they like the sweet white wine a lot, but technically they are optional)
- Seasonings

OPTIONAL ITEMS ARE:

- A meat grinder
- A stand mixer, like a KitchenAid, with a meat grinder attachment.

excellent producers. Then we suggest referring to the chapter Olives, Almonds, and Cured Meats with Sherry (see page 55) when you do.

Country Style Pâté

In the realm of French charcuterie, the simple country pâté remains its cornerstone preparation. The cool thing about pâté is that the gateway version is called *pâté de campagne*, or country-style pâté, and this thing is super easy to make. If you get into it, you can go more complex and more expensive, but pâté de campagne, despite its fancy name, is not difficult to produce in a home kitchen.

Buy a Terrine

There are a few things in the world of cuisine that have the unique characteristic of sharing the name of the vessel with the name of the dish. Those that come to mind are terrines, tagines, casseroles, cassoulets, and hot pots. And it's no coincidence that if you actually buy the correct vessel, the dish will turn out much better. I really recommend buying an enameled, cast-iron terrine if you want to make an incredible pâté.

There is a rule with making pâté and sausage: One-third of the weight should be fat, and two-thirds of the weight should be meat. If you are going to make a pâté with a meat that is really intensely flavored, you can divide the amount of that meat with an equal amount of pork, which would be a ratio of one part pork, one part other meat (such as mild-flavored lamb or venison), one part fat. Pork meat and fat are the chameleon of meats. They change their flavor to match the flavor of the meat being featured.

If you're a home cook, you've got another choice. You can grind your own meat, in which case you can follow the rubric above, choose your preferred meats, and really control your own style of pâté. Or you can just buy ground pork, which is usually around 70/30 lean to fat, and make the pâté out of 100 percent pork. It's how you handle that pork that makes the difference between a good pâté and a tough, dry one.

4 pounds ground pork

½ pound chicken livers, trimmed and finely chopped (optional)

¼ pound shelled pistachios, toasted and cooled

2 shallots, minced, sweated, and cooled

2 cups breadcrumbs

½ cup milk

½ bunch parsley, finely minced

2 to 3 gratings of whole nutmeg

Kosher salt to taste

Fleur de sel or other crunchy sea salt, for garnishing

It's ideal to let any pâté mature for two to three days before serving, although it's not absolutely necessary; it can be served right away once it cools completely.

Pâté de Campagne with Pistachios (and Chicken Liver, for the Brave)

Serves 16 to 20, depending on how thick you slice the pâté

1. Put the well-chilled pork in a large bowl with all of the other ingredients. Chill again to ensure that everything is very cold. Mix thoroughly. You can do this in a stand mixer with a dough hook. Otherwise, use your hands. DO NOT use a food processor or a stand mixer with the paddle attachment; they will overwork the meat mixture. As soon as the meat and the rest of the ingredients are mixed, STOP. It is better if the ingredients seem less than thoroughly mixed rather than starting to get sticky and shiny. Agitating ground meat is an undesirable but necessary evil to make a nice pâté. The more we agitate ground meat, the more we force moisture out of its structure, prior to ever cooking it. We need to mix the ingredients together, but not a bit more.

2. Heat the oven to 325°F.

3. Take a small piece of the mixture and form a little patty. Heat a sauté pan and cook the patty until cooked through. Cool it slightly and then taste. This is how we determine if the pâté needs more salt. It should taste slightly salty when warm, because cold food tends to have less flavor intensity than warm or hot food does. DO NOT skip this critical step. Many charcuterie products have been ruined by not tasting the mixture before cooking it, rendering the finished product irreparably bland.

4. Adjust the seasoning if needed, then press the meat mixture into a ceramic terrine or meatloaf pan.

5. Boil some water separately.

6. Put the terrine in a shallow roasting pan and pour boiling water into the pan until it is halfway up the side of the terrine. Put the lid on the terrine and place the roasting pan in the oven. (Note: If you don't have a lid for the terrine, cover it with plastic wrap and then with foil. Aluminum foil can sometimes leach onto the top of the terrine if you put it in direct contact with the meat.) Bake the terrine for about 45 minutes to an hour, until it reaches 155°F internal temperature.

7. Cool the terrine on a rack with the lid on until it reaches room temperature. Then place it in the refrigerator to cool thoroughly.

8. Slice and serve with mustards, pickles, and crusty bread. Garnish with fleur de sel.

Wine Wardrobe Bottle #8

LIGHT-BODIED RED

If it wasn't for that movie about loving Pinot Noir and hating Merlot, light-bodied red wines might still be marginalized by big fruit and oak. So while I may publicly kvetch about the snubbing of Merlot, I will secretly thank Alexander Payne for making Pinot Noir one of the most requested wines in American restaurants.

He didn't do it single-handedly, though—Pinot Noir has been around for a while and has always been on people's pedestals.

The French have been making the world's best Pinot Noir for centuries in Burgundy—and still do. The Grand Crus of Burgundy are the most amazing, life-changing Pinot Noir experiences on the planet, and are priced accordingly. Even Premier Cru Burgundy (one step down from Grand) sports a hefty price tag. The only Burgundy within reasonable financial reach leaves us with rather variable wines labeled Bourgogne, and they can be a huge disappointment.

Then there are the Pinot Noirs of California—specifically the Sonoma Coast, where winemakers are taking their cues from Burgundy and putting them toward a uniquely California flavor spectrum. But those are the exception, and the finest examples are costly. If it's from California and it's cheap, there's a good chance that you're not drinking 100 percent Pinot

Noir, but something that has been boosted in flavor by a more robust variety. (In California a wine needs to contain only 75 percent of the grape stated on the bottle.)

The Willamette Valley of Oregon is a place that strikes a perfect balance between the bombast of California and the gravity of Burgundy. The law in Oregon is that the wine has to contain 90 percent of the stated grape—but the act of blending heartier varieties into Pinot Noir is rare, because those more robust grapes don't perform as well in the cooler climate of the Willamette Valley. That said, Oregon Pinot Noir comes with a range of price points that tend to be higher than average as well.

In fact, I'd say that most quality Pinot Noir—whether it be from Burgundy, Oregon, or California—is priced beyond something we can advocate as everyday wine. It's out there, but my personal research on Pinot priced in the twenty-dollar range shows it's hard to find. (So if you do

This is Rachel Hubbard and her daughter, Holly. Their kitchen was great, as was the grilled salmon with various light-bodied reds. We might have broken an expensive glass, but don't tell Rachel's husband Mike.

find one, we recommend picking up a number of bottles.)

I love Pinot Noir. I love Burgundy. But I can't afford to drink it every day. Which is why you'll find my Wine Wardrobe regularly stocked with the *underdog*. Read on.

Beaujolais

Of all the gross misconceptions in the world of wine, perhaps none has done more to muddy the understanding of a wine as the creation of Beaujolais Nouveau.

Beaujolais Nouveau is at once a brilliant marketing construct and a devastating reprogramming of the world's perception of a place and a grape (even more than the invention of Fumé Blanc or the annexation of the name Chablis by American jug wine producers).

So in the spirit of setting things straight, we're going to insist on highlighting Beaujolais—specifically Gamay Noir produced in the ten crus (reminder: "cru" is a vineyard or group of vineyards) that make up this under-appreciated part of Burgundy.

Beaujolais Nouveau was at one time a simple celebration of the end of the harvest—a local tradition that involved rolling out barrels of barely fermented grape juice as a reward for a job well done. This practice eventually spread from the bistros in Lyon to the restaurants of Paris, where producers became increasingly clever in their methods of delivering their wine to the glasses of thirsty Parisians.

The race to deliver Nouveau (and the parties that sprung up around it) garnered increasing attention from the world during the '70s—but it wasn't until 1985, when the release date was changed to the third Thursday of November, that things went awry. Placing it in the wheelhouse of enthu-siasts willing to take a long weekend to party (along with the convenient marketing tie-in of Thanksgiving) catapulted Nouveau to the conscious-ness of the American people, erasing whatever conception of Beaujolais may have existed before.

We love a good party—and have no beef with Beaujolais Nouveau beyond the overarching misconception it wrought. When people hear *Beaujolais*, they only think of Nouveau—a simple drink meant to be consumed once a year to celebrate the end of harvest.

What should come to mind when the world thinks of the Gamay Noirs of Cru Beaujolais are wines of complexity and character well suited to anybody who appreciates Pinot Noir.

Here is a list of the ten crus of Beaujolais. For now, these represent the best light-bodied reds in the world:

- Brouilly
- Chénas
- Chiroubles
- Côte de Brouilly
- Fleurie
- Juliénas
- Morgon
- Moulin à Vent
- Régnié
- Saint-Amour

Each cru has its own personality to explore, but they all share an energy and a fruit spectrum that can easily stand in for the more famous Pinot Noir.

Another great resource for light-bodied red wines: Italy. In the north, look for Schiava from Trentino-Alto Adige. In Sicily, keep your eye out for Frappato.

Then there are the reds of Austria and Germany—both these parts of the world are known more for their white wines, but the reds are distinct, underappreciated, and food friendly. Varietals we recommend include Zwiegelt, Blaufränkich (also known as Lemberger), and Dornfelder.

Light-Bodied Red Pairing Exploration

SALMON:

(Unfortunately) Salmon Comes with Some Baggage

Living in the Pacific Northwest, Chris and I actually hear people speak about being "tired of salmon" or that salmon is "boring." I've heard that people in Maine say this about lobsters. I personally have never tired of salmon when it is fresh and in season. In fact, I think that it is one of the most delicious animal proteins on the planet. It is at once oily, intense, rich, metallic, and reminiscent of the sea. It also takes on an incredible, almost crème brulée–like texture when cooked properly: crispy flesh or skin yielding to a custardy interior as each flake slips away from the next. Salmon is not just fish, it is special. It is salmon.

Sadly, salmon has become a very complicated thing. If you talk about it long enough you won't be able to help but get political. All of this could be solved if we all agreed to not eat too much of it and buy it from responsible people who believe strongly in ocean stewardship. If the fishmongers are telling us that there isn't much available, make the portion smaller, or serve something else. The peace of mind is worth the extra couple of dollars to buy it from the right person and adhere to their advice when it comes to scarcity. We want this beautiful animal to be available for decades to come. It is OK—actually, it's imperative—to make it a treat instead of a nightly ritual.

If you feel like you want to really do your part environmentally, don't buy farmed salmon—with two exceptions: Scottish on the East Coast, and Skuna Bay on the West Coast. Both of these farming styles are known for their high water-to-fish ratio, and the farms are huge pens in the open ocean, rather than landlocked cesspools of disease that less-humane fish farming is known for. These types of salmon are going to drive the marketplace for years to come because we as a nation are just plain eating too much of it. I highly recommend eating some every year, but maybe less than you used to, and making a special occasion about it when you do.

The thing that is so fascinating to us about salmon in the Pacific Northwest is that it goes so perfectly with one of the other great products of our region: Pinot Noir. Red wine with fish is absolutely perfect if it is the right fish. With salmon and Pinot Noir, it's almost like the two were devised at the same time in some extraordinary food lab that was hell-bent on coming up with a perfect food and beverage pairing. They taste that delicious together. This isn't just a "grows together, goes together" thing either, as French red Burgundy from half the globe away is equally good with the fish. There are also a ton of other light-bodied red wines that go very well with salmon, as my associate will discuss further.

Get Your Grill On

The cooking method for salmon really matters for this pairing. The application of dry heat, whether it be from a pan or a grill, seems to highlight the nuances of this pairing best. In fact, if I had to pick one method for a light-bodied red, it would likely be grilling. The char on the fish is reminiscent of the char of oak barrels, a beautiful, complementary flavor. Charring also produces slightly bitter notes, which contrast with the rich fruit of the wine very well.

Cooking fish on a grill can be tricky. Many people solve this by placing the fish on foil (not really grilling it), or placing the skin side on the grill grates, and then scraping the fish off of the skin (leaving behind most of the grill flavor). To properly grill salmon, one

has to be comfortable with the idea of extremely high heat, committed to not fondling the fish as it cooks, and understand that fish is usually (professionally) cooked most of the way on one side.

For this method, we will presume thick-cut pavés (blocks) of king salmon. The first choice in the matter is whether or not to leave the skin on the fish. A few things should influence this decision: 1) can your grill reach a hot enough temperature to properly crisp the skin? 2) has the fish been properly scaled? 3) do you like the flavor and texture of crispy fish skin?

The first question is easy to answer. Generally a stainless-steel grill grate will not retain enough heat to properly char and crisp the skin of fish, though it can be done. The process is far easier if the grill grate is cast iron, which retains a whopping amount of heat. Also, if your grill doesn't reach at least 550°F with the lid on, it isn't hot enough for this method. No worries—just remove the skin before you cook it, as your particular grill will probably leave it soft and slightly difficult to cut or bite through.

If the fish hasn't been scaled properly you'll know right away, as there will be loose scales in the paper that it is wrapped in. These scales can be removed, but ideally this is done when the fish is still whole, using a special tool made for the job. I personally would remove the skin at this point, because one missed scale can remain stuck in the back of your throat or teeth for much longer than you like. Very unpleasant.

Crispy fish skin can be one of the greatest things on earth, but it's an acquired taste. To those of us who love it, it adds a whole new dimension of texture and intense flavor to the fish. But for some it is very unpleasant texturally, and can sometimes even cause difficulties emotionally. Some people just find that eating the skin of fish is weird. In such a case, remove it. (The point of these "can't miss" pairings is pleasure. Set yourself up for success and do whatever makes you and your guests happiest concerning the skin.)

If your grill can't be set up to have two zones, you will need to perform a little bit of fancy footwork at the end of this process, but it is possible. Let's assume, though, that you can construct a really hot zone and a less hot zone in your grill. The hot zone should be very, very hot. As hot as you can get it, whether it be raging hot charcoal or the gas turned all the way to high. The other side should be off, again whether it is devoid of hot coals or just turned completely off.

Yep, We Even Brine Fish

Grill is fired up. Let's get the fish ready (these instructions are for fish fillets that have had the skin removed, by the way). Don't be cowardly about seasoning. There is no other way to put it. In the great words of the one of the best cooks in history, Madeleine Kamman, "There is no altruism in blandness." Your fish should taste excellent with no sauce or accompaniments whatsoever. There is no way to achieve that without salting the fish, and it will seem like you're salting it heavily until you get used to the appropriate amount.

Here's the basic method: First, you'll make a brine, cool it, and submerge the fish in it. I aim for a brine of 3.6 percent salinity, which is approximately the salinity of the ocean. This turns out to be two tablespoons of salt to a quart of water. It will seem like a lot. Adding sugar will help make sure things caramelize beautifully, so you'll add a little brown sugar too. Bring this to a boil and cool it down to room temperature. Even better, leave it a little bit warm.

Submerge the fish in this solution. If it's cold fish going into cold brine, leave it for 1 hour. If it is cold fish going into room temperature brine (better), leave it for 30 minutes. The amount of flavor transfer in this short amount of time is going to absolutely shock you. We can't do this at the restaurant because we don't know how many people will order salmon that far ahead of time. This method is superior to what we can produce at the restaurant. The fish will be at the right temperature for grilling too.

Pat the fish dry. Thoroughly. It is really important that you do this step, even if you don't have time to brine the fish, because wet surfaces prohibit crispy, seared product. Then you're going to do something that will surprise you. You're going to season the fish with salt and fresh cracked black pepper. It won't be too salty. It will be crisp on the surface. Much of this salt falls into the grill itself.

Putting It All Together

Oil is a key element of grilling fish. Oil the grates on your grill, and then oil the side of the fish that you're going to grill first. Lightly. The key to fish not sticking to the grill is not about using a ton of oil, but about being patient enough to let the fish cook until it releases from the grill grates.

Look at your piece of salmon. One side will be flat, but have some unsightly grayish-brown flesh running through it. This is the skin side. The other side will be sort of rounded off. This is the side that was once up against the bones. It should have no discoloration. We call that the *presentation side*, and it is the side you always place on the heating element first. Now find that hot spot you made—it should be right over the coals or the element. Set the fish on the grate and back away slowly. If you're the fidgety type, find something to do with yourself for the next 4 to 5 minutes. Sit on your hands if you have to. Run around the block a couple times. Whatever you do, don't touch that piece of fish. Don't do it. Don't even lift the grill lid to look at it. I implore you. Your desire to mess with it is why you've found grilling fish to be difficult up to this point. You are your own worst enemy if you can't resist these urges.

The next step also requires discipline. Get a metal spatula, not tongs, and slide it under the fish on one corner. Gently, gingerly try to just barely lift it from the grill. Does it want to release, or does it want to stick? If it releases, give it a quarter turn and then put the lid back down and walk away again. If it doesn't, wait in 1-minute increments until it does. Many an overzealous backyard grillmeister has attempted the previous instruction with all of the grace of a stampeding buffalo, and left a leathery flap of fish flesh stuck to the grill, and a mutilated piece of fish fillet on their spatula. Fish is delicate; treat it that way. You don't want to leave the tastiest part, which is that beautifully charred crust, sitting on the grate to burn and be scraped

away by a grill brush the next time you grill. That part should be on your plate, then soon in your mouth, chased down with an Oregon Pinot Noir.

After you've turned it that quarter turn, you don't need to wait nearly as long—probably just 2 to 3 minutes, depending on the thickness of the fillet. It shouldn't stick at this point no matter what, as a crispy, charred crust has formed. Brush the top side with a little oil and turn it over at this point, then move it over to the cooler side of the grill. Admire your handiwork. If your grill has cast-iron grates, you should have those signature restaurant cross-hatch marks staring back up at you, on your very own grill, in your very own backyard. If you had to cook a piece of salmon on the stainless grates because your cast-iron grates have yet to arrive in the mail, then you will have a nicely caramelized surface on your fish. While it won't be a deep char like cast iron gives you, it will still be pretty damn tasty.

Now that the fillet is on its back, lovingly staring up at you from the grill, you should baste it with some tasty fat. Butter is great. So is olive oil. We've even brushed salmon fillets with duck fat at the restaurant. (It seemed like the right thing to do, and it would be my pinnacle fatty medium for pairing with light red wines.) Butter will do, though. Just melt it and brush it on the fish after you've turned it over. Again, not too much or you'll have flare-ups that will put a sooty veneer over your near-perfect masterpiece.

Why only near-perfect at this point? Because you need to make sure it is done properly. Salmon is best served at an internal temperature of around 130°F to 135°F. This is going to be what we call medium-rare fish. If you like it done a little more, bump it up to 140°F for silky, flakey, medium fish. If you cook it to the FDA-recommended 145°F, you'll have dry, overcooked fish. These 5-degree increments actually matter that much. My best suggestion: Pull it off around 130°F and it will finish cooking itself to the perfect 135°F. Fish doesn't need to rest like red meats, but do put it in a warm spot while you get your accompaniments, sauce, and family together.

This fish, for this exercise, will just be served nakedly with the Oregon Pinot Noir. Normally, though, you'll have accompaniments and maybe even a sauce. Just make sure that these elements make equal sense with a light-bodied, fruit-driven red wine. Mushrooms really come to mind here. A simple ragout of mushrooms can serve as both a vegetable side and a sauce at the same time.

2 quarts water

¼ cup kosher salt

2 tablespoons brown sugar

4 (6-ounce) king salmon fillets, skin on

1 pound mixed fresh wild mushrooms, or even cultivated mushrooms (these could include morels, porcinis, chanterelles, crimini, shiitake, portobello, oyster, and many others), sliced ¼-inch thick

1 tablespoon neutral oil

2 tablespoons butter

2 shallots, minced

½ bottle red wine (do the right thing: drink the other half while you cook)

2 cups chicken or beef broth (mushroom broth works too)

2 tablespoons roughly chopped fresh parsley

2 tablespoons minced chives

1 tablespoon thyme leaves

3 tablespoons cold, cultured, or sweet finishing butter

Grilled King Salmon with Wild Mushroom Ragout

Serves 4

1. Make the brine by bringing the water, salt, and sugar to a boil. Set aside to cool. If you need to brine fast, boil half of the water and then add the other half as ice.

2. When the brine is at room temperature, place the fish in the brine for 30 minutes.

3. Light the grill and build two zones: One should be almost oppressively hot, the other should be medium hot. On a gas grill this is easy; on a charcoal grill you will need to build a hot zone with the coals leaning toward one side. You need to be able to get the hot zone to a minimum of 550°F.

4. While the fish is brining and the grill is heating up, make the mushroom ragout. (Note: If you like, you can make the mushroom ragout up to 3 days in advance—just don't add the finishing butter until you reheat it, as it will "break" when reheated, which means it will have a bunch of grease sitting on the top of it rather than a creamy texture.)

5. Bring a large sauté pan to medium-high heat. Make sure the mushrooms and the shallots are ready and nearby. Add the neutral oil to the pan. It should smoke almost immediately. Then add the butter. This will slightly cool the pan, but the butter will begin to bubble and melt very quickly. If the edges of the melted butter look like they're going to burn, lift the pan off the heat and swirl the butter around.

6. Place the pan back on the heat and add all of the mushrooms at once. Let the mushrooms sear for at least 2 to 3 minutes before tossing or stirring them. This will build a nice, brown caramelization on the mushrooms. If you toss them too early, the pan will cool way too quickly and the mushrooms will belch out liquid and never brown.

7. Add the shallots. (We know that most recipes would have you add the shallots at the beginning, but with this much heat, they would definitely burn. Adding them later in the process allows you to put a nice amount of heat on the shallots without burning them.) Sauté this mixture for at least 7 to 10 minutes before adding any salt. Then reduce the heat to medium and add several large pinches of salt—at which point the mushrooms will usually release a ton of liquid.

8. Reduce this natural liquid by half, then add the wine and reduce it until almost dry.

9. Add the broth. If using homemade broth, the liquid will slightly thicken as it reduces. This comes from the natural gelatin in the broth. If using

store-bought broth or mushroom broth, you will end up having a bit thinner ragout. It will still taste fantastic.

10. When the liquid has reduced to a sauce-like consistency, remove the pan from the heat. If you are serving the sauce right away, add the parsley, chives, and thyme. Slowly stir in the butter (off-heat). The butter will slightly thicken the ragout and give it a creamy consistency. It will also enrich the sauce tremendously. (If you are saving the sauce for later use, add the herbs off-heat and begin cooling it now.) Taste the ragout for salt and adjust. Place it in a warm place, but do not reheat it using direct heat.

11. Place the fish skin side down (if grilling skinless salmon, place the nicer-looking side down first) over the hot zone you built up earlier. After 3 minutes or so, rotate the fish a quarter turn to make those nice hatch marks. After another 2 to 3 minutes, turn the fish over and place it on the cooler zone of the grill.

12. Cook the fish to 130°F for medium rare. If you like your fish a little more done, cook it to 140°F. We don't recommend cooking it more than that or it will be dry.

13. To finish, put a generous spoonful of the sauce on the plates first, then serve the fish on top of the sauce, along with whatever accompaniments you wish.

Pinot Noir and Salmon

If I were to subject myself to deep hypnosis in order to delve into the fuzzy depths of my restaurant memory, I would probably stumble on the first instance of standing next to a table of people and making a wine pairing recommendation. I suspect the wine recommendation was Oregon Pinot Noir and salmon.

Better, I'd like to get into a time machine and find the person who first threw a glass of Pinot Noir next to a perfectly grilled salmon and declared the two united forevermore.

It is so natural a flavor marriage that I have all but declared a moratorium on pairing salmon and Pinot Noir, challenging myself and the sommelier team to explore all other conceivable options in the wine pairing wardrobe before succumbing to the obvious.

But we often just shrug our shoulders and succumb.

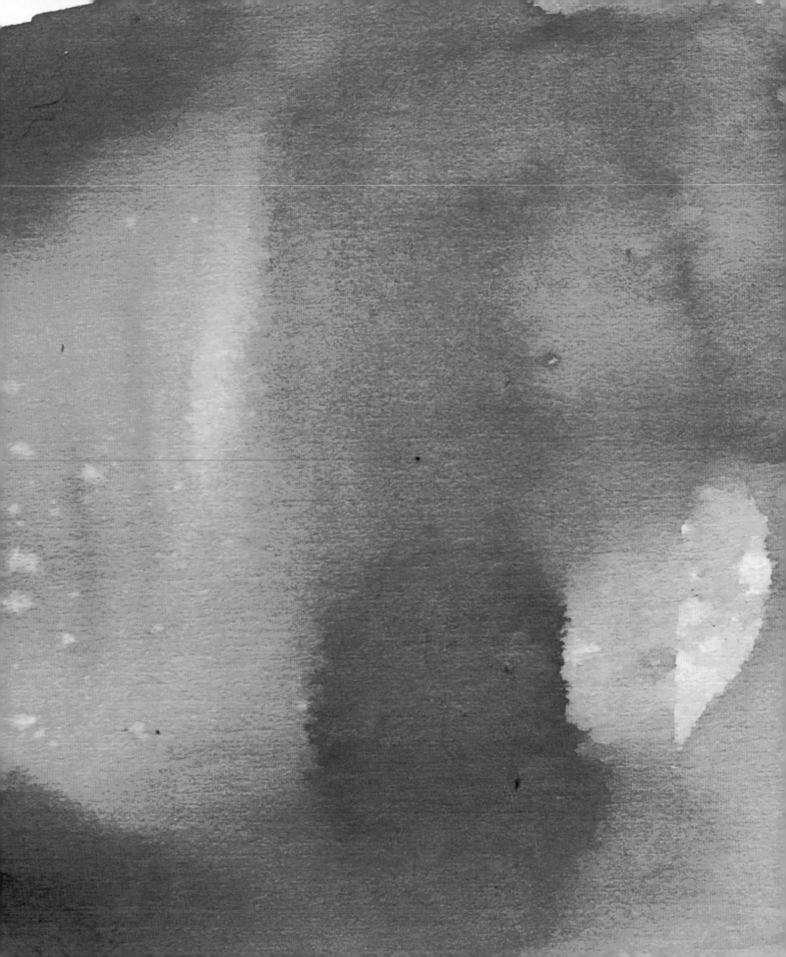

MEDIUM-BODIED RED

Medium-bodied red wines don't get the attention that the full and tannic wines do—there's less overt flash and bang. They don't boast and brag. They don't have to. Proof is in the pairing, I guess you can say.

Point of honesty: When tasting one hundred wines in a day as I sometimes do, it's difficult to not be attracted to full-bodied and tannic wines. It's also hard not to be drawn to the color and acidic shock of light-bodied wines. The medium-bodied wine needs us to pay a little more attention to it.

Medium is not to be confused with the middle—it's a top priority when it comes to pairing with food. If there is a red wine to stock in excess, it's this one. (Otherwise you might find yourself heading to the wine store more than once a week, which is not necessarily a bad thing.)

What's great about medium is that it's where we tend to find a lot of examples of the ever-catchy and often accurate mantra, "What grows together, goes together." Classic and familiar dishes from Italy, France, and Spain end up being coupled with medium-bodied classics like Chianti, Côtes du Rhône, and Rioja.

It is also the category of wine that has the most variability—this is where you're going to see the benefit of getting to know the people at your local wine shop. Classic, Old World regions of France, Spain,

and Italy are influenced enormously by vintage—irrigation is either not practiced or downright illegal, so the weather makes its mark, for better or worse.

Scanning my tasting notes for examples of medium red wines, the descriptions are less colorful and more attitudinal:

- Even-keeled
- Balanced
- Confident

The light-bodied wine shocks you with acidity, the tannic wine shocks with astringency, the full-bodied red shocks with viscous booze and fruit—but the medium-bodied wine

confidently steps into the room and takes care of business.

It's almost like a medium-bodied wine fits one's mouth in a way that makes it more about the flavor than the weight impact, which explains why it tends to get along so well with food—never demanding the spotlight.

MEDIUM-BODIED RED WINE REGIONS:

- Côtes du Rhône
- Chianti
- Rioja

MEDIUM-BODIED RED WINE GRAPES:

- Grenache
- Dolcetto
- Barbera
- Cabernet Franc

Medium-Bodied Red Pairing Exploration

RAGOÛT, RAGÙ, STEW

One of the most important cooking methods on earth is stewing. It is economical, free of strict rules like those for pastry or charcuterie, and produces some of the deepest, richest flavors in all of cuisine.

The terminology for these delicious items is often confusing, so let's sort that out first. *Ragoût* is the French word for stew. It can be a main dish or a side dish. For example, if I was going to serve a stew of pork with white beans and sage, the French would refer to the dish as *ragoût de porc avec haricot blanc*. However if I was going to serve a seared pork chop with stewed white beans in the restaurant, I'd probably call those beans a white bean ragout. The French, oddly in this case, are far less specific about the term.

The Italians, on the other hand, are very specific about what makes a *ragù*. In the purest sense, ragù is a pasta sauce, almost always based on meat. This sauce is slow-cooked with flavorful liquid until the meat becomes velvety tender. In northern Italy, they usually use the meat sauce to dress a pasta dish. In southern Italy, they often simmer a large piece of meat in liquid, then dress the pasta with this flavorful liquid, and serve the meat as a separate course with vegetables. In both cases, the methodology is nearly identical. Tough meats, aromatic vegetables, flavorful liquid, and long, slow cooking produce exquisitely complex flavors that become far more than the sum of their parts.

As with many things in this text, we'd like to focus on the methods used to make master recipes, and then let your imagination take over to personalize those recipes. The key here, whether you serve a stew as a main dish or a pasta sauce or both, is that you follow a basic set of methods to achieve success, no matter what your final seasonings are.

Browning, Caramelizing, and a Man Named Maillard

The most important task that one can perform when preparing a stew, ragout, or ragù is to take the time to properly brown the meat. This cannot be stressed enough. There is a magical chemical reaction that takes place when meat is exposed to high heat and a little bit of fat. It is called the Maillard reaction.

It was discovered ages ago, but first discussed scientifically by a French physician named Louis Camille Maillard in 1910. Also known as browning or caramelizing, this reaction takes advantage of the fact that with enough heat, sugars turn into caramel, and with meats and vegetables there are additional reactions occurring because of amino acids present in the food. In summary, browning equals flavoring. There is a list of the flavors that are produced by these reactions in Harold McGee's opus *On Food and Cooking*. We'll spare you the scientific names of the compounds that create these flavors, but here's a list of the flavors themselves:

- Sweetness
- Acidity
- Bitterness
- Fruitiness
- Sherry-like flavors
- Butterscotch
- Caramel
- Nuttiness
- Savoriness
- Floral flavors
- Meatiness
- Green vegetable flavors
- Chocolate flavors
- Earthiness

Quite complex indeed. All of these flavors are created above and beyond the flavor of the product itself. We are chemically creating new flavors with heat.

Dry heat is what we use to brown things. This reaction is simple, and should be understood in the most basic way so that it can be successfully employed. So here's the straight dope: Sugars caramelize at around 330°F, while water vaporizes at 212°F. If something is going to brown, it can't be wet or it will steam—which is why we pat it dry just before searing it. If you are going to brown something with a lot of water content, like ground meat or vegetables, you need to cook a lot

of the water out first before it will start to brown. This also means that your pan has to be hot, hotter than you are likely to be comfortable with if you're new to cooking. This includes keeping that pan hot once there is food in it.

Hot Pans Solve Problems

It's simple math. If your pan is 375°F before you put any meat in it, it cannot possibly still be 375°F afterward. The meat you are adding to the pan is likely to be cold, say 40°F to 50°F. That's a full 325 degrees colder than the pan! If you were to touch something 325 degrees colder than you, I assure you that you would not remain a balmy 98.6°F on the surface of your skin where you touched it. If you put too much in the pan at once, or add things too quickly, you will drop the heat of the pan down to a temperature so low that you are no longer browning, but rather steaming. This is why heavy-gauge, thick-bottomed pans work so well to brown foods. The piece of metal in question holds its heat longer.

The same goes for over-agitating things once they are in the pan. Don't peek underneath things. Don't jostle them around, and don't turn them over too fast. When you do these things you cool the pan, which, again, is getting you back to that steaming temperature and further away from that magical Maillard temperature.

Another mistake that people make when it comes to browning is that they get the pan too hot. They hear that the method is best done with extremely high heat, and they just frankly overdo it. The result is that the surface of the product goes straight from brown to black, especially out on the edges, as the meat curls under the intense high temperature. The oil you're browning in likely cannot take the onslaught either, and will begin to smoke violently, and potentially could light on fire if you've really gone too far. There are a couple of ways you can solve this. First, you can take advantage of the exact situation above that you were trying to avoid by just adding more and more product to the pan until the heat comes back down from a smoking inferno to a nice firm sizzle. The other way is to drop the heat under the pan. The problem is that if you're not using gas, that heating element is still hot as hell. Lift up the pan or move the pan to another burner. Generally at these temperatures, only 15 to 20 seconds are necessary to take it from ridiculously hot back to the temperature you wanted in the first place.

The Sound of Flavor

The hope is that after a fair amount of practice, you will feel the sensation of transferring heat through a pan to be a powerful, controllable process, and one that you can shape and manipulate to your will. This allows you total control over browning things. Generally, a good start is to turn your pan (hopefully a heavy-gauge one) to about medium high, say seven out of ten. All stoves vary, so you'll need to find this sweet spot on your stove over time, but medium high is a good starting place.

Get the pan hot, but don't add the oil yet. Heating the pan and the oil at the same time can unnecessarily denature the oil. Once the pan is at the right temperature, drizzle in the oil; you'll need about ⅛ inch of oil covering the bottom of the pan. Let the oil heat up for 10 to 15 seconds. If you're at the perfect temperature, small wisps of smoke will come off the oil at this point. Don't let it sit and smoke like crazy. That's when you add the product you're planning to brown (and not all at once if there's a big batch to do).

Then you're going to do something that you probably wouldn't expect: you're going to listen to your food. Specifically you're going to listen to what I refer to as "the sound of flavor." There is a very specific sound that is created when food is heated in fat and proper browning is occurring. It is a crisp, sizzling sound that says to you, the cook, that moisture is rapidly evaporating, sugars are caramelizing, and amino acids are bonding. In other words, the food is getting brown, under your confident command and control (that Maillard dude was right). If you hear nothing, you're in big trouble. Pull the meat out immediately and wait until the pan is actually hot. If you hear a low, gurgling sound, the meat is starting to steam and simmer in its own juices. Pull some of the pieces out of the pan and let what remains in the pan get up to temperature and begin browning. Then return the extracted meat to the pan and carry on.

Proper Browning Takes Time

This is not a process to rush. Many people think that they should brown things very quickly, and they are disappointed with their results. To the contrary, if I were making a stew with diced meat, I would take approximately 2 to 4 minutes to brown *each side*. That's 12 to 24 minutes to brown all six sides of the cubes. If you're wondering whether I would actually turn each individual piece of stew meat with tongs to ensure that it is browning properly on all sides, I can tell you that I would. The reason is that each bite of that meat later on would be that much more intensely delicious.

An analogy, if you will. Years ago, when I was a teenager, I was an avid skier. My pops and my brother and I all had season passes to a local ski resort, and we'd ski forty to fifty times a winter—easily more than twice a week. When we were this crazy into skiing, we watched a lot of VHS tapes of Warren Miller films. We'd watch maniacal, extreme skiers like Glen Plake and Scot Schmidt hike up to crazy peaks, way out of the bounds of manicured ski runs. I'll never forget hearing Warren Miller talk about how when you hiked up to your starting point, each turn was that much sweeter coming back down the mountain. That you'd really earned those turns by virtue of all those miles you'd hiked.

Browning a stew is like hiking in backcountry for skiers. You know, as each of your guests puts a bite of meat in their mouth, that you spent those extra minutes making every one of those bites as flavorful as possible. The extra time spent cooking is rewarded by the extra enjoyment of those eating the dish.

Now the Aromats

Every ragout contains vegetables, but whether they are added at the beginning (what we call the bottom of the pan) or later on to preserve their color, texture, and integrity is a very important distinction. Often, we add vegetables that come from bulbs first, like garlic, onions, shallots, leeks, fennel, etc. We also tend to add tough, fibrous vegetables like celery and carrots at this early stage. These are known as aromatic vegetables (*aromats* for short). We sweat or caramelize them so they'll release a lot of flavor when they are eventually smothered in liquid.

Most of us have heard of deglazing a pan, but just in case you haven't, this is simply the act of using a liquid to dislodge crispy, caramelized bits from the bottom of a pan. This happens to be a cornerstone of Western cooking methodology, so much so that the French call these crispy bits *fond,* which translates to bottom, deep, background, and foundation.

Pro tip: Aromats are mostly water, and you can actually deglaze with them. After you've browned all of your meat, take it out of the pan and set it aside. Add a little bit of fresh fat to the pan and turn the heat to high. Don't let the fond burn! Just as you see the fond start to darken, dump the aromats into the pan and stir vigorously, scraping the bottom of your pan with your spoon. The moisture that is almost immediately released from the vegetables will deglaze the fond, and then this delicious, flavorful compound will be thoroughly coating your vegetables. The smells released at this stage of cooking are incredible. I've always liked to think of them as a little gift for the cook. If you have people over, take note of when they start to say, "Smells good in there!" from other parts of the house. It's usually not when you're browning the meat. It's when you add the aromats to the pan. They represent the smell of delicious, savory food. That's why we call them aromatics.

1 Get all your ingredients ready. Start by searing the beef.

2 Make sure to sear all sides. (This could take a while.)

3 Fond.

4 Add aromatics to deglaze.

5 Further deglaze by adding red wine.

6 Add broth.

Don't Just Add Water

There are some stew recipes that call for water, but they can almost always be improved by adding something with more flavor. This liquid can have alcohol in it, like wine or beer, but generally we also use some broth. I find stews made from 100 percent wine, like classic boeuf bourguignon, to be a little strong. I almost always cut back the wine and use some broth too.

Broth and booze are not the limits. There are classic stews made with milk, coconut milk, or fruit juice like apple cider. On some occasions we add no liquid at all, if we know that the ingredients of the stew are going to release a ton of liquid themselves.

Reduction

If you're using a liquid that benefits from being reduced, like wine or broth, it will really improve the stew to let it reduce as the meat cooks. It is important to never boil meat or it will get tough, so this can be a slow and tedious process that cannot be rushed. The stew needs to be kept at a bare simmer, under a watchful eye. As the liquid increases in viscosity, its boiling point will reduce, meaning you need to be vigilant about continuing to reduce the heat. The rewards are immense, however, as the liquid that you are developing in the pan will not only be concentrated in flavor, but will be exchanging flavor with the meat as well. Some liquids, like dairy or coconut milk, have too much fat in them to reduce. They tend instead to break, which means that the fat separates from the liquid. There are ways to re-emulsify

these liquids if this happens, but it is a practice that's just better avoided.

Finishing Veggies

There are other vegetables that are not aromats, but are pretty darn good in a stew. These would include any kind of wilting greens, potatoes, baby spring vegetables, etc. Basically if the vegetable would not benefit from long cooking, we add it closer to the end. Potatoes or noodles are a special case, as their starch will also thicken the stew. This requires the cook to be observant once they're added. The newly thickened liquid loves to burn on you and ruin your last two to three hours of work. Don't let it. Be present once starchy things are added to ragouts.

The Final Steps

There are some ingredients that should only be added at the very end, such as citrus zest and fresh herbs. These ingredients produce incredible aroma for the stew, but their pungency deteriorates quickly. Save them for the very last minute to get the most out of them. The same goes for if you're garnishing the stew with any cheese. Add it at the very end or put it on the table for guests to add themselves. Cheeses tend to break when cooked for a long period of time as well.

The finished stroganoff

Almost Classic Beef Stroganoff

2 pounds beef (a tough, marbled cut like chuck or even brisket), cut into 1-inch cubes

Sea salt and freshly cracked black pepper

All-purpose flour, for dredging

About ¼ cup neutral oil

2 yellow onions, diced or sliced (it will feel like a lot)

1 pound mushrooms, sliced (morels would make an absurdly good beef stroganoff)

1 cup red wine

1 tablespoon Worcestershire sauce

1 tablespoon soy sauce

2 cups beef stock

1 cup sour cream or crème fraîche

1 teaspoon Dijon mustard

½ cup chopped parsley

Classic beef stroganoff is made with just-cooked beef tenderloin. This is an expensive method that doesn't yield nearly the results that tough beef stew meat and the braising method can accomplish. Serve this version with egg noodles, boiled potatoes, mashed potatoes, or rice.

1. Generously season the beef with salt and pepper and then dredge the pieces in flour. Pat all excess flour off of the meat. Heat the oil in a 12-quart Dutch oven or other deep, heavy-gauge pot over medium heat. Sear the meat on all six sides. The heat doesn't need to be high—just make sure the beef is always sizzling and you are fine.

2. Transfer the beef to a plate and sauté the onions and mushrooms together over the remaining crispy bits, also known as the fond. Cook them, stirring, until they are thoroughly wilted and starting to brown.

3. Add the red wine, burn out the alcohol, and then add the Worcestershire and soy sauce. Reduce until almost dry.

4. Add the beef stock and return the meat to the pan. Cover and gently simmer. Even better, put the covered pot in a 250°F to 300°F oven and cook until tender, checking it occasionally to be sure that the liquid is not simmering too vigorously. This will usually take about 2 hours. The meat is ready when fork tender.

5. Look at your sauce. If it is too thin, strain out the meat, onions, and mushrooms and reduce the liquid by up to half. The sauce should coat the meat and mushrooms, not sink to the bottom of the pan. It needn't be as thick as gravy, as you will be adding ingredients that further thicken the sauce.

6. Remove ¼ cup of the liquid and whisk it into the sour cream to temper it. Whisk the sour cream mixture back into the rest of the liquid, then whisk in the Dijon mustard. Taste and adjust for salt.

7. Spoon the stroganoff over your chosen accompaniment and garnish each serving with lots of chopped parsley.

large yellow onion, thinly sliced

2 carrots, thinly sliced

1 rib celery, thinly sliced

1 head garlic, cloves separated and peeled

1 bunch parsley

½ cup olive oil

3 pounds ground veal (or choose a combination of pork, beef, or veal)

¼ pound pancetta, finely minced

1 (6-ounce) can tomato paste (San Marzano brand, if possible)

½ bottle white wine (red is OK too, if that's what you're drinking while you make the sauce)

2 quarts meat broth (beef, chicken, homemade, or store bought—it honestly doesn't matter that much)

2 quarts whole milk

1 cup heavy cream

Salt and pepper to taste

Balsamic vinegar to taste

¼ cup chopped fresh herbs (we use sage, rosemary, and parsley in the winter; we use basil, oregano, and parsley in the summer)

This is the most arduous recipe in this book. It is actually one of the most arduous recipes in my entire culinary repertoire. You will be at the stove for a while. Spend the time, though, and you will be rewarded with one of the greatest sauces in all of Western cuisine.

This is a great Sunday afternoon project. Sports on the tube. Spoon in one hand and glass of nice wine in the other. This is cold weather cooking for the most part, so plan a chilly fall or winter weekend around it. You will want to serve

continued

Neo-Classic Veal Bolognese

Serves an army

1. Pulse the onion, carrots, celery, garlic, and parsley in a food processor until you have a coarse paste. Reserve.

2. Get the sturdiest, thickest, deepest saucepan you have (a 12-quart saucepan or dutch oven is perfect) and heat it to medium-high heat. Nonstick will not work for this recipe. You need to form a fond in the pan and nonstick will not do this. Add the olive oil and let it come just to a smoke.

3. Add the pancetta to the pan. Brown until crisp and rendered. Then remove the pancetta to add later. You will be using its valuable fat to sear the meat. Place about one-third of the ground meat into the pan in small, hand-formed nubs. You will eventually be browning and breaking up this meat as much as possible, so the key here is to not overload the pan. Once the meat starts to brown, add little bits more. You will eventually overwhelm the pan, but the more caramelization you can form at this early stage the better.

4. Eventually the liquid in the pan will reach a point where the meat will no longer brown. At this point, add the rest of the meat to the pan and start stirring, vigorously. For 20 minutes to 1 hour, you will stir and stir and almost nothing will happen. Then you will notice a crispy brown fond forming on the bottom of the pan. Now you're getting somewhere.

5. Add the tomato paste. Keep stirring. It will try to burn on you. Don't let it. Immediately reduce the heat to medium low. As you turn the tomatoey mixture over and over onto the fond, it should deglaze the pan. The liquid will also start to reduce.

6. Just when the fond seems like it is going to burn, add a few tablespoons of wine. It will loosen the fond significantly. Stir and wait for the meat to brown again and produce another fond. Deglaze the same way until you run out of wine.

7. Add the vegetable paste. It will almost immediately deglaze the fond. It will also smell ridiculously good. Stir and scrape. The vegetables will belch out an absurd amount of liquid, but that's OK. Keep stirring until the liquid has evaporated and a fond is starting to form. Keep the heat at medium-low. Many people get impatient at this stage and try to rush it. Please don't.

8. Keep doing the same thing with broth until you run out of broth, just ¼ to ½ cup at a time, loosening the fond, evaporating the broth, and re-forming the fond. This is concentrating the flavors in the sauce in an incomparable way.

continued

this sauce on everything! In Italy you'd serve it on fresh tagliatelle, and we agree with this choice, but gnocchi, polenta (hard or soft), or other noodle shapes work well too. We've even served it on flatbread. The sauce is awfully heavy to put on stuffed pasta like ravioli or tortellini, but the combination will still work—and if you really want something to stick to your ribs, don't let us tell you not to. The sauce is rich and intense, though, and a little goes a long way, so dress your pasta delicately with it. You can always add more.

9. Add the milk all at once, stir well, and bring everything to a simmer. Return the pancetta to the sauce at this stage. Simmer on low heat for at least 1 hour and up to 4. Stir often. If the mixture seems to be getting too dry, add more broth, or milk, or even water. The simmering and mellowing is more important at this point than the specific type of liquid added. Essentially it is impossible to overcook this sauce, and it tends to improve from long cooking. It will certainly be done after 1 hour, but if you have the extra time . . .

10. When the sauce is velvety and thick, add the cream and the chopped herbs. The sauce should not have any watery liquid separating from the meat.

Taste carefully for salt. You will likely need some at this stage. We wait until the end to add it because all of the reduction could make the sauce extremely salty if we added it earlier. Give the sauce a few turns of fresh ground pepper at this stage as well. If the sauce is way too rich, or flat in flavor, add a few teaspoons of balsamic vinegar to perk it up. Toss with freshly cooked egg pasta and garnish with grated Parmigiano-Reggiano cheese, more chopped herbs, and possibly a sprinkling of crisp breadcrumbs.

FULL-BODIED RED

Scanning my tasting notes for examples of full-bodied red wines (what I call the Gateway Reds) I found the words:

- Voluptuous
- Hedonistic
- Zaftig
- Boozy
- Blammo
- Running mouth-first into a flavor wall
- Mouth burden
- Thick, rich, fun

The first red wines I drank were all of a certain boozy and fruity intensity, and I have no shame in loving them. A time machine trip to the wine rack in the kitchen of my apartment I shared with my friend Grant back in my twenties would have been a greatest hits of all the wines that have fallen (to a certain extent) out of vogue.

And really, it's just a little unfair. For some reason it's OK for the world to consume a bazillion gallons of cheap Malbec every day, but Old Vine Zinfandel is somehow avoided? We are slaves to fashion, but I encourage all thoughtful drinkers to at least visit the wines of their otherwise misspent youth. They will surprise you. (Or at least dislodge memories, like hearing a song you haven't thought about for a number of years.)

So how can you spot a full-bodied red wine on a shelf? One shortcut:

alcohol by volume. Just like you can spot a wine with residual sugar by finding a bottle with 12.5% or less ABV, look for a bottle of red with an ABV of at least 14.5%. It isn't obvious, but alcohol has a higher viscosity that translates in the mouth as *weight*.

So why have a high-alcohol red in the Wardrobe? Most of what you will read about alcohol and wine pairing is that higher alcohol levels make things more challenging—and it's true to a point. The weight and the intensity of high-alcohol wines can stomp on more delicate and detailed dishes—but we don't always put together delicate and detailed things.

One place these wines perform well: the backyard BBQ. Many barbecue sauce recipes contain a little bit of sugar in the form of molasses, brown or white sugar, honey, or otherwise. Commercial sauces often advertise *smoky and sweet* because we love those two things together. The full-bodied red wine, while not technically sweet, comes with maximum ripe fruit flavors; sometimes we describe them as having a brambly fruit character, like pulling berries right from the vine. These ripe fruit flavors are often mistaken for sweetness—so pair these wines with smoky flavors and enjoy that yin and yang.

This is Amy and Brandon Screen: two of the nicest people on earth. We spent a long afternoon at their place with full-bodied red wines while pan-roasting pork tenderloin and producing a decadent reduction sauce.

Another surprising area for the full-bodied red wine: spicy food. Having spent many years working with the cuisines of Southeast Asia, I've found that many of the dishes that have a full-bodied mouth experience jive well with full-bodied wines—the trick is to *avoid tannin*. The tannins in wine tend to pick up on heat spice and intensify the flavors, throwing the dish out of balance. But a rich Panang beef curry with a fruity Australian Shiraz? It's a savory peanut butter and jelly reaction—peanut-based curry with jammy Shiraz is a dramatic departure.

One last reason to have the full-bodied red wine around: it's a great cocktail. These round and rich numbers don't have challenging acids and tannins—they are smooth operators that function nicely when you don't want to do anything beyond putting *flavor* in your mouth. (Just watch your intake—it'll hit you harder than you think . . .)

**SHOPPING LIST FOR
FULL-BODIED REDS**

- Zinfandel
- Syrah
- Shiraz
- Malbec
- Merlot

Full-Bodied Red Pairing Exploration

ROASTED LEAN RED MEATS:

Tenderloin Steak and Cabernet Sauvignon? Not Really . . .

I remember when my dad started collecting wine. My family and I were enamored with the amazing labels he was acquiring. They were mostly very rich, very tannic red wines. Back then we thought it was a good idea to serve grilled beef tenderloins with these wines, because we thought they would hold up to the "monster wines" we were drinking. They didn't. In fact, we didn't know what we were talking about back then at all. We were enraptured by the idea of serving really expensive, big wines with equally decadent and expensive cuts of meat like beef tenderloin or rack of lamb. We should have served those wines with rich and sticky, braised beef short ribs.

The tenderloin and lamb racks would have been better served by a soft, rich, full-bodied red wine. Tannins want fat, and most loin cuts are trimmed almost entirely of it. The lean, minerally protein of medium-rare roasted beef or lamb, or even pork, tends to be beautifully contrasted by the voluptuous fruit of a big, full-bodied wine, where the tannins have fallen off from age, or were never there in the first place. If you have old wine, roast some lean beef, lamb, or pork, then pair it with your aged treasure.

Which Cuts Are We Talking About?

If you hear the word *loin*, that's what we're talking about here. Loin cuts are very tender, with more pale, delicately flavored meat and little fat. This is perfect for a full-bodied red without a lot of tannin. Here are some examples:

- Beef: tenderloin, New York strip steak, flank steak, hanger steak, flat-iron steak
- Veal: tenderloin, chops
- Pork: tenderloin, loin, chops

- Venison: loin, saddle, backstrap
- Lamb: loin, chops, rack of lamb
- Duck: breasts (with properly rendered skin)
- Squab
- Quail

There are also a few cuts that don't work as well for this type of wine, as they are fattier and are better served by tannic reds from the next section. Avoid them for this pairing. They are:

- Beef rib eye steak
- Beef bavette steak
- Wagyu or Kobe beef
- Veal breast
- Pork shoulder (roasted very slowly)
- Pork belly (roasted very slowly)
- Leg of lamb
- Duck legs (roasted very slowly)

Roasting: Two Methods for Success

When we roast something, we are cooking it with air. Really hot air. Stop and think about this for a moment. As a medium for transferring heat, air is highly inefficient. In fact, of all the methods we use to transfer heat, roasting is by far the least efficient. Imagine a 212°F oven. You could stick your hand into it and hold it there for quite a while before you got burned, but if you touched the metal sides of this oven, you'd get burned rather quickly. If you stuck your hand into boiling water (also 212°F) you would get burned very, very badly, as you would with steam or oil at the same temperature.

It is this inefficient heat, though, that we are actually thankful for when we choose to roast something. Take the example above and imagine putting a whole chicken through that rigmarole. The boiled chicken would cook the fastest, followed by the steamed bird, then the metal, then the oil. In fact, it would be *dangerous* to roast a bird at 212°F. Bacteria would grow too quickly at this low temperature before the meat got fully cooked. Now imagine cranking

that oven up to 400°F. You could still put your hand inside it, but not for very long. Roasting allows us to cook large things without just burning the outside and leaving them raw on the inside. When we cook something entirely in the oven, from its raw state, it's called oven-roasting.

There is a seeming paradox for oven-roasting: The less done you want the interior of your product, say medium rare rather than well done, then the hotter you want the oven to be. This is because you have less time to get the exterior caramelized before the interior overcooks. Remember our friend Maillard from the ragout chapter. We need sustained high heat to produce that caramelization. Otherwise we end up with a gray, insipid-looking roast with none of the nutty, brown flavors that we associate with roasted meats.

If well done is desired, you need to drop the oven temperature in order to keep the outside from burning while you grossly overcook the interior of the roast. In fact, if you prefer your meat to be well done, there is a magnificent solution to that: braising, which is a flavorful way to purposefully "overcook" something but retain its moisture and succulence. Skip to the next section and treat yourself to some far less expensive braised meats, rather than obliterating an expensive loin cut. By definition (because of the cut's inherent leanness) if you are cooking a loin cut to well done, you are going to dry it out. Conversely, we never braise anything to less than well done. You won't hear about a braised dish cooked to medium rare.

Sometimes, even at 500°F, the piece of meat in question is just too small to get it browned by oven heat alone. This is when we ramp up our manipulation of heat transfer even further. We're going to pan-roast. This allows us to apply direct heat to the exterior of the product with a pan or the grill, but then slow things down by placing it in the oven to finish. This is the most popular cooking method used in restaurants. It allows us to quickly produce something that is beautifully caramelized on the outside, but precisely cooked to the right doneness on the interior.

Pork is Not White Meat

The National Pork Board is genius. They hired a top-flight PR firm back in the late 1980s to create a better image for pork, which during the fat-free craze of that era was considered a pariah. This firm came up with the slogan *Pork: The Other White Meat.* This same firm came up with the *Got Milk?* campaign, and forever confused a generation (mine) into thinking that *Corinthian leather* was an actual thing beyond upholstery for a Chrysler Cordoba. They were attempting to capitalize on the perception of healthy eating that chicken was enjoying at the time. In fact, part of their campaign included recipes that were traditionally made with chicken breasts, such as Pork Cordon Bleu.

The colloquialism stuck. In fact, I've had numerous, lengthy, and often heated discussions with people that pork is not white meat, and they remain convinced otherwise. For the purposes of cooking, and certainly for this text, we are going to go with the USDA definition that pork is, indeed, red meat. This discussion is largely semantic, but it is important that we have our ducks (speaking of red meat) in a row when discussing wine pairings.

1 Start by trimming off the tail and head pieces of the pork tenderloin to get an evenly sized cylinder of pork.

2 Trim away all silver skin, first by making a flap of silver.

3 Then by reversing direction and pulling the silver while cutting as little meat as possible.

4 Trimmings should all go in the bowl with the reserved pork.

5 Cut the cylinders in half so you have four evenly-sized portions.

Ingredients

2 whole pork tenderloins (about 2 pounds total)

3 to 4 tablespoons all-purpose flour, for dredging

6 tablespoons neutral oil

2 large yellow onions, sliced very thin

1 carrot, cut into ¼-inch coins

1 rib celery, cut into ¼-inch slices

1 tablespoon tomato paste

½ bottle red wine (drink the other half while you're cooking)

1 quart beef broth (store bought is fine)

1 bay leaf

12 sprigs thyme

1 pound yellow potatoes (like Fingerlings, German Butterball, Yukon Gold, or Yellow Finn), sliced in half lengthwise

4 tablespoons finishing butter, cold

A few drops of red wine vinegar (optional)

Full-bodied red with "white meat"? Yes indeed. Although pork tenderloin can also go with white wine (hint: so can filet mignon), we're going to make this pairing work by adding a very nice red-wine pan sauce to the equation. Coupled with a deep sear and some earthy ingredients like potatoes and onions, this will work quite well with a voluptuous red.

We will also use a technique to make the sauce more intense: we're going to use some of the pork for the sauce, then strain that meat out. And yes, some people may object because it will seem costly or wasteful. But believe us, this is a great method; you'll be getting the flavor out of the pork and at the same time avoiding the traditionally very overcooked tail end of the loin.

Roasted Pork Tenderloin with Onions, Herbs, and Yellow Potatoes

Serves 4

1. Trim the pork of all silverskin and fat. Keep the silverskin and discard the fat. Cut both pointed ends off of the loins. Then cut each remaining loin in half; you will end up with 4 perfectly cylindrical pieces of pork, about 5 to 6 ounces each. I will refer to the portioned pieces as the loins, and the trimmed pieces (the pointy ends) as the reserved pork.

2. Salt the pork loins thoroughly as early as you can. Alternatively, you can brine the pork loins in a zipper-lock bag containing 2 tablespoons of salt and 2½ cups of water. Do not brine them for more than 24 hours (keep refrigerated).

3. Cut the reserved pork into ½- to 1-inch pieces. The point here is that these small pieces will create a lot of surface area on the reserved pork, which will translate into a delicious sauce.

4. Heat the oven to 400°F.

5. Dust the reserved pork with flour and pat off all of the excess. There should be a very fine veneer of flour over the pork.

6. To make the sauce, heat 1 tablespoon of the oil in a medium saucepan until it begins to smoke. You want to get the reserved pork just short of burned, so you will be browning the pieces for quite a long time, dropping the heat often until you still hear sizzling at medium-low heat, and the meat is a deep chestnut brown. Transfer the pork to a bowl.

7. Add another 2 tablespoons of neutral oil. Add half of the onion plus the carrot, celery, and the tomato paste to the pan. The vegetables should start to pick up the fond—but if not, add just a few splashes of red wine. Cook the vegetables until they start to brown and the tomato paste has changed color from bright red to a deep crimson.

8. Add the reserved pork back to the pan and add the wine. Bring to a full boil. Skim any foam that comes to the surface of the liquid and discard it. Once the alcohol has burned off and the wine has reduced by two-thirds, add the beef broth and bring to a boil. Next, add the bay leaf and half of the thyme sprigs. Reduce the heat to a simmer; you're going to simmer this mixture for the next 45 to 60 minutes. When there is about 1 cup of sauce left in the pan, take the pan off the heat.

9. Toss the potatoes in salt to taste and 2 tablespoons of the neutral oil. Place them all cut side down on a sheet pan and put them in the oven. Do not even think about them for the next 20 minutes. They will form a delicious brown crust on the cut side if left unmolested. So leave them be!

10. Heat an ovenproof sauté pan to medium-high heat. Add the last 2 tablespoons of neutral oil and let it come to a smoke. Pat the loins dry and add them to the pan one at a time. The first one should be vigorously sizzling before you add the next one. DO NOT agitate any of them at this point. Resist every urge to move them around at all. Carefully sear the pork on all sides as nice and brown as you can. Remove them from the pan and take the pan off the heat. Save the pan, which should have a nice fond in it, for finishing up the onions and the sauce later.

11. Spread the reserved onions in a roasting pan, then put a roasting rack over the onions and place the pork loins on the rack (they'll be suspended over the pan).

12. Meanwhile, check the potatoes. Poke them with a paring knife, toothpick, or cake tester. If the knife or the tester picks the potato up off the pan, they still have uncooked starch inside and are not done. Roast them for another 5 minutes and repeat this process until they are cooked through.

    Let's take a minute to summarize! You now have sauce simmering away, cooked potatoes on a sheet pan, and seared but uncooked pork loins over onions on a roasting rack. Remove the potatoes from the sheet pan and arrange them on the rack with the pork loins. We're now going to finish cooking the pork, reheat the potatoes, and par-roast the onions—all at the same time. Shove the whole thing in the oven for 10 to 15 minutes.

13. Heat the reserved sauté pan to medium heat (do not burn the precious fond that is in it). Strain the sauce from the saucepan into the sauté pan. Press lightly on the veggies and meat to extract all their juices. Discard the strained vegetables and pork; they have done their job. Scrape the fond vigorously with a wooden spoon.

Amy did a great job with these potatoes.

14. Quickly rinse the saucepan and then place the unused thyme sprigs in the strainer. Strain the liquid from the sauté pan back into the saucepan over the thyme sprigs. This puts a nice, fresh thyme flavor back into the sauce. If you have a degreasing pitcher, strain the sauce into the degreasing pitcher first, then pour the pure liquid off into the saucepan, leaving the fat behind. Otherwise you'll need to skim the fat from the top of the sauce.

15. Bring the sauce to a simmer. Skim any fat or scum from the sauce that comes to the surface. The goal is a sauce that is clear, shiny, and has the viscosity of whole milk.

16. Check the pork. You want to cook pork tenderloin to no more than 145°F. We recommend going as low as 135°F or 140°F, because it's so easy to overcook this lean cut of meat. When the pork is at the desired temperature, transfer the loins to a plate and tent them lightly with foil; let them rest for about 10 minutes. Return the roasting pan to the oven to finish heating the potatoes and onions. (The onions under the pork have likely started to brown and collect some of the pork juices, so they don't need a long time in the oven.) Now you have rested pork, a near-finished sauce, and cooked vegetables.

17. Remove the sauce from the heat and add the cold butter, one tablespoon at a time, whisking thoroughly. Do not let the sauce reboil or it will break. Taste the sauce, adding salt if necessary. Also, the sauce might seem a little one-dimensional and flat. If so, add just a few DROPS of red wine vinegar to perk it up. The sauce should now have the viscosity of half and half, and easily coat the back of a spoon.

18. Place a nice pile of the onions, plus any other vegetable you are serving, in the center of some warmed plates. Slice the pork into 5 or 6 slices each. Fan the pork around the vegetables. Spoon the sauce around the whole presentation and serve.

1 Heat the pan to medium high; then add neutral oil.

2 Dredge the reserved pork pieces and trimmings in flour. Shake the excess flour off in a sieve.

3 Gently, evenly place the reserved pork pieces in the pan.

4 Deeply sear the reserved pork pieces. Don't worry about overcooking them, they won't be eaten directly.

5 Add vegetables and red wine to deglaze.

6 Scrape the fond with a wooden spoon to dislodge all of the tasty bits.

7 Bring to a boil, and then add broth.

8 In a separate pan, sear the tenderloins on all sides over medium high heat.

9 Spoon fat over the top of the tenderloins as they're searing for an even better crust.

10 Place some onions on a sheet pan and a roasting rack over the onions.

11 Place the seared tenderloins over the onions.

1 Strain the liquid from the saucepan into the still raging hot pan that you seared the tenderloins in. Be careful of steam burns!

2 Dislodge the fond and then strain back through a sieve into a degreasing pitcher.

3 Gently pour the sauce back into a saucepan, leaving the fat behind.

4 Carve the pork, and then solicit friends to help with the plating. Plating is fun, and should not be attempted sober if you have a sommelier handy.

5 Spoon the sauce around your presentation, but don't cover up your perfectly cooked pork with sauce.

6 Final garnish with herbs just before serving.

TANNIC RED

If you have a friend with an abrasive personality and a tendency to talk at high volumes, then you know you tend to invite your loud friend to only very specific social situations. Super Bowl Sunday isn't the same without the Loudmouth—Easter Sunday, not so welcome.

Tannic reds can be the boors of the wine world, and are so wildly popular you would think that everyone was eating medium-rare rib eye steaks nightly.

Here are the words that I use when describing tannic red wines:

- Astringent
- Cotton mouth
- Mouth drama
- Tongue squeezer
- Sandpaper tongue
- My lips are sticking to my teeth
- Sucking on the business end of a blow-dryer

None of that sounds particularly appealing, but there are reasons we sometimes need the mouth-drama queen. For one, we do eat a lot of steaks, and many cuts of meat need a little tannin to handle the fat. It's a cliché for a very good reason—it works.

It will also give you an ongoing excuse to purchase and consume triple-cream cheese. Once you've had something like Délice de Bourgogne with a tannic red, you'll understand. (The tannins and the fat in the cheese cancel each other out in the best way, and all the hedonism of the wine is released into the open arms of the dairy. It will make you think about skipping dessert entirely and just having cheese for the rest of your life.)

And sometimes we just want something to drink that will bite back a little. Think about black coffee and hoppy beer—we like a little bitter in our glass from time to time. So that particularly hard day at work? Pull the cork on your most tannic red and call it a mood pairing.

All right, so how can you tell if a wine is tannic? It's not like beers that list the IBUs (international bitterness units) on the label. (Beer labels are officially a thousand times more helpful than wine labels based on that inclusion.)

Certain grapes are naturally more tannic—they have developed thicker skins over the millennia—and most of them happen to be on the top of the popularity charts. There are always exceptions to the rule, but generally

Here we all are at the Kezner's house hanging out while the short ribs were braising. The adults: Jamie and Dan Kezner on the left, Keita and Chris Horn in the middle, Coach and wife Kristin Mills on the right. The two hams (Jack Kezner on the left and Silas Horn on the right) are clearly having more fun than the adults. Or at least having more fun getting their picture taken.

speaking, the following grapes tend to have more pronounced tannins. Also: look for something young. As a bottle ages, the tannins eventually bind and soften. The youth of a tannic red wine ensures a more dramatic mouth.

Shopping List for tannic reds (safe bets by grape):

- CABERNET SAUVIGNON—The sheer volume in the world guarantees quality variability. Also, the popular kid demands higher prices.

- CARMÉNÈRE—At one point planted throughout Bordeaux, proper Carménère is a delightful mix of blackberry and blueberry fruits and tannins. Chile is currently the best source, but it's being planted in more places as of late.

- PETIT VERDOT—Rarely seen as a stand-alone variety on account of its wicked tannic structure. That said, there are some brave people willing to put it center stage.

- NEBBIOLO—The sneak attack, insofar as Nebbiolo tends to be a more medium-bodied affair. Only one place to look: Piedmont. You can spend a lot on Nebbiolos from Barolo and Barbaresco—look instead for Langhe Nebbiolo.

- PETITE SIRAH—Also spelled Petit Sirah, Petite Syrah, or Petit Syrah—which is funny, since it turns out that it should be called Durif. (It was developed by one Dr. François Durif back in the 1870s.)

- TANNAT—The name actually stems from the tannic nature of the grape. Grown in southwest France in an area called Madiran, Tannat is often blended with Merlot to soften its blow. It is also widely planted in Uruguay.

- AGLIANICO—Arguably southern Italy's greatest grape, Aglianico, grown in the volcanic soils of Vulture and Taurasi, can be profoundly complex and engaging.

- NEGROAMARO—Hailing from the heel of Italy's boot, the direct translation of Negroamaro is Black Bitter.

- MOURVÈDRE—The tannic backbone of many wines in the Southern Rhône Valley and the star of Bandol, Mourvèdre is a sturdy grape. It can also be found in Spain under the name Monastrell.

- ALICANTE BOUSCHET, TOURIGA NACIONAL, TOURIGA FRANCA, BAGA—These grape names may not be familiar but are just a few of the many used throughout Portugal. It's unusual to find single grape expressions there, so look for the regions Douro, Dão, Beiras, Alentejano. The wines from these places tend to be structured and surprising.

Tannic Red Pairing Exploration

BRAISING:
How to Properly Braise a Cut of Meat That Would Suck Any Other Way

A long-lost friend of mine (now an accomplished chef) was once asked the following interview question: "What do you like to cook and eat on your own time?" His answer? "*Anything braised.*" He got the job.

I feel the exact same way about braising. There is something beautiful, simple, and almost miraculous about braising. Through the use of liquid and patience, we can convert something ordinary into something remarkable. There's a part of me that wishes I'd never studied the science of braising, so that it would still seem like magic to me. When I cook with friends, I braise.

A long-lost friend of mine (now an accomplished chef) was once asked the following interview question: "What do you like to cook and eat on your own time?" His answer? "*Anything braised.*" He got the job.

Long, slow-cooked meats are part of the cuisines of every meat-eating culture. There are parts of every animal, such as the shoulders of four-legged animals and the hind-quarters of birds, that are very well suited to being cooked this way. Slowly browning tough cuts of meat in fat, then allowing them to luxuriate with wine, rich broth, and aromatic vegetables makes for some of the best cooking we do on earth. Almost every culture does it in one way or another. Sometimes that liquid is coconut milk, or fortified wine, or even water, but

the basic method is simple: brown everything deeply, add liquid and aromatics, cover, and cook very slowly.

There is no other method of cooking more economical than braising. Most often it involves taking cheap cuts of meat and marrying them with tough, fibrous vegetables. Braising requires very little technical cooking skill, but it does involve following the method precisely and having patience.

Many of you have likely begun to notice the similarities between making a ragout and a braise. They are indeed close cousins, and the methodology that both share is known as combination heat or combination cooking. This simply means that we start out with one method, searing, and finish with another method, slow simmering in liquid. With a stew or ragout, the difference is only in the size of the product and the amount of liquid.

Step 1: Seasoning

No matter what the meat is that is being braised, it is critical that the seasoning (kosher salt at a minimum) be applied at least 20 minutes before searing. This is even better if done two

> "We hear of the conversion of water into wine at the marriage in Cana as of a miracle. But this conversion is, through the goodness of God, made every day before our eyes. Behold the rain which descends from heaven upon our vineyards, and which incorporates itself with the grapes, to be changed into wine; a constant proof that God loves us, and loves to see us happy."
>
> **—Benjamin Franklin**

to three days in advance, as the meat will benefit from the tenderizing and seasoning properties of salt. Plus the exterior of the meat will start to dry a little, which is ideal for searing.

Step 2: Pat it Dry

Do this step. We implore you. Pat all of the excess moisture off the meat with an impeccably clean kitchen towel or paper towels. This will get you searing quickly. If moisture is on the surface of the meat, you will have to boil that moisture away before the meat will start to brown. Drying the surface is a really important step. Even if you are going to dredge the meat with flour, this prevents you from collecting too much flour on the surface of the meat and getting a gummy texture.

Step 3: To Dredge or Not to Dredge?

You have a choice whether to dredge (very lightly coat) the meat pieces in flour before browning them; these same rules apply to a stew as well as to a braise. To summarize: Dredging the meat in flour helps thicken the sauce, albeit clouding it more like a gravy. It also creates nice, toasty flavors in your braise. Not dredging results in a thin-ner sauce, but leaves it much clearer and shinier. Not dredging requires a bit more skill to properly brown the meat, as flour browns quickly and easily, whereas the surface of the meat itself can take a little longer.

Step 4: Sear the Meat

Generally, you will be browning larger cuts of meat when braising. This could be as small as one-bone beef short ribs, or as large as an entire pork shoulder. It honestly doesn't matter—you still need to take the proper amount of time and brown *every* side deeply and evenly. Counterintuitively, this does not require extremely high heat. In fact, I usually brown using medium-high heat to start, but by the time I'm searing the last side and the product has really warmed up, I'm usually at medium low.

The point of all of this browning is that it provides flavor for your sauce. This is critical to a properly executed braise. Much of the crust that forms during this process will actually dissolve into the liquid and produce an incredibly flavorful sauce. If you poorly caramelize the meat at the beginning, your sauce will lack depth of flavor, and will be underdeveloped—even insipid. Browning is the most active part of the whole braising process. Take your time with it. Once the meat is in the liquid, you're free to head for the living room, glass in hand, to spend time with loved ones, only checking occasionally. Right now, you need to be deeply browning (glass can and should still be in hand).

Step 5: Add Aromatic Vegetables

This step can vary greatly. I've braised with only onions. I've also braised with a combination of shallots, garlic, lemongrass, galangal, young ginger, shrimp paste, chiles, and cilantro roots. The only similarity is that all of these vegetables are known for their extraordinary aromatic value. The individual dish will tell you which of these aromats to use, but the manner in which you add them is important.

After browning, remove the pan from the heat and transfer the meat from the pan. Pour out any spent oil

that remains in the pan, as it is likely to have done its job and is probably starting to wear out on you. If you browned properly, there should be a richly browned, crusty fond on the bottom of the pan. You want to avoid burning this fond at all costs, as it cannot be replaced if you do. Make sure you have fresh oil, a wooden spoon, and your fully prepped aromats at the ready.

Put the pan back on the heat. The fond will start to sizzle just a tiny bit from the trace of residual oil left in the pan. It is also likely to start darkening, rapidly. Don't let it. Add the fresh oil, wait for it to shimmer, and then add the aromats all at once. Immediately stir with the wooden spoon. The moisture present in any chopped aromatic vegetable will begin to release very quickly from the heat. It is this liquid that you will use to deglaze your pan.

Don't worry, I've watched cooking television shows too. I know I'm supposed to add liquid at this stage. Don't. There is plenty of water in those vegetables, and you won't ever be able to fully and properly caramelize them if you add liquid first. Stir frequently and vigorously until all of the fond is dislodged. If you'd like to put some additional color on your vegetables, you now have the power to do so, by sautéing them until they reach the desired color. For classical French and many Italian dishes, you will want to develop as much color on the vegetables as the meat. For lighter-style braising, you will just kiss the vegetables to the fond to release it, then immediately add liquid.

Step 6: Add Liquid

This step is super easy. You just want to make sure that you add anything with alcohol first, burn the alcohol off, and then add any other liquids. Unless you have a gas stove, the word *burn* is going to have less excitement for you, as you will actually just *evaporate* the alcohol out. This is a common courtesy to those dining with you who do not wish to consume alcohol, such as children or those with health concerns. If the alcohol is diluted with other liquids and ingredients, it will evaporate much more slowly. Remember, this cooking method also involves a lid, which will further retard the process of alcohol evaporation, so take care to get the booze out first. A good way to check: use your nose. If it smells boozy, keep simmering.

The liquid that you add should be as flavorful if possible. You can braise in water. It actually works fine, but in my opinion it is always a wasted opportunity to bring more flavor to the party. Without a doubt, we braise in stock more than anything else. Even store-bought, commercial broth is better than nothing.

The worst mistake that people make with braising, short of poor browning, is adding too much liquid, or using too big of a vessel, or both. Just think of the physics for a second and it will make sense. If you add a lot of liquid in a vessel too big, your ratio of liquid to product will be really high. This will perfume the sauce less than if there's a tight vessel that just holds the product, the aromatics, and less liquid.

Step 7: Put Everything Back in the Pot, Cover Tightly, and Simmer

Fairly self-explanatory step, but a few additional techniques can help you with the process.

The liquid should be halfway up the side of the meat, meaning the vegetables will be entirely submerged. When you open the pot the next time there will be quite a bit more liquid.

Bring the liquid to a simmer just before covering the pot, then drop the heat to low. The liquid should never boil, just gently simmer for the entire cooking process. Using direct heat to get the liquid up to temp will save you a lot of time in the long run.

You can continue with your pot on the stovetop; it's a perfectly satisfactory method of braising, and works very well when done properly. The problem is that every time you peek inside the pot to make sure it is not too hot, you release a huge amount of steam and heat. This dramatically slows down the

overall process. When braising on the stovetop, you will need to diminish your heat further and further throughout the process as the product heats up and the liquid gains viscosity. This means a fair amount of peeking, or you risk burning the bottom of the pot, or boiling the liquid—both ruinous outcomes.

When you braise in the oven, you apply even, continuous, low heat to the entire pot, rather than direct heat from the bottom, which is where the meat and vegetables happen to be sitting. Remember, this is a preference, and I've done both methods hundreds of times. But I do think that oven-braising is less tedious, more predictable, and likely to yield the best results.

Step 8: Remove Solid, Refine Liquid

Once the meat is done, meaning that it's fork tender but still holding its shape, you should remove the meat from the liquid and aromatics. Place the meat on a plate or shallow bowl so that any liquid that comes off of it can be recaptured and added back to your sauce. Cover loosely and keep it somewhere warm.

Strain the liquid through the finest sieve that you own. If you have cheesecloth, line your sieve with cheesecloth as well. The point is to get the liquid as free of debris as humanly possible.

Taste your sauce. It is likely to be fairly thin, and somewhat lacking in flavor at this point (although I have gotten lucky on occasion and found an almost fully finished sauce at this stage). Now we go to a branching set of instructions:

- **SAUCE TOO SALTY?** This is the most challenging contingency. You need to quell the salt but give the sauce more body. First, add a few drops of acid, be it vinegar or citrus, which as we learned in the Mind Mouth chapter will diminish the impression of saltiness.

- **SAUCE TOO THIN?** Reduce the sauce, but DO NOT add more salt at this point. Keep tasting as the sauce reduces. If it gets to the appropriate body without getting too salty, you're in luck, as no further refinement will be necessary. If it still seems too thin, we might need to thicken the sauce with a *slurry*, which is a combination of pure starch (like corn starch, arrowroot, or potato starch) and liquid. Bring the liquid to a full boil, add little bits of the slurry at a time, and let the sauce return to a boil. Once a liquid boils, the full potential of the thickener will be realized, which is why we add only small amounts at a time, and let the sauce fully reboil in between additions of slurry. Once the sauce has the appropriate body, taste it one more time.

- **SAUCE TOO THICK?** This can happen if you dredged the meat. Sometimes the liquid will look like a thick country gravy from the starch used during the dredge. If this happens, you have to thin the sauce down with more broth. Then taste again and reseason with salt and acid to get the flavor back in balance.

- **SAUCE HAS VERY LITTLE FLAVOR?** This is often the case, as the seasoning from the meat will not have fully leached into the liquid. Start with reducing the sauce. Again, DO NOT add more salt at this point because you'll concentrate the salt in the liquid by reducing it. If you get the right body but not enough seasoning, add salt. If you get too salty, follow the instruction here.

Add the juices that have exuded from the resting meat back into the sauce. This will thin the sauce somewhat, but that's fine, as it will reduce a bit more during the reheating and glazing process. At this point you should have a perfectly braised piece (or pieces) of meat, along with a delicious, clear sauce that has been seasoned and is the right body for the dish.

Step 9: Glazing, Finishing, and Serving

Glazing is a step that enhances the flavor and texture of a braise tremendously. Place the meat and liquid in an uncovered pan and put it in the oven. Every 5 minutes or so, pull the pan out and baste the meat with the sauce. Your objective here is to reduce the sauce to a glaze right over the surface of the meat. You will end up with a shiny, sticky, enriched piece of meat that has sauce glazed all over it.

Once the meat is properly glazed, then add your finishing ingredients such as butter, herbs, or citrus zest to the sauce. Take a final taste and adjust with a bit more fat, acid, or salt as necessary. Garnish each serving with colorful, fresh-tasting ingredients such as chopped fresh herbs, lemon zest, cheese, crushed nuts, etc.

You have just served a perfect braise.

Opposite, bottom: Short ribs, just out of the oven, with some additional seasonings at the ready.

2 pounds bone-in beef short ribs

Flour, for dredging (optional)

4 tablespoons olive oil

1 bottle full-bodied red wine

1 yellow onion, cut into large dice

1 carrot, cut into large dice

¼ cup tomato paste

1¾ cups to 2 cups beef stock (store bought is fine)

1 bay leaf

½ bunch thyme

1 teaspoon black peppercorns

Braised Beef Short Ribs with Gorgonzola Polenta

Serves 4

Short Ribs

1. Heat the oven to 300°F.

2. Salt the short ribs as far in advance as you can (up to 3 days). Store them unwrapped in the refrigerator, ideally on a rack, until you're ready to use them.

3. Pat the beef dry with paper towels. Dredge them in flour if desired. Dredging will produce a thicker sauce with more body. If a thinner, jus-like sauce is desired, or if gluten intolerance is an issue, simply omit this step.

4. Heat half of the oil in a dutch oven to medium-high heat, and sear the beef on all sides except the bone side (sometimes searing the bone side can weaken the tendon holding the bones to the short ribs). Sear the beef in small batches and remove each piece when it is thoroughly browned. Discard the fat in the pan, but not the crispy brown bits that have formed on the bottom. Add the rest of the oil and bring the heat back up. Don't let the bits (the fond) on the bottom of the pan burn.

5. Add the onion and carrots and cook vigorously, stirring, until the onions and carrot begin to brown. The moisture in the veggies will cause the fond to dislodge. If it doesn't, add a splash or two of wine to loosen it.

6. Add the tomato paste and stir; cook for an additional 3 to 4 minutes. Add the wine and bring to a full boil. After several minutes, most of the alcohol will have burned off.

7. Add the bay leaf, thyme, and peppercorns to the wine. Return the short ribs to the pan and add just enough beef stock to come to the top of the short ribs. Return to a simmer. Do not completely submerge the ribs, or your sauce will lose concentration. Cover the pan very tightly and place it in the oven. Cook for 2 to 2½ hours, checking occasionally to be sure the liquid is simmering gently, not boiling (reduce the oven temperature if it's cooking too vigorously). The ribs should cook until they're fork tender.

8. Remove the pan from the oven and raise the temperature to 375°F.

9. Carefully remove the ribs from the pot and, using a fine-mesh sieve, strain the liquid into a saucepan. Press all of the extra liquid from the vegetables and then discard them. Simmer, skim, and reduce the sauce to a nice, glossy consistency that coats the back of a spoon, about 10 to 15 minutes.

For the Polenta

2 cups chicken stock

½ cup coarse cornmeal polenta (grits)

4 tablespoons (½ stick) butter, at room temperature

4 ounces Gorgonzola dolce cheese (avoid Gorgonzola piccante; it is too strong)

For the Final Garnish and Plating

½ cup minced flat-leaf parsley

1 small shallot, finely minced

Zest of one lemon

2 tablespoons high-quality olive oil

Pinch of salt

10. Taste the sauce for seasoning. It is still going to reduce a bit more, so it shouldn't be salty at this point. If it is, add a little more beef stock (or water, if your stock is salty) to decrease the salinity. The sauce should be rich and slightly reminiscent of red wine.

11. Place the ribs in a baking dish and pour the sauce over them. You are going to glaze them by repeatedly basting them with the sauce while you make the polenta. Pull the pan out every 5 minutes or so and baste the meat. The sauce will slowly reduce to a glaze right on the surface of the meat.

Polenta

1. In a medium saucepot, bring the chicken stock to a boil. Slowly whisk in the cornmeal. Return it to a boil, then reduce the heat to low. Boiling polenta can be dangerous, in that large bubbles will form and spit magma-like polenta at you. Be careful, and use a long-handled spoon.

2. Continue to whisk the polenta until it achieves the consistency of mashed potatoes. This can take anywhere from 10 to 20 minutes, depending on the brand. Keep glazing your short ribs every 5 minutes in the oven while you're doing this process. So long as the liquid surrounding them does not boil, you would be hard pressed to overglaze the short ribs.

3. When the polenta has achieved the right consistency, remove it from the heat and take a taste. Be careful, as it is going to be hotter than Hades. If the polenta is still gritty but has reached the right consistency, then whisk in more liquid (water is fine) and continue to cook. The polenta should be smooth, so you just need to cook that cornmeal a little longer so it gets soft. It will reduce some and the meal itself will also absorb more liquid, which will return you to that perfect consistency.

4. Whisk in the butter, then the cheese. Taste. You may need to add a lot of salt at this point, depending on how salty the cheese and butter are.

1 Once your polenta is fully cooked, start adding gorgonzola.

2 Whisk to thoroughly incorporate.

3 The cheese should be fully blended into the polenta. Taste for salt.

4 Add herbs and whisk some more.

5 Slowly add cold butter one pat at a time to further enrich the polenta.

6 Put the lid back on; this stuff will stay hot for quite a while in a heavy gauge pan.

Final Garnish and Plating

1. Do not use a machine to make this garnish or it will be absurdly strong. It should be delicate, bright, and very citrusy.

2. Fold all of the ingredients together. Place a mound of polenta in a large, warmed dinner bowl.

3. Place a piece of the now-glazed short rib on the polenta. Give the sauce a final taste and add salt if necessary.

4. Spoon the sauce around the base of the polenta, then spoon the garnish over the top of the short ribs.

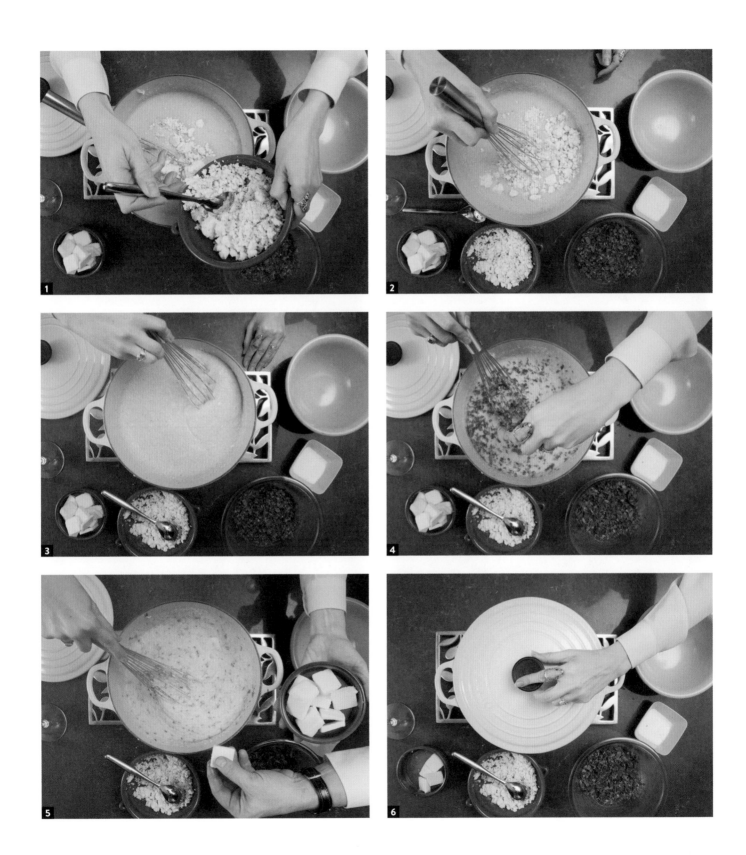

Wine Wardrobe Bottle #12

DRY ROSÉ

I've looked into it, but I can't seem to determine exactly where or when the gross misperceptions concerning rosé came from. It wasn't the invention of White Zinfandel—that was somewhat recent in the history of wine—though I'm fairly confident that it only added to the overall opinion that rosé was a throwaway wine of questionable quality, consumed by people who didn't know anything about wine.

Back even a few years ago, it was impossible to get people to consider drinking rosé outside of the context of a summer picnic. (And looking over old wine lists, it looks like maybe we wine folks weren't taking rosé very seriously either; our opening wine list had but three rather uninspiring choices.)

But fashion has changed things drastically. Each year as spring approaches, millions of cases of rosé are preordered by retailers and restaurants in anticipation of the seasonal rush. Twenty years ago, little thought was given to the stuff—now it's the wine world's Groundhog Day.

For anybody in the business of selling wine, rosé is impossible to ignore. Since the millennium, the consumption of rosé has risen: we will soon see a day where one out of every ten wines consumed on the globe is pink. And I'm all for it.

That said, I still think there's something attitudinally incorrect about how we consume rosé: it's perceived mostly as a seasonal beverage. We only think about pink wine when it's hot—somewhat akin to listening to reggae only in Jamaica.

Here's one great reason to have rosé in your fridge: it makes for a great winter attitude adjustment. It's the *only* positive result of the connection of summer to rosé—you crack a bottle and it will smell like summertime in your glass.

But the omelet recipe on page 256 is not necessarily seasonal. (We recipe-tested it in February using parsley still growing in our backyard.) Putting rosé on the sidelines when the days get short is like refusing to ride your bike on an unseasonably warm winter day.

The most common method for making quality rosé introduces the unavoidable wine term **maceration**. Most red grapes produce white juice—color is obtained by allowing the fermenting juice to steep (macerate) with the skins of the grape. If the maceration process is brief (anywhere from

a few hours to a day), only a little bit of the color of the grape skin is imparted to the wine. Voila, rosé.

The other method for producing rosé brings up another unavoidable wine term: **saignée**. The saignée method is employed by wineries seeking to make their red wines more intense. By bleeding off a portion of liquid early in the fermentation process, the winemaker creates both a rosé and a potentially more intense red wine.

Rosés are produced all over the world, but it's in the south of France where you will find the finest examples. France produces over one-quarter of all the rosé in the world—but also consumes more rosé than any other country. It stands to reason that the highest quality is found where the demand is highest.

Provence is inarguably the quality epicenter. Over 140 million bottles of rosé are produced in Provence each year—almost 90 percent of all the wine made in Provence is rosé. Look for these regions on the bottle:

- Côtes de Provence
- Coteaux d'Aix en Provence
- Coteaux Varois de Provence
- Bandol

Other parts of France worth seeking out:

- TAVEL—The only wine allowed in this area of the southern Rhône Valley is rosé.
- LANGUEDOC-ROUSSILLON—The largest producer of rosé in France.
- MARSANNAY—For the Pinot Noir lover, this is the best address for rosé in Burgundy.

There are other parts of the world making world-class rosé, but start with France. If you grow bored with French rosé, give me a call.

The many beautiful shades of rosé .

Age is Only a Number

I have heard wine professionals I love and respect proclaim that rosés are to be consumed within a year of their vintage date. And yes—as a general rule of thumb, what we love about rosé is the fresh and lively fruit experience that will, sadly, diminish over the course of time. (And with the state of rosé in the world today, there's an abundance of the fresh stuff at hand, so it takes no effort to equip yourself with the latest release.) But I'm going to go against the trend on this, and hopefully some will follow.

I think the idea of a twelve-month expiration date on wine is arbitrary—and if you stretch that arbitrary expiration date by just a few months, you will likely stumble on some awesome wine at steeply reduced prices.

Price is set on demand. Demand is the result of perception. And we all perceive last year's rosé to be over the hill when the new stuff starts hitting the shelves in late winter/early spring. (This is also the result of distributors slashing prices to make room for new shipments—it's rather hard to sell last year's wine at the same price as the recently arrived vintage.) But do know that there are certain regions and producers that not only buck the trend, but are the sort of exception to the rule that calls into question the veracity of the rule itself. (And they all seem to be either made by a French person or made in France.)

In the spring, you'll see the prices slashed on all manner of Marsannay, Bandol, Tavel, and Provence rosé—grab a bottle and open it immediately. (Maybe wait until you get home.) If you find that bottle to represent the sorts of things you love in rosé, then go back and get a few more bottles.

I once had a ten-year-old bottle of rosé from a certain producer in Marsannay. It changed my mind.

Dry Rosé Pairing Exploration

THE ZOMBIE APOCALYPSE MEAL

This dish uses every ingredient in the One Dozen Essential Items for Your Pantry detailed in the next chapter. So, if you're looking for a quick nosh and you've stocked your pantry with everything we've recommended, then you've always got a sophisticated meal available to you that can be put together and inserted into your face in less than twenty minutes. This is also your go-to meal if you're snowed in, or you've just arrived home from the bar, or if there's a herd of animated dead wandering the streets. Don't let the breakfast moniker of omelets hold true for you here either. French people wisely enjoy omelets at all hours of the day, and for good reason. If you don't want to run to the store, make this and crack open a bottle of rosé, or cheap sparkling, or even Champagne if you're feeling saucy. But we love this most with rosé.

If you're anything like me, you never quite use up the fresh herbs that you bought for the last recipe you made, so throw some of those in the omelet too if you've got them. They are certainly not a requirement, but a great addition.

The omelet you can make every day of your life if you have a properly stocked pantry. And rosé.

For the confit shallot:

1 shallot, thinly sliced

1 tablespoon mild olive oil

¼ cup water

A tiny pinch of red chile flakes (piment d'Espelette would be even better)

A tiny pinch of kosher salt

A few drops of sherry vinegar

Minced fresh herbs, optional (stick to just one type, as some herbs interact poorly with others)

For the vinaigrette:

1 teaspoon Dijon mustard

½ teaspoon honey

1 tablespoon sherry vinegar

1 tablespoon grapeseed oil

1 tablespoon extra-virgin olive oil (your best stuff)

For the omelet (makes 1, so you'll need to make this part twice):

2 eggs

1 tablespoon butter

Pinch of salt

Confit shallot (recipe above)

1 tablespoon grated Parmigiano-Reggiano

Zest of lemon (just a swipe or two across a microplane)

1 to 2 tablespoons vinaigrette (recipe above)

A Rolled Omelet Filled with Confit Shallot, Parmigiano-Reggiano, and Sherry Vinaigrette

Makes 2 omelets

Making the Confit Shallot

Don't be put off by the term *confit*; it just means shallots that have been cooked down until they're very soft and sweet. Here's how to make it.

1. Slice the shallots as thin as you can. Even drag out a mandoline to do this if your knife skills aren't quite up to the task. Note that if you are just returning from the bar, your mandoline should remain in your cupboard. Inebriated people and mandolines are a precursor to an ER visit.

2. Add all of the ingredients except the fresh herbs to a small (preferably nonstick) sauté pan. Bring them to a simmer. What you're going to do here is simmer the shallots in the water on very low heat until the water evaporates, leaving behind just the olive oil, which you are then going to slow-cook the shallots in for an additional 5 to 10 minutes, until they just start to turn golden. You could take this even further and make caramelized shallots if you wish; just keep cooking them at low heat until they get as dark as you like.

3. Add the fresh herbs, if using, right at the end. Remove the pan from the heat but keep it warm.

4. If you're using a small, nonstick sauté pan, don't wash it out! It will now have some delicious remnants of confit shallot oil glistening across its surface. This flavor will permeate your omelet that you, coincidentally, will be making in the same pan.

Making the Vinaigrette

This vinaigrette is simple to make and will be used right away, so we highly recommend the "jar method" rather than getting out some sort of mechanical appliance to combine the ingredients. It is quite simple. Place all of the ingredients in a jar, put the lid on tight, and shake like a demon. The emulsion will hold for a few minutes. Shake it once more, like a crazed maraca player, right before you use it, and then plate it gently with a spoon.

Making the Omelet

Writing words to describe the process of making an omelet puts me into the rarified territory of some of the greatest culinary writers of all time, the likes of Auguste Escoffier, Julia Child, Madeleine Kamman, and Jacques Pepin. As a chef caught somewhere between the age of chefs as blue-collar, workaday drones and chefs as celebrities, I truly feel the weight of this attempt. The names above are still revered by my generation.

Because expressing in words something that is almost always better demonstrated (like how to make a rolled omelet), I highly recommend watching the menagerie of YouTube videos out there on the subject. If you have access to a person who really knows how to do this, I even more highly recommend blowing $4 on a carton of eggs just to learn the process from a master. However, we will illustrate the technique on the following pages.

1 Crack your eggs into a bowl. Remove any bits of shell.

2 Whisk eggs with a fork just to get them evenly yellow. Try to incorporate as little air as possible.

3 Add eggs all at once to a medium hot pan. Lift the pan off of the heat to control the temperature if necessary.

4 Stir the eggs vigorously with a rubber spatula until they are about three quarters set.

5 Spread the remaining liquid eggs out to form a thin, even layer of egg.

6 Add shallots.

7 Add herbs.

8 Tilt the pan away from you and begin to roll the omelet with the spatula.

9 Keep tilting and rolling until the omelet is almost completely formed.

10 Make the final turn out of the pan onto the plate.

11 Shape the omelet once it is on the plate to a perfect roll.

One Dozen Essential Items for Your Pantry

To get a wine-friendly meal on your table with relative frequency, it really helps if you keep these few inexpensive ingredients around—they'll give you a head start. If you cook a few times a week, you should never worry about throwing these items away, so it just makes good sense to have them at all times.

The main question I get asked more than anything regarding these ingredients is, "Where do I buy all of this stuff?" It depends on where you live, but to be honest, even though I live in a city where all of these things are available in a retail shop somewhere, I still find myself mail ordering a lot of them. Some of our favorite mail-order sources are listed on page 281. You should be able to get most of these items no matter where you live.

For the grocery items like eggs, butter, shallots, and citrus fruits, you should find them in almost any supermarket. As we've mentioned before, a busy store is a store that's turning things over faster. Keep that in mind as you decide where to shop.

1. Salt

The most important tool chefs have at their disposal is not a knife, not a fancy immersion circulator, not a 38,000 BTU stove; it is simple kosher salt. In the great words of Chef Thomas Keller of The French Laundry:

> The ability to salt food properly is the single most important skill in cooking. . . . It heightens the flavor of everything across the board, no matter what you're doing—even some sweets. . . . But if you taste salt in a dish, it's too salty.
>
> —French Laundry Cookbook, 1999

Salt, the Politics

Salt has gotten a bad reputation over the years. People fear it. Most recipes say, "Add salt and pepper to taste." While not every dish needs pepper, every dish does need salt. Unfortunately this is the one ingredient that most cooks could really benefit from learning more about. Far too many cooks put too little salt in their food, and very few put too much. How does one determine what is too much? Mr. Keller said it perfectly above: If there's too much salt, it will actually taste salty.

If you are afraid of salt, you will never realize the full flavor potential of a dish. That's right, salt is a flavor enhancer. So is sugar. Think about how awful having a teaspoon of salt in your mouth at once would be. How about sugar? All at once. Terrible. Yet both of these ingredients powerfully season our food. If you wish to truly assuage your fear of salt, then just avoid processed foods, especially fast food. Fast food is like the Dead Sea. They use salt and sugar in everything, and in high quantities: the bun, the meats, the sauces, the cheese, the tortillas, the breading, and especially the desserts.

So picture the average American, who eats fast food once or more a week, being skeptical about the amount of salt that they personally have to add to a dish to make it taste good. In the presence of a professional chef, they usually freak out when they see the chef amply salting a dish, thinking that the seasoning is way too much. That tiny bit of additional salt that you use in your own cooking will not even come close to the sodium load taken on by fast food or processed foods. In fact, if we handed you the amount of salt present in the average fast food dish and forced you to season your food with it, you'd likely object to the practice on the premise that adding that much salt to a dish is absurd.

Enhanced Flavors

Think about salt being used to flavor some beautifully prepared, crystal-clear chicken broth. It would take a fair amount to accomplish the task. Think of sugar flavoring a chocolate mousse in the same way. It takes tablespoons, not pinches. Now think of both preparations without the addition of sugar or salt. There's a reason we call them sweets and savories. These two categories of food are defined by sugar and salt respectively. The absence of these two ingredients is quite simply what blandness is.

Now think of both of these ingredients put together. Some of your favorite foods are salty-sweet. I've never even met you and I already know this about you. That's because the flavors of salty and sweet are so powerful when linked together. Think of caramel corn, prosciutto and melon, ketchup and french fries, Thai food. And there are many more examples. These flavor powerhouses are truly the opposite of bland.

Do I Really Need to Have More Than One Salt?

So yes, salt is very important, but there are so many kinds available on the market today that it must seem terribly confusing. Here's what you need to know:

- TABLE SALT, or iodized salt, is only useful for those tiny restaurant salt shakers. If you have any, do away with it. It is chemically processed, and far too finely textured to season precisely with. In fact, if you taste it side-by-side with other salts, it will taste sharp and chemical rather than smooth and round.

- KOSHER SALT is essentially mass-produced, flaky sea salt. Contrary to popular belief, it has not been blessed by a rabbi or met certain specifications within the Torah. In fact, kosher salt is short for "koshering" salt, which was traditionally used to make meats kosher by precipitating meat juices, allowing cooks to wipe the surface blood and juices away, thereby desiccating their surfaces

and preparing them to become kosher.

If you are Jewish and would like to ensure that your salt is, in fact, kosher, then you are looking for a product called Kosher Certified Salt, which is produced in accordance with the Orthodox Union.

If you are just looking for good salt to season with, there are two major brands of kosher salt in the United States: Morton's and Diamond Crystal. Morton's is smaller flaked than Diamond Crystal. Most chefs I know prefer Diamond Crystal, as larger flakes produce more control when seasoning with the fingers, a practice you should develop as soon as humanly possible. I've used Morton's in my kitchens many times as well, and it is a fine product; it just requires an adjustment in feel. On the occasion that you are measuring salt, however, the brand is critical, since coarser grains will measure differently than finer ones. It is why we rarely tell you how much salt to put in a recipe, and if we do, it's usually a ratio with water or meat, by weight.

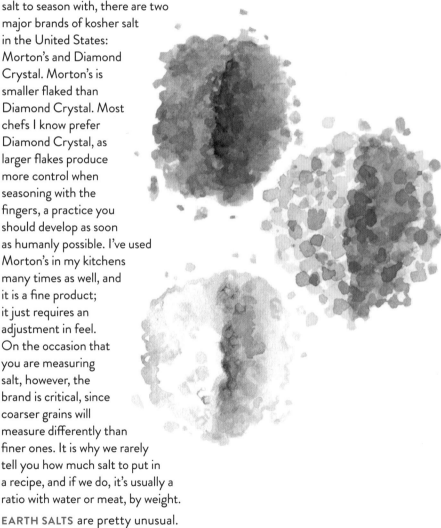

- EARTH SALTS are pretty unusual. They are harvested inland from salt mines rather than seaside salt flats. These salts are often very earthy, and sometimes stink of sulfur, literally like rotten eggs. They are only useful on rare occasions for certain ethnic recipes, and in general I would avoid them. A seeming exception to this is Himalayan salt, but believe it or not this is actually ancient sea salt that is millions of years old. It involves plate tectonics, faith in science, and circumstance, but the salt found in the Himalayas is actually salt from the ocean.

- **SEA SALTS** are their own vast category, so we're going to keep it very simple for this text. Remember, the most common sea salt is kosher salt. Colloquially, sea salt generally refers to specialty salts that are unprocessed.

    Crystalline, hand-harvested sea salts bear names such as fleur de sel, sel gris, flaky Maldon salt, or even more exotic varieties like rose-tinted Australian Murray River, bright red Hawaiian Alaea, or Mediterranean Cyprus Flake. These are known as finishing salts, which means they're generally used on dishes that are ready to be eaten—never for seasoning something prior to it being cooked. For all intents and purposes, one need only have one finishing salt in their pantry, although you can really geek out and take it much, much further. We have lots of different salts that we like to play with, but the key word here is *play*. There is no dish on earth that would be ruined by not having the "correct" finishing salt. In fact, there are very few dishes where finishing salt is remotely close to being a requirement—but this shouldn't deter you from having some, because it's fun, and it can vastly improve many dishes, including desserts.

- **FLAVORED SALTS** can also be really fun, and to me the most important one is truffle salt. Truffle salt is a great finishing salt, and it provides a great way to infuse something with truffle flavor when fresh truffles aren't available. It is certainly superior to petroleum-like truffle oil, which often doesn't contain any real truffles at all. Other flavored salts like rosemary salt or lemon salt can quickly and easily be made on one's own.

- **SMOKED SALTS** can also be an amazing addition to one's culinary repertoire. They are smoked with varying degrees of intensity and different types of wood, all of which can be perceived on the palate in the right dish. They are great on grilled foods to further intensify the grilled flavor. They can also be delicious on or added to slightly sweet foods (like scallops) to get that smoky-sweet flavor profile jacked up.

2. Olive Oil

Terroir, It's Not Just for Wine

Olive oil is one of our favorite ingredients. It is a food that bears many similarities to wine, in that there are widely varying levels of quality, because there are those who make it for huge corporate profits as well as those who make it with passion and intent. Olive oil also has "vintage variance." The words *vintage* and *single vineyard* are used for olive oils because they are so similar to wines. (But olives don't grow on vines or in vineyards; instead they grow on trees, in groves. I have yet to hear about an olive oil's grove-age or see them referred to as *single grove*.) The point is that the highest-quality oils will have a year on the bottle somewhere, and, like wine, the really good ones will vary in flavor from year to year. Also similar to wine, the finest olive oils are small production, rare, expensive, and often come from a single estate, which gives them a real sense of terroir.

Wine and olive oil are also similar in the way we use them in the kitchen. We aren't going to heat up something and sear it in our finest olive oil any more than we'd make a red wine reduction using a bottle of fine Bordeaux. This means that you should probably have at least three olive oils in your home: One for cooking and searing, one for dressings and emulsions, and one for what we call finishing, which is that final drizzle over a dish that allows us to experience the impeccable quality of the oil at its finest. Crusty, peasant bread is perhaps the best minimalist vehicle for finishing oils and is an excellent appetizer in and of itself—and a sprinkle of any of the coarse finishing salts previously mentioned takes it over the top.

When it comes to finishing oils, there are a myriad of different styles and flavors, and you should select one that you like the most. If you are a totally socially maladjusted food nerd like me, you will have several different finishing oils of varying flavors and textures. Then you will have choices when it comes to what kind of oil you feel is best for the dish you've just prepared.

Lastly, every year in late fall, you can invest in *olio nuovo*, freshly pressed oil from that season's harvest. These oils are special for about three to four months and then lose their quality, as well as their extremely vivid color and intensity. These oils are generally very raucous, peppery, and can even promote glandular activity in the back of one's palate because they are so astringent and bitter. In a word, they are delicious—but when purchasing such an oil, one should know that they are not purchasing a subtle or delicate experience.

How Can One Be an Extra Virgin?

The term *extra-virgin* can be confusing. Obviously, most oil producers would like to put this label on their bottle, as it has come to be known as the finest quality, most desirable olive oil. The problem is that there is no universal governing body that regulates the use of this term. In fact, the International Olive Council has set up high standards, but the United States (among many other countries) does not legally recognize those standards. In a perfect world, extra-virgin olive oil is derived from the first, cold press of the olives, and it will contain no more than 0.8% acidity (specifically oleic acid, a fatty acid with a moderate pH). But due to the lack of standards, so-called extra-virgin olive oil might contain as little as 10% true first-press oil and a huge percentage of low-quality cooking oil of almost

any type. So, as with many things in the world of gastronomy, you need to do your research and buy from a trusted source.

Searing with Olive Oil

When it comes to searing, there are varying schools of thought. There are those who say that you should never use high heat with extra-virgin olive oil, and there are those who say that you can, but you should never let it get so hot that it smokes. In the restaurant we do apply heat to extra-virgin oil, as the alternative is to use olive oils that have been chemically treated or are of vastly inferior quality. What we don't recommend is using your expensive, estate pressed and bottled, ultra-premium oil for searing. This is where we reach for a quality, large-production extra-virgin oil that still tastes good, but is not quite at the finishing level.

Emulsifying with Olive Oil

When you agitate olive oil with a very rapidly spinning blade, you expose it to a large quantity of oxygen at once, which robs it of its fruity specialness. This is why we really don't make vinaigrettes or aiolis in machines (blenders, stick blenders, or food processors) with our good olive oils. If you want a really high-quality vinaigrette or aioli, we recommend whisking the sauce together by hand.

3. Butter

Butter is often the first thing in a pan, but it is also quite useful when it is the last thing in the pan. Not terribly different than salt, we use butter for both cooking and finishing. You've probably guessed the next tip: it behooves you to have two types of butter in the house. The first, for sautéing, roasting, or anything you're going to do where the butter is brought up to high heat, can be far less expensive and more utilitarian than the butter that you use for finishing. Finishing butter is always left "whole," meaning that it is never pre-melted or clarified. It is added to dishes cold and with care to not break its natural, tenuous emulsion.

Finishing with Whole Butter

So what do we mean by finishing with butter? Quite simply, we are using the unique properties of butter in a variety of ways and seeking to get the richest buttery flavor into the dish. Pastry- and sauce-making are the two most important categories for this kind of butter, but mashed potatoes, polenta, or puréed vegetables really benefit from the addition of whole butter as well.

Cooking with Butter

The good news is that the butter you use for most cooking need not be expensive. It's best that you buy it as fresh as possible, and we always recommend unsalted (also known as sweet butter, especially in Europe). The amount of salt in a dish should always be your choice, unless you are using something like bacon or anchovies, which you then need to "season around" (meaning you need to take into account the amount of salt these items have in them already before you add more). You can definitely season around salted butter, but again, we really prefer to control the salinity of every dish if we can. Many finishing butters are only available in salted form. We still recommend these, especially if you've found a little number from France, or Italy, or Ireland that you absolutely love and it is not available in unsalted form.

There is a myth out there that butter companies take the unsalted butter when it is about to reach its expiration date, and then salt it and put on a new expiration date. This is patently untrue. Salt is a preservative, and will extend the life of your butter, so there is going to be a longer shelf life on that salted butter label no matter what. We recommend just buying less of the very freshest sweet butter, and buying it more often.

Additionally, you shouldn't really store butter in the refrigerator. We recommend keeping a small amount of butter (say, one stick) at room temperature for spreading on toast, making sauces, and other things where soft butter is preferable. Otherwise the freezer is best. Then pull out what you need when you need it. Butter picks up superfluous odors very quickly, and we all know that the refrigerator can be filled with all manner of various smells. Some of them are wonderful, like that takeout curry from the Thai joint that you properly cooled down, with the lid off, in your fridge. However, you might notice the next day that your butter has a slight curry-like aroma to it. This goes for other things in there too, like the beautiful, properly wrapped-in-paper piece of Saint Agur cheese that you didn't quite finish. Think of butter as an aroma sponge. Even if the individual aromas in your refrigerator are wonderful, the combination of Saint Agur Cheese and Thai curry is not enhancing the flavor and freshness of your butter.

There is another kind of butter to hit the US market relatively recently, and we couldn't be more excited about it. "European-style" cultured butter is essentially made from crème fraîche instead of fresh sweet cream. Let's back up for a second. In the United States, dairy products have long been preserved by pasteurization, a process where the milk or cream is heated to 161° Fahrenheit for 15 seconds to kill most of the bacteria. Prior to this process, most dairy products were cultured, meaning that they were fermented as a way to extend their shelf life. Culturing dairy products takes advantage of their inherently beneficial bacteria and gives them a slightly sour tanginess. Often the cream thickens as well. The good bacteria eclipse the bad bacteria, and the result is dairy products that won't perish in two or three days like raw sweet cream would. This process is employed to make yogurt, kefir, crème fraîche, sour cream, and cultured buttermilk. In a way, cheese is made in a similar fashion, although the milk solids are separated from the whey first. Essentially, our most intelligent and clever ancestors figured out that if bacteria were going to propagate in dairy products, they were going to make sure those bacteria actually made us healthier instead of making the products go bad. And—bonus!—cultured products often tasted better than their less complex pasteurized counterparts.

Summary: If you take crème fraîche and churn it up, you will have cultured butter. The complexity of flavor is comparable to the difference between whipping cream and crème fraîche. While it's not great for everything, cultured butter is a worthy addition to your pantry.

4. Vinegar

Vinegar is, in the simplest sense, spoiled wine. The word is derived from the French phrase *vin aigre* which means sour wine. It is wine that has been inoculated by a bacteria known as an acetobacter, which converts the alcohol, in the presence of oxygen, into acetic acid. Acetic acid is somewhat sharp, and causes the characteristic crinkling of the nose when one takes a giant whiff of it. Vinegar is made in a number of different ways, but it tends to happen rather naturally in the right environment. Fortunately, the necessity of oxygen in this process is why wine with a sound cork can last for years, even a century or more, without converting into vinegar.

Not all vinegar is made from wine. Some comes from fermented fruit juice, rice, and beer (malt vinegar could just as easily be called beer vinegar). I'd like to highlight two very special types of vinegar made by unique processes: balsamic and sherry vinegars.

Balsamic, the Non-Vinegar Vinegar

Balsamic vinegar has technically never been wine. It is trebbiano grape juice that has gone through what is known as a *batteria* of barrels of varying sizes and wood composition, and naturally reduced over eons. The result is a syrupy, sweet, extremely complex elixir that is not like any other vinegar on earth. It is also hideously expensive, and should be. We recommend that you make the investment to get the nicest balsamic that you can afford, and then use it simply, when you can really show it off. This is not vinegar you make a salad dressing out of, or acidulate a sauce with. It is its own thing, and should be the main focus of the dish when it is served—if only out of reverence to the artisans who spent ten, twenty-five, or even one hundred years meticulously caring for it and aging it. In Modena, Italy, where balsamic was born, there are people who start batches of *balsamico* knowing that they will be long dead by the time it is ready to be consumed. These kinds of traditions are rare in the world of food and wine anymore, and when you find one, it is hard not to be enraptured by the romance of it.

Pro tip: One of the most delicious combinations on earth is a chunk of Parmigiano-Reggiano cheese with a drop or two of *balsamico* on it.

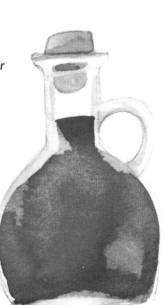

Sherry Vinegar, Nutty and Sweet

Sherry vinegar is very special as well. Making sherry wine is a complex process of its own, and making the vinegar is essentially picking up where the winemaker left off. First, sherry is blended with batches of sherry vinegar and then aged in barrels. Some of that is used to top off other sherry vinegars, and some of it is sold. The barrels provide more flavor to the vinegar, and over time it concentrates through evaporation. This process continues, whether the old vinegar is blended and the process is continued or the final product is achieved. In the former case, there can be parts of the vinegar that exceed fifty years old. Sherry vinegar is far more acidic than balsamic, but it is much richer and more savory than normal wine vinegars.

5. Neutral Oil

Olive oil is all the rage. Has been for at least twenty years. If you watch cooking shows, they will use olive oil for pretty much everything: for Cajun dishes, for soul food dishes, even Asian dishes. The problem is that olive oil tastes reminiscent of olives. Even the silkiest, most buttery olive oils taste more like olives than butter. Granted the oil can be mild, but the good ones, the ones you should buy, have a ton of flavor. Hence the need for neutral oils.

Does the Dish Go with Olives?

In fact, though olives tend to go with food from the Mediterranean, the Middle East, and California, they tend to NOT go with foods from most of the rest of the world. That's our litmus test for using olive oil: Would the dish go with olives? For a puttanesca sauce, or a lamb *tagine*, or hummus, olive oil makes sense. In fact it would be silly to use any other oil. But what about a well-made New England clam chowder? Or a Reuben sandwich? Or phad Thai noodles? These dishes could actually be ruined by a strongly flavored olive oil. The point? Don't use an oil made from a fruit that would be incompatible with your dish.

High Heat? Grab the Neutral Oil

As we've noted, olive oil is very special. It has distinctive flavor, a low smoke point, and it changes dramatically when high heat is applied to it. The last point is the most important. When we want to use very high heat, which we should when searing something, olive oil is a terrible idea.

This is why neutral-flavored oils are so vital to your everyday pantry. The point is to have as little flavor as possible. These oils are used as a medium only. Whether that medium is to neutrally, richly carry other flavors to the palate, like a vinaigrette, or whether it is a medium to cook things at high heat, like sautéing or searing.

There are several neutral-flavored oils that we like, but ultimately the two best are canola and grapeseed. Canola oil is inexpensive, has a high smoke point, and almost no flavor at all. Grapeseed has an even higher smoke point, and is virtually flavorless as well, but is quite a bit more expensive than canola. Both of these oils are amazing for searing fish, scallops, steaks, or whatever you like.

So we add another oil to our pantry. With these three fats—olive oil, butter, and neutral-flavored, high smoke-point oils—we can certainly produce thousands of wine-friendly dishes.

6. Parmigiano-Reggiano

The King of Cheeses

We could suggest many different cheeses for you to always have on hand. There are many very versatile cheeses out there too, like Gruyère, or good cheddar, or fresh goat cheese like chèvre. While any of those would have been fine choices, there is simply no other cheese on earth that is as versatile, noble, and, most importantly, flavorful, as well-made Parmigiano-Reggiano. It has been called the King of Cheeses by cheese experts all over the world, and with good reason.

It almost feels like a bit of a trope to say that this cheese is so special, but the fact of the matter is that it is very, very special. It can be broken into chunks and eaten plain, or with a drop of good balsamic. It can be used to finish a pasta, a polenta dish, or risotto. It can be used to flavor a potato gratin. It is absolute magic on scrambled eggs. It's even good on Mexican food in a pinch, if you don't have any queso añejo around. We've been putting it on family meals of tacos and chilaquiles in the Purple Café kitchen for years.

Parmigiano-Reggiano is special for many reasons. The great chef Massimo Bottura of the famed restaurant Osteria Francescana in Modena, Italy (as of this writing, one of the top ten restaurants in the world), served a very famous dish back in 1995 called "Five ages of Parmigiano-Reggiano in different textures and temperatures." He has since evolved this dish to be known simply as "Five textures, five tempera-tures, and five levels of umami." He believes, as do we, that

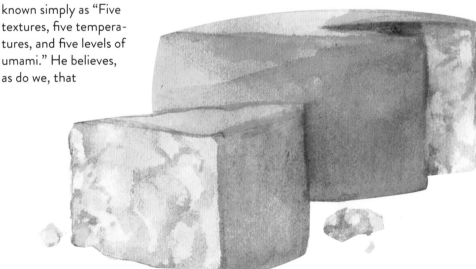

Parmigiano-Reggiano is the most umami-rich ingredient in Western cooking. Umami, the Japanese word for "the fifth taste," a meaty, savory taste, has been linked to the presence of glutamates in foods. Parmigiano-Reggiano has a whopping 1.2 grams per every 100 grams of cheese. Although Roquefort cheese has a slightly higher glutamate content, its pungency and other compounds in the cheese give it a diminished taste of pure umami than you taste in Parmigiano-Reggiano.

We have discussed umami throughout this text, as we feel that it is equally important to the tastes of sweet, acidic, bitter, and salty when it comes to the complex flavors of food and wine. You want umami in your food. Trust us.

Good Parmigiano-Reggiano has a flavor reminiscent of pineapple. It is also salty and sharp, with a crystalline texture that is formed by concentrated amino acids and salt. They add to the pleasure of the cheese, giving it a gritty, almost crunchy texture when eaten in chunks. The aroma of Parmigiano-Reggiano is very nutty and almost sweet. When grated it takes on a fruity aroma and flavor. It is truly an incredible product, and should be in everyone's refrigerator at all times. Just wrap it in slightly damp paper towels and put it in a zipper-lock bag. It will last for months, but you should be going through it much faster than that.

7. Mustard

A Mustard for Every Occasion

Mustard is a super versatile ingredient, and one enjoyed by nearly every culture on earth. Think about it: From Germany to China, from the United States to India, the mustard seed is a popular and widely enjoyed spice and condiment. Latin cuisine seems to have a diminished appreciation of mustard, but even they have their *mostaza*, which they use on some grilled meats. Northern European countries absolutely adore this ingredient, and it is fundamental to Indian cooking, yet the most famous mustard is from France and the city it is named after: Dijon.

If you have no other mustard in your fridge, you should have some decent quality Dijon mustard. It has so much versatility and it can always be diluted with mayonnaise or aioli if its strength needs to be tempered. I admittedly have a mustard problem, as I presently have eleven jars of the stuff in my refrigerator: Dijon, whole grain, extra hot, sweet-hot, fig-balsamic,

Raye's classic yellow, Annie's yellow, maple, sweet and smoky, Chinese, and violet. I can stop any time, I swear . . .

There's Science in That Jar

Regardless of how tasty mustard is, we also love the chemical properties of mustard. Mustard contains lots of mucilage (we'd prefer any other name too), a sticky substance found in its seeds. This substance happens to hold emulsions together beautifully, whether they be oil and vinegar, meat and fat, or the components of a butter sauce like hollandaise. This emulsifier also tends to thicken beautifully, and helps make aiolis and mayonnaises extra stable.

Beginning Your Collection

As far as flavors go, which mustard (or mustards) you choose is truly a matter of preference. I feel like I need them all, but I am a bit of a lunatic when it comes to my pantry. You could probably get by with a nicely made Dijon and be just fine. The thing about mustard is that it lasts pretty much forever, so every time you buy a new one, the other ones are still in that fridge. Don't let anyone tell you that you have enough—they just don't understand. Over a year or two, you may have amassed the maniacally large collection that I have too. Just be careful of revealing too much to your friends and family. I personally feel a mustard intervention coming sometime soon.

8. Honey

Even More Terroir

The world of honey is a rabbit hole. Once you are willing to go beyond the clover honey in the little plastic bear, you have entered a realm of varietals and terroir not terribly dissimilar to wine. Honey is made from bees, and those bees are pollinating flowers, and those flowers come from a specific place. Sound familiar? The only thing that is similar about every single wine is that it is made from grapes. The type of grape and the place where it was made are critical to its final flavor. Honey is exactly the same. There are mass-produced, homogenized, blended honeys from huge farms, and there are varietal-specific honeys made from one type of flower in a specific part of the world. These are referred to as monofloral honeys.

Our favorite example of this is fireweed honey. The Pacific Northwest has a lot of forest fires, and the first plants to pop up the following year are often fireweeds. They have big, beautiful, purple flowers, and they tend to grow best at higher

altitudes. Beekeepers bring their bees to the foothills to pollinate the wild-flowers and make this very special honey. Imaginably, it sells out from almost every source very quickly. The flavor is not what you'd expect either, as it would seem that a big, raucous, robust honey would come from such a plant. Oddly, paradoxically, the honey is very delicate, with a slightly spicy backbone to it.

Another favorite of ours are bitter honeys. The most prevalent variety is chestnut honey, although *mānuka* honey from New Zealand, Japanese knotweed honey, and the very rare *corbezzolo* honey from Sardinia are also incredible examples of honeys that have a bitter finish to them. Doesn't sound like your bag? Think about bittersweet chocolate and the complexity that the bitterness provides. It is good stuff.

9. Shallots

A Ubiquitous Aromatic

In years past, I'd likely have had garlic on this list instead of shallots, but I honestly feel like shallots are a more versatile pantry ingredient. They can also function as a vegetable in and of themselves, which garlic cannot to any but the most ardent of fanatics. Shallots are very versatile, used extensively in French, Southeast Asian, and Indian cooking, and most American chefs are using them in huge quantities as well. The Italians have a term called *insaporire*, which translates as "to bestow flavor"—a term that certainly applies to shallots.

Chefs love shallots. Before I worked in the industry I really didn't use shallots unless I was following a specific recipe, and back then I didn't know why. I wasn't really sure what they tasted like or were supposed to taste like. People say that they taste like a combination of garlic and onion, but I've never felt that way. Shallots taste like very mild onions, but also have a uniqueness to them that really has no substitute. This mildness is actually an advantage. Where the flavors of onions are intense and pungent, shallots are subtle and polished. This vegetable very gently perfumes sauces, vegetables, starches, and pastas and is incredibly versatile. On the grand stage of flavorful food, shallots often work behind the curtain.

The last role that shallots play is to infuse their flavor and then actually be removed from the preparation. Many classic French sauces call for simmering chopped shallots in a flavorful liquid like wine or broth and then straining those shallots out once they have expunged their delightful flavor.

A Touch of Sass

Sometimes you want a dish to have an extra little kick. Not necessarily spiciness. In fact, often you don't want the heat to be directly perceived, but you want to stimulate the palate in the way that only chiles can. This is where red chile flakes come in. They are simply dried, hot peppers that have been crushed.

If you want a truly spicy hot dish, we actually recommend that you diversify your approach and draw from the galaxy of fresh and dried chiles available in today's markets. You will produce more complex chile flavor this way, which is really great for dishes that you want to drive with heat and big, punchy flavors (these might include Thai dishes, or Mexican, or even Indian or Moroccan). We use chile flakes like an Italian would, or the French would use *piment d'Espelette*, just to subtly nuance the heat and give the dish more complexity. This is achieved with mere pinches of this ingredient. Measuring it would almost always be in the eighth- to quarter-teaspoon range unless you were making a really large quantity.

Basque Heat

If you really want to spend some money, and you can find a good source, the piment d'Espelette mentioned above is a game changer. It is a slightly smoky, sweet-hot chile powder from the French Basque town of Espelette. It is quite simply amazing. Unfortunately because of its scarcity, and the fierce tradition surrounding both its production and export, you are going to have to dig deep into your wallet if you want some of this stuff. I recommend it, not in lieu of other varieties of chile flakes, but in addition to them.

11. Eggs

Worth the Search

Good eggs. A chef's obsession. We all want that light-green mixed pack of farm eggs that we get out of a local farmer's barn, leaving a few bucks behind on the honor system. In fact, those are the best eggs you can get, period. On the few occasions where I get my hands on them, at a farmers' market or when I'm brave enough to venture out of the city, I am always rewarded with pornographically orange yolks that stand at attention like a boot camp recruit, and whites that are not the slightest bit runny. Just thinking about them almost makes me want to drive out to the country right now to get them. Then reality takes hold. I am an unapologetic, highly enthusiastic food dork—but I'm still not going to drive to the country every weekend for eggs, so I have to make some concessions.

The concession, which seems to continue to improve on an annual basis over the last decade, is cage-free, organic eggs. They are the closest commercially produced product to farm-fresh eggs. There are all kinds of them available, and we've seen little difference in brown vs. white, vegetarian diet vs. regular organic, and omega-3 enhanced vs. not. Just make sure they're cage-free, organic, and as fresh as possible.

12. Citrus Fruit

Just a Drop Can Change a Dish

For both their juice and zest, I always have a lemon, lime, and orange around. The visceral freshness that a quick spritz of lemon juice or zest can impart to a dish is amazing. During the cold winter months, we are lucky enough to have a bevy of citrus fruits available, such as blood oranges, Meyer lemons, clementines, tangerines, Minneolas, cara cara oranges, and many, many more. When I first became a chef I always felt like citrus was a summer thing, since it is so bright and fresh. Paradoxically, citrus is a deep winter fruit. Now I've embraced this fact as a blessing. Since most winter foods are so heavy, starchy, and rich, citrus fruits are a shining beacon to cut through that heaviness and keep dishes balanced. I also love what pastry chefs are able to do with citrus fruits.

We live in the jet-fresh age, and while I love to buy local and seasonal foods, I acquiesce when it comes to fresh citrus. Their quality does go up and down somewhat throughout the year, but only the most ardent locavore will refuse to use lemons in the summer

because they aren't in season. The navel orange, the Persian lime, and the Eureka lemon—our common, grocery store lemon—have been genetically engineered (in an orchard, not a lab) to fruit and flower all year-round. I highly recommend keeping a variety of citrus in your fruit bowl all year. And when winter comes along, venture out into the world of specialty citrus. Many of them are delicious and unique.

Preserved Lemons, More Than the Sum of Their Parts

Lemons (especially Meyer lemons, which have a spicy perfume and beautiful, almost orange skin) have the unique property of being easily preserved with salt. The French call this lemon

confit. In Morocco, where lemons preserved in this way likely originated, they are called *l'hmad marakad*. We like to call them preserved lemons, and they are ridiculously easy to make. Every year during the peak of Meyer lemon season, when Meyers are almost the same price as regular lemons, we put up over forty quarts of preserved lemons at the restaurant so we can use them for the rest of the year. The preserved lemon has a flavor that is not duplicable with any quicker method, so make sure you make enough to last, as you will certainly become addicted once they enter your culinary repertoire.

We've had some success applying this method to tangerines too, as their skin is thin enough to fully cure without getting too bitter. Our attempts with limes, navel oranges, and grapefruits have been less successful, although the bitter quality of the finished product might be of interest to craft bartenders.

Here's how to make preserved lemons:

- Cut some lemons into quarters, but don't go all the way through; it should look almost like a flower. Reserve all of the juice from this process.

- Pack kosher salt into the cut parts of the lemons. You cannot put too much salt inside the lemons, so really pack it in there.

- Pack the lemons into a jar, salting between each layer. When we say pack, we mean PACK them in. You should cram as many lemons into the jar as possible, short of cracking the glass. This will release a lot of the juice in the cut lemons and create a brine of pure lemon juice and salt, which is what you want.

- If the juice does not reach the top of the jar, add the juice of a few fresh lemons in order to cover all of the salted lemons.

- We keep the jars in the refrigerator, but you don't have to. Assess where you have more space. As long as the jars are very tightly sealed (use a mason jar with a screw-top lid to ensure this), you can hold preserved lemons in a cool, dark place like your pantry or a closet.

- The lemons should be ready in about six weeks. When you use them, trim the white pith away. The rind itself is now completely edible. Make sure to rinse the rinds to remove any excess salt.

- Don't forget how much salt you used! You need to adjust the seasoning of any dish you are using these lemons in, or you will over-salt it.

- To date, we've found no good culinary application for the juice. It is appallingly salty, highly acidic, and fairly bitter from the oils extracted from the pith. We've tried brining shrimp and chicken in it but it was awful. We just discard it once the last lemon is used.

Honorable Mention: Fresh Herbs

There's Always Some Leftovers

Fresh herbs provide a kaleidoscope of flavors and aromas that we can add to dishes on a year-round basis now. Fresh herbs are available at nearly every grocery store as well, which allows us to use them whenever a recipe calls for them, unlike in the past when we had to substitute nearly flavorless dried herbs. However, unless you have a vibrant herb garden, we cannot recommend that you keep every fresh herb that you might ever use in your fridge like the other ingredients we recommend for your pantry. When you do have them, don't ever throw them away if they're still good. You never know when you might find them useful. Some of them will dry in your fridge quite nicely, like fresh bay leaves and thyme.

Others will turn black or slimy, or wither away. That's OK, but it never hurts to have a few herbs in the fridge if you're making a broth, or an omelet, or a quick pasta dish.

Fresh herbs are often game changers when it comes to wine pairing. That herbaceous Sancerre or Chinon might benefit tremendously from a fistful of chopped parsley and chives added to your dish at the last second. We love using them, but they need to be really fresh, so herbs only get an honorable mention as far as your everyday pantry goes. Obviously, if you live somewhere where you can plant an herb garden, absurdly fresh herbs will be available to you at all times.

Mail Order Sources

AMAZON.COM

Believe it or not, almost everything on the list is available through Amazon. However, there are other sources where you can get even higher-quality or scarcer items. Should you find yourself in a pinch, you can fulfill this whole list with this online megastore in about ten minutes of shopping.

ZINGERMANS.COM

Based in Ann Arbor, Michigan, Zingerman's is my favorite specialty food store in the country. The meticulousness with which they source their products is unmatched, in my opinion. Plus in this day and age of wanting to understand our food's exact provenance and pedigree, Zingerman's provides you with a great deal of lore about every product they sell. Be warned, Zingerman's is not trying to be a discount store. They carry only the best, and the best tends to cost a fair amount.

DEANDELUCA.COM

Dean and DeLuca is the granddaddy of specialty food stores. In business since 1977, they've stayed relevant and well stocked ever since. Lots of rare, specialty products are available through D&D.

SALTWORKS.US

There is no peer. If you want specialty salt, there is simply nothing like Saltworks. I've personally toured the plant several times throughout their growth and they run a first-class operation. They're also obsessively passionate about salt.

MARXFOODS.COM

Marx Foods is a very upscale shop in our hometown of Seattle. The quantity of rare inventory carried there is mind-boggling. Sourcing and maintaining that inventory—weird and interesting things like extraordinary Moroccan olive oil, authentic French cassoulet beans known as Tarbais, fresh truffles when they're in season—is pure art. Great shop.

MURRAYSCHEESE.COM

If I didn't have the luxury of working directly with a cheese importer and two wholesalers, I would probably order a lot of my cheese from Murray's. They are incredibly passionate. They even cave-age some of the cheeses themselves, in the true French *affineur* tradition. This allows them to offer cheeses that are truly unique to their shop only.

IGOURMET.COM

I get lost in there, but there are a ton of different products available at this site. Their honey selection is mind-boggling. The butter selection is also a thing to behold. Simply massive.

Wine Wardrobe Cheat Sheet

Shopping List for the Wine Store

- **CHAMPAGNE:** Look for a Champagne you've never heard of before. If a wine shop is occupying shelf space with something other than a large, well-known Champagne house, there's a likelihood that it has somebody's strong personal endorsement.

- **INEXPENSIVE BUBBLES:** Get to know the Crémants of France: Bourgogne, Bordeaux, Alsace, and the Loire. But also seek out Extra-Dry and Dry Prosecco—keep in mind the extra few grams of sugar are a flavor booster. If there is a retail price tag on the bottle, don't scrape it off. Knowing what you paid for it will encourage you to make Mimosas.

- **LIGHT-BODIED WHITE:** Know the classic Sauvignon Blancs of the Loire Valley (Pouilly Fumé/Sancerre) and the new classic of New Zealand (Marlborough). But when you're done with those, explore Muscadet, Grüner Veltliner, and dry Rieslings.

- **MEDIUM-BODIED WHITE:** While the majority of white wines produced in the world fall under this umbrella, do yourself a favor and purchase any Italian white wine employing a grape other than Pinot Grigio. Coach would also advocate seeking out white blends of Sauvignon Blanc and Semillon from Bordeaux.

- **WELL-SEASONED WHITE:** When we talk about well-seasoned wines, we're more or less talking about oaked Chardonnay. However, this might be the number-one reason to strike up a relationship with the local wine shop: ask for a well-oaked wine other than Chardonnay, and you should be introduced to all sorts of interesting wines from Portugal, Spain, Australia, Chile, and Argentina.

- **FULL-BODIED WHITE:** Head to the varieties of the Rhône Valley: Viognier, Marsanne, Roussanne, and Grenache Blanc. These grapes (especially those grown in the south of France or in Spain, Washington, and California) don't need the oak—their gregarious personalities make it unnecessary.

• **SWEET WHITE:** German Riesling is on the top of our list, though there are many Chenin Blancs from Vouvray that are hard to argue with. And as long as it's from Asti, Moscato is a handy and delicious thing to have in the Wardrobe.

 • **LIGHT-BODIED RED:** Pinot Noir will always be expensive—treat yourself from time to time, but arm yourself with Cru Beaujolais. Forget whatever bias you have—Cru Beaujolais is where you will find the most surprise and pleasure.

 • **MEDIUM-BODIED RED:** There are a great many classics, generally from Europe, to fit the bill. Chianti, Côtes du Rhône, Bordeaux, Rioja, on and on and on.

 • **FULL-BODIED RED:** Hedonism is where we're at on this, so no need to find a wine up for a complexity award. Shiraz and Zinfandel come to mind first, but it's difficult at times to find much better than bulk wine–production examples of these wines. Look at Malbec, red blends from America, wines of the Languedoc-Roussillon, and modern Spanish wines from Toro and Priorat.

 • **TANNIC RED:** Know your target on this one, since you have a couple of different paths. If the wine is necessary in order to hang out with fatty steak in an ersatz sauce role, you might be heading to tannic Cabernet Sauvignons from the West Coast, Australia, or South America. For more complex fare, blended wines or Nebbiolo from the Piedmont region of Italy are high on our list.

 • **ROSÉ:** Make this easy. Look to southern France: Tavel, Provence, Bandol. You won't get bored.

You Can Have a Bigger Wine Wardrobe If You Like

You probably noticed that there are a couple of wines highlighted in this book that are not included in the Wine Wardrobe: Tawny Port and Fino Sherry. That was on purpose. We believe that once you have Fino Sherry with cured meats, olives, and almonds you won't need reminding—you'll always want it around. Or that you'll never bother with blue cheese without Port ever again because the thought of one without the other is an incomplete sentence.

The more you play with food and wine, there is a strong chance that your Wine Wardrobe will grow—that you'll discover specific food and wine experiences that you'll want to repeat. Go for it.

Index

Note: Images are indicated by *italics*.

Oven-Roasted Asparagus
with Blistered Shallots and
Sunny-Side Farm Egg, 144,
145
Rolled Omelet Filled with Confit
Shallot, Parmigiano-Reggiano,
and Sherry Vinaigrette with dry
rosé, 256–59, *257–259*
scrambled. *See* scrambled eggs
emulsifying, 266
estate, 93
"European-style" cultured butter,
268
Extra Brut Champagne, 105
Extra-Dry Prosecco, 118–19
extra-virgin olive oil, 266
Fanny Bay oysters, *51*, 53
fat, 129
fennel, pickled, 134
fermentation
Champagne, 104, 107
Chardonnay, 162–63
malolactic, 68, 163
fettuccine Alfredo, 165–66, 168
finishing, 265, 267
Fino Sherry
cured meats and, 55–56,
59–62, *60*
flavor of, 62
flor, 61
fortify of, 60–61
origins of, 60
oxidation of, 61
fireweed honey, 273
fish
frozen, 124
raw. *See* crudo
refreshed, 124
salmon, 194–202
slicing of, 125–27, *126*
white. *See* white fish
fish roe, 108
fishmongers, 123
flavor
buttery, 68, 163
contrasting of, 47
description of, 36–37
oak barrel effects on, 161, 173
salt used for, 39, 262–63
sound of, 209
sugar effects on, 39
techniques that alter, 46
flavored salts, 264
flor, 61
food
acidic elements of, 46–47
fatty elements of, 46
salty elements of, 46
spicy elements of, 46
texture of, 37
wine pairings with. *See* wine–food
pairings
fortify, 60–61
fractional blending, 61
Franklin, Benjamin, 237

French-style scrambled eggs,
112–13, *114*
Fresno chile, 132
front-label deception, 93
frozen fish, 124
fruit, citrus, 277–78
full body, 33
full-bodied red wines
alcohol by volume for, 219
barbecue food and, 219
descriptive terms for, 219
pork and, 226, *227–233*,
228–29
roasted lean red meats and,
221–29, *224–233*
shopping tips for, 283
spicy food and, 220
types of, 220
full-bodied white wines
grapes used in, 173–74
regions for, 174
shopping tips for, 282
white fish and, 175–78
Fumé Blanc, 192
Gaeta olives, 58
German Prädikat System, 182–83
German Riesling
alcohol by volume of, 183
Auslese, 183
description of, 71–72, 182
Kabinett, 182–83
Spätlese, 183
ginger, 132
glazing, 243
gorgonzola polenta, 245, *246–248*
Grand Cru wines, 161
Grand Crus of Burgundy, 191
grapes
acids in, 34
Grüner Veltliner, 138
medium-bodied red wines, 206
Melon de Bourgogne, 138
tannins in, 35, 235–36
Viognier, 173–74
grapeseed oil, 271
Grenache Blanc, 174
Grenache Blanca, 174
Grenache Noir, 174
Grilled King Salmon with Wild
Mushroom Ragout, 201–02
grilling
of asparagus, 141, 143
of Dungeness crabs, 67
of hot dogs, 71
of salmon, 195–96, 198
Grüner Veltliner, 138
Halibut, Pan-Roasted, 178, *179*
ham, 57, 58–59
Hawaii, 121
Hearty Burgundy, 117
heat, 37
herbs, 279
Himalayan salt, 264
honey, 273–74
horseradish heat, 37
hot dogs

boiling of, 72
braising of, 71–72
cooking of, 71–72
grilling of, 71
microwaving of, 70–71
pan-searing of, 71
Riesling and, 69–72
toppings on, 70
Hurricane Island oysters, 53
inexpensive bubbles. *See* sweet white
wines
international bitterness units, 235
International Olive Council, 266
Jamón Ibérico, 58
Jamón Ibérico de Bellota, 58
Jamón Serrano, 57, 58
Jerez, 60–61
Kabinett, 182–83
Kalamata olives, 56, 57
Kamman, Madeleine, 196
Keller, Thomas, 262
kosher salt, 263
Kumamoto oysters, *51*, 53
Kusshi oysters, *51*, 53
labels, wine, 91–93
Languedoc-Roussilllon, 253
layered, 93
lees
Champagne, 104
Chardonnay, 163
leftover wine, 87
lemons, 277–78
Lewis Bag, 53
l'hmad marakad, 278
light body, 33
light-bodied red wines
Beaujolais Nouveau, 192–93
Italian, 193
Pinot Noir, 191–92
salmon with. *See* salmon
shopping tips for, 283
varietals of, 193
light-bodied white wines
asparagus and, 139–45
description of, 137–38
Sauvignon Blanc, 137–38
shopping tips for, 282
lime, 132
limes, 277–78
liquid
for braising, 240–43
reduction of, 212
loin, 131, 221–22
Loire Valley, 138, 183
long, 93
macaroni and cheese, baked, 165,
169–71
maceration, 251
Madiran, 236
mail order sources, 281
Maillard, Louis Camille, 207, 209,
223
malic acid, 68, 163
malolactic fermentation, 68, 163
Manzanilla olives, 56
Marcona almonds, 55, 57, 59

margarita, 34
mark-ups, 94
Marsannay, 253
martini, 75
McGee, Harold, 208
meat
Almost Classic Beef Stroganoff
and medium-bodied red wines,
214
braising of, 223, 237–48,
238–248
browning of, 207–10, 238–39
dredging of, 238
glazing of, 243
loin, 131, 221–22
sausages, 59, 70, 187
searing of, 238–39
veal Bolognese, 215–17, *216*
medium body, 33
medium-bodied red wines
Almost Classic Beef Stroganoff
and, 214
description of, 205–06
grapes used in, 206
Neo-Classic Veal Bolognese and,
215–17, *216*
ragoût and, 207–12, *211*
ragù and, 207–12, *211*
regions for, 206
shopping tips for, 283
stew and, 207–12, *211*
medium-bodied white wines
grapes, 148
overview of, 147–48
shopping tips for, 282
steamed shellfish with, 149–58
Melon de Bourgogne, 138
Merlot, 78, 236
Mermaid Cove oysters, 53
microwaving of hot dogs, 70–71
milk, 27–28, 33
Mind Mouth
description of, 31–32
exercising of, 43
purpose of, 42
Monastrell, 236
Montrachet, 161
Moscato D'Asti, 183
Mountain Chablis, 117
Mourvédre, 236
mouth. *See also* Mind Mouth
abilities of, 33
acid testing in, 34
mouthfeel, 37
multi-vintage Champagne, 104
Muscadet, 138
mushrooms, 199
mussels, 150, 152–53
mustard, 272–73
Naked Cowboy oysters, 53
Nebbiolo, 236
negociants, 105
Negroamaro, 236
Neo-Classic Veal Bolognese,
215–17, *216*

Acknowledgments

Chris and Coach would like to thank the following people:

Keita Horn—menu tester, grammar consultant, humor editor, motivator. (Wife.)

Kristin Mills—chef consultant, product tester, proofreader, motivator. (Wife.)

Larry Kurofsky—the guy that gave us jobs, and the guy who let us do this thing. Without him, this wouldn't have happened.

The wonderful human beings that opened up their homes, cooked these recipes, and let us take their pictures—Jim Benoit, Grace and Hun Kim, Rachel and Mike Hubbard, Eric Rabena and Adrienne Kimberley, Brandon and Amy Screen, Dan and Jamie Kezner. Sorry about the mess.

Coach's crew—the ladies and gentlemen who do the real heavy-lifting in a busy kitchen (Chefs, Sous Chefs, Lead Lines, Cooks, Professionals): Andy Wagenbrenner, Micah DeNunzio, Jon Langley, Kyle Cole, Megan Erickson, Omar Salazar-Cruz, Devin Adams, Felipe Salazar, Zach King, and Ben Williams.

Horn's team—the people that make me look good every day, and the people that took care of business while we hashed this out: Tyler Alden, CT Doescher, Ryan Bolin, Janice Dean, Christian Douthitt, Nick Blewett, Adam Galbraith, Eli Traverse, Aaron Reeves, Ben Denton, Scott Thompson, and RJ Arnold.

And to our teachers and mentors. We didn't come up with all this in a vacuum.

And to our parents who taught us to love things like food and wine.

About the Authors

CHEF HARRY "COACH" MILLS almost accidentally had a career in politics. That would have been a disaster. However, he did enjoy what he remembers about college.

His first restaurant job was at the drive-thru window at a now defunct fast food restaurant. (He takes no credit for its demise.) His next step up in the culinary world was washing dishes, which eventually led to a degree at the Art Institute School of Culinary Arts. He graduated in '97, worked as Sous Chef in several small European bistros where he learned the then obscure art of charcuterie. It was this specialized skill that earned him a faculty position at his alma mater, a position he held for seven years.

A lifetime of wine enthusiasm made working at a wine focused restaurant appealing. His tenure at Purple Café and Wine Bar began in 2006.

He has spent the last decade working with Chris Horn, which is clearly the highlight of his career.

He lives in Magnolia with his wife Kristin.

CHRIS HORN was once the world's greatest country club bus boy. Just ask him. His college days (Whitworth University) included many jugs of "Hearty Burgundy" and other alleged wine.

Post college, having studied "English Writing" Horn went right back to bussing tables. After many years in this coveted position, he was finally allowed to interact with guests beyond clearing plates and filling water glasses.

His resumé includes a giant seafood restaurant and a giant Asian restaurant.

A lifetime of wine enthusiasm made working at a wine focused restaurant appealing. His tenure at Purple Café and Wine Bar began in 2006.

He has spent the last decade working with Harry Mills, which is clearly the highlight of his career.

Chris was named the Washington State Wine Awards Sommelier of the Year as well as the *Seattle Magazine* Sommelier of the Year in 2015.

He lives in Ballard with his wife Keita and son Silas.